D1605786

Southern Literary Studies

FRED HOBSON, EDITOR

The Kingfish in Fiction

Huey P. Long and the
Modern American Novel

Keith Perry

*PING + SHARON —
THANKS FOR HELPING MAKE
MY FIRST ELDERHOSTEL
SUCH A GREAT EXPERIENCE!

Keith*

LOUISIANA STATE UNIVERSITY PRESS
BATON ROUGE

Copyright © 2004 by Louisiana State University Press
All rights reserved
Manufactured in the United States of America
FIRST PRINTING

DESIGNER: Andrew Shurtz
TYPEFACES: Adobe Caslon, Clarendon Bold Condensed
TYPESETTER: Coghill Composition Co., Inc.
PRINTER AND BINDER: Thomson-Shore, Inc.

Library of Congress Cataloging-in-Publication Data

Perry, Keith.
The Kingfish in fiction : Huey P. Long and the modern
American novel / Keith Perry.
p. cm.
Includes bibliographical references and index.
ISBN 0-8071-2942-9 (cloth : alk. paper)
1. Political fiction, American—History and criticism.
2. Politics and literature—United States—History—20th century.
3. American fiction—Southern States—History and criticism.
4. American fiction—20th century—History and criticism.
5. Long, Huey Pierce, 1893–1935—In literature.
6. Political corruption in literature.
7. Southern States—In literature.
8. Politicans in literature.
I. Title.
PS374.P6P47 2004
813'.5209351—dc22   2003025464

for my mother—

and in memory of her father,
EARL G. HARRELL, 1914–1999

You throw a rock in a pond and it don't make but one splash but they is ripples runs out from it.

—"Statement of Ashby Wyndham," *At Heaven's Gate*

Contents

Acknowledgments

WERE IT NOT FOR THE GENEROSITY AND ENCOURAGEMENT
of the professors, colleagues, editors, friends, and family who have offered me such constant support over the past several years, this project
would have remained—at best—a possibility.

I first have to thank Jean W. Cash, professor of English at James
Madison University, for allowing me to sit in on the graduate seminar
in the Fugitives and Agrarians she taught toward the end of my two
years as an adjunct instructor there. Mentor and friend since my days
as an undergraduate, she has done more for my career than anyone
outside my immediate family—in this case offering me an excuse to
reread *All the King's Men* during the spring of 1993. If it were not for
that reading and the argument I first tested as a guest in her seminar,
this book would probably not exist.

I next have to thank those who, four years later, made sure my further development of that argument passed muster as a dissertation for
the Ph.D. in twentieth-century American literature at the University
of South Carolina. A. Keen Butterworth served as my dissertation director. In addition to advising me on content and style and shepherd-
ing me through the process of completing both dissertation and
degree, he—alongside his wife, Nancy—ran the warmest, most open
house I found in Columbia. Patrick G. Scott served as its second
reader, as well as my most constant advocate from my first day on the
USC campus. Ashley Brown served as both its third reader and as my
only living link, however tenuous, to the study's center. He seemed to
have known half the writers my classmates and I could only read—
Pound, Eliot, and O'Connor among them—and, as a grade-schooler
on a field trip to Washington, D.C., in the mid-1930s, he had watched
as a certain young senator from Louisiana addressed the packed galleries of the U.S. Senate. . . .

I next have to thank those friends—fellow graduate students and instructors of English—who not only endured more talk of this project than all those above put together, but offered me the day-to-day support it took to help me keep putting one sentence, one paragraph, one page after another. At the University of South Carolina, there were Dale Harter, Robert Trogdon, and Lucy Morrison. At Auburn University, there were Dan Albergotti, Marian Carache, Jacqueline Foertsch, Patsy Fowler, Gary McDonald, Tony Perrello, David Peterson, and Joe Walker. Special thanks also go to Tom O'Shea for pointing out to me a novel that, until that point, seems to have escaped the notice of all who had taken up this subject. Were it not for his commenting on the dime-store paperback of *A Lion Is in the Streets* I happened to be carrying past his office one day, *President Fu Manchu* would probably have escaped my notice as well.

I also have to thank those at LSU Press who have done so much to help me turn a dissertation into a monograph. John Easterly, now associate editor of the *Southern Review*, was equal parts kind, accommodating, and patient; Sylvia Frank Rodrigue, since John's mid-2002 departure, has ably and amiably taken over where he left off; George Roupe has skillfully copyedited the final draft, catching each of my stylistic shortcomings before other readers had to suffer through them. I am also indebted to the anonymous outside readers for their suggestions for expanding the breadth and depth and overall direction of each successive draft.

Most, though, I have to thank my family for their love and support, much of which came during an incredibly tough time in all our lives. My parents believed in me when others had yet to, lending me the money for graduate school when mine ran out and I had yet to earn my first assistantship—and then, a few years after I'd graduated, forgiving the debt altogether. My wife, Nicole—my girlfriend when I began writing, my fiancée while I revised—has watched countless hours we could've spent together become hours I've spent alone with this book. For that I thank her and apologize to her, and I hereby promise to ask Mr. Long to excuse us if we ignore him more in the future.

Without any one of the friends and family listed here—and many of those who were neither when I began have since become both—this book would be less than what it is. I thank them all.

The Kingfish in Fiction

Introduction
The Facts and the Fiction

THE STORY BEHIND THE STORY BEGINS IN THE SPRING OF 1932 on a front porch somewhere in the suburbs of New Orleans. Sketchy though they may be, the details tell us a great deal about their subject at age thirteen—and, more importantly, at something closer to thirty. Russell Long, then a pensive, perhaps uncommonly reticent high school student, had just moved to town from Baton Rouge. With him on the front porch that afternoon were a handful of his new friends, at least one of their fathers, and a few of that father's friends. Hardly had the adults opened the afternoon paper when one of the men among them began belligerently denouncing an almost perennial target of nearly every newspaper in the state: Louisiana's former governor and now its new U.S. senator. The specifics of the man's outburst have been lost, of course, but according to one of the teenagers present, they created a "terribly embarrassing" situation for Long and his friends. They knew what the man and his friends did not—that his son's new acquaintance, now standing within sight as certainly as earshot, was none other than that same senator's son. Stunned beyond comment, Long's friends turned toward him as, with characteristic tact but uncharacteristic boldness, he heard himself assert, "Pardon me, sir, that is not the way it happened. . . . What the papers said is not what my father did."[1]

Fifteen years later, much, but not all, had changed for Russell Long. His father had been dead more than a decade, the victim of an assassin's bullet fired one night in September 1935, but the late senator was still anathema enough to many to remain almost as much a target for such tirades. His son, moreover, still found himself defending his

---

1. Robert Mann, *Legacy to Power: Senator Russell Long of Louisiana* (New York: Paragon House, 1992), 41.

father from them. Hence his late-1946 request to friend and U.S. senator John H. Overton: not yet a U.S. senator himself, Long had to ask Overton to present before the Senate a motion proposing that "In Defense of My Father," a rebuttal he had written to formally respond to his father's critics, be entered into official Senate proceedings. Overton agreed, the motion passed without objection, and on January 20, 1947, the essay was printed in the *Congressional Record*. Its first sentence reads: "I venture the assertion that no man of our times has been more abused, vilified, and misrepresented by the American press to its reading public than my father, Huey P. Long." It was as if assassination had not been enough, Long implied, as if the press were single-mindedly determined to depict his father's accomplishments as "the means of fostering fiendish purposes," as if, as a result, American history were now destined to portray him as "a legendary character of the underworld." The press, the son charged, had characterized his father as a "ruthless dictator," a "noisy low-grade rabble-rouser," a politician fit to play only the role of Satan in "the epic of American democracy." What Long saw, in sum, as he recollected the decades of articles about his father, was "a campaign of steady and constant derogation," an obvious and outright perversion of fair comment that first "turn[ed] freedom of the press into freedom of libel," then, worse, led "the average disinterested reader"—his friend's father, perhaps, on that front porch in New Orleans some fifteen years before—"to accept deliberate falsification and imaginative assertion as truth."[2]

Even more objectionable, Long continued, was a then-recent rash of novels that, though they never so much as mention his father's name, often render innocuous even the most negative journalistic assessment. He charged that, in addition to magnifying his father's reputation as a dictator and rabble-rouser, the novels stoop still lower, indirectly depicting him as a man who used language "that would be an injustice to the most illiterate man in America," a man "possessed," moreover, of "an obsessive lust for sexual indecencies." Even more than the "fallacious" newspaper and magazine articles he first decried, what had prompted Long to write "In Defense of My Father" was the publication of four such novels during the previous five years. According to

2. *Congressional Record*, 80th Cong., 1st sess., 1947, 93, pt. 1:438–39.

the note that prefaced his essay upon its appearance in the *Congressional Record* and, concurrently, in various Louisiana newspapers, the incident that most immediately set his pen to paper was *Life* magazine's December 9, 1946, publication of Hamilton Basso's "The Huey Long Legend," an article analyzing the four most recent fictional incarnations of his father. Though nothing indicates that Long read the novels themselves, he had certainly read the article: a family friend would say several years later that doing so had "hurt Russell terribly." Clearly the source of his father's characterization as a latter-day American Satan, the article is also, more than likely, the source of Long's comments regarding the characters' grammatical and sexual proclivities.[3] More than just the one article out of thousands to push a son to again defend his father's name—and not, as on that afternoon in 1932, on a friend's front porch, but in no less an arena than the U.S. Senate—Basso's was the most comprehensive and widely read of several to declare that, despite the fact of his 1935 assassination, the Kingfish, by way of fiction—and much to his eldest son's continued offense— was still fair game for public vilification.

Just as the occasion for "In Defense of My Father" was the publication of "The Huey Long Legend," the occasion for "The Huey Long Legend" was the publication some two months earlier of Robert Penn Warren's *All the King's Men* (1946). Contrary to much popular and even a good deal of scholarly assumption, however, Warren's first Pulitzer Prize–winner is only the best-known and neither the first nor the only American novel to fictionalize the life of Huey Pierce Long. As many as twelve years earlier, Basso himself—soon to emerge the most forthright voice in the ensuing debate—had forced a Long-like character into *Cinnamon Seed* (1934), his second novel. Harry Brand, the novel's so-called King-Frog, moreover, was only the first of what would become a half-dozen such characters. The following year, Sinclair Lewis's *It Can't Happen Here* (1935) became the second American novel to fictionalize Long, and, in that Berzelius Windrip, unlike Basso's Brand, stands just off the narrative's center, it also became the first Huey Long *novel*. Its successor, perhaps because of Long's 1935 assassination, would not follow for another seven years—but, as Gilgo Slade

3. Ibid., 438; Mann, 66.

occupies one of the most central positions in *Sun in Capricorn* (1942), it would constitute Basso's own, and was to remain his only, Long novel. The following year, John Dos Passos set a by now familiar character, one this time named Chuck Crawford, near the center of *Number One* (1943). Adria Locke Langley's *A Lion Is in the Streets*, initially the most popular of the lot, followed in 1945, only to see Hank Martin overshadowed in 1946—and, indeed, for at least the next six decades—by the entrance of *All the King's Men*'s Willie Stark. Though first on the list of the most fully realized, best-known fictional incarnations of Long, Warren's Stark thus emerged a perhaps surprising sixth among the six thus far created.

Perhaps the best way to introduce these characters is to put to the test one of Basso's most paradoxical assertions. Since "the known facts of Long's life" read "so much like a disguised rendering of [the] fiction"—not vice versa—that all distinction between them is easily, if not frequently, obscured, we should first focus not on the fictional characters but on the historical figure who so clearly inspired them. The facts that gave birth to the fiction are as follows: According to T. Harry Williams, author of the most exhaustive of the more than half-dozen full-length Long biographies, Huey Pierce Long, Jr., was born August 30, 1893, the seventh child of Huey Pierce Long, Sr., and Caledonia Tison Long of Winnfield, Louisiana. Poor seat of the even poorer Winn Parish, Winnfield was at the time an unincorporated northern hamlet of perhaps two thousand. Few if any were the Creoles and Cajuns for which Louisiana is better known, most of its inhabitants instead being the descendants of Scots-Irish settlers who emigrated from surrounding states only after the Louisiana Purchase. Contemporary Long biographer Carleton Beals, in an unusually sympathetic passage, described these people as

> common sturdy folk who built the nation but have remained stepchildren of the prosperity they helped create, the forgotten men of the South. All this folk—those not in the slave-holding aristocracy—had been shoved off upon marginal lands too worthless to be absorbed into big estates. For generations they had been out of touch with even provincial centers of civilization—lost souls in the

folds of dismal low hills. Ignorant, superstitious, bigoted, inarticulate, they could not improve their lot or lift their swarms of progeny into the professional or business world. Their only outlets were sex, corn whiskey and religion. The Bible was their sole intellectual nourishment; they looked with dark suspicion on wider learning, rarely even read a newspaper. Mostly Baptists . . . they were, like their obstinate red hills, their sun-baked fields and brittle cornstalks, dry, uncompromising men, who took life seriously and lived by Puritan morals.

For the most part, they farmed what little local land was arable. Winn Parish's harvests were "scrawny," its livestock "scrawnier," its people "scrawniest" of all.[4]

According to Forrest Davis, another contemporary biographer, Winn Parish "raised only one crop in abundance: dissent." In 1861, shrugging off concern for what they considered a rich man's war, citizens charged their parish delegate to the state convention with a relatively rare vote against secession; in 1892, trusting their economic futures to neither of the more conventional parties, they voted into office the entire Populist slate; in 1908, inspired by a recent visit from Eugene Debs, they voted into office nearly half the Socialist ticket. Winn, in short, was the "most radical" parish in Louisiana, a reputation that soon earned it the nickname "Winn Free State."[5] The Longs, however, lived a bit above this ornery discord, bred as it was in abject exigency. Williams explains that Huey Junior could claim part in at least one American political tradition by recalling his birth in a log cabin, but that it was far more substantial than the derelict shanty he often turned it into on the stump (*HL* 20). Upon moving to Winn Parish, Huey Senior had bought a tract of land that, after the lumber boom that followed the 1901 arrival of the Arkansas Southern Railroad, became the new center of an expanding town. Land prices rose, and

4. Hamilton Basso, "The Huey Long Legend," *Life*, 9 December 1946, 108; T. Harry Williams, *Huey Long* (1969; reprint, New York: Vintage, 1981), 20, 29, hereafter cited parenthetically in the text as *HL;* Carleton Beals, *The Story of Huey P. Long* (Philadelphia: Lippincott, 1935), 28; Harnett T. Kane, *Huey Long's Louisiana Hayride: The American Rehearsal for Dictatorship, 1928–1940* (1941; reprint, Gretna, La.: Pelican, 1971), 36.

5. Forrest Davis, *Huey Long: A Candid Biography* (New York: Dodge, 1935), 45.

the Longs became not just financially independent but relatively af-
fluent. Members of the local intellectual elite as well, they saw that
each of their nine children attended at least a few semesters of college
(*HL* 21). Williams warns against making too much of this information,
though, for what was upper-class in Winnfield would have been something somewhat less almost anywhere else (*HL* 22). His family may
have been well-off by local standards, but Huey Junior would soon realize that the patricians to the south, particularly in New Orleans,
would look upon him as "a hillbilly or a hick, as somebody who did
not quite belong." Williams concludes that, amidst the rigidly defined
social strata of the early-twentieth-century South, Huey Junior and the
rest of the Longs were approaching but still stood appreciably outside
the most select of Louisiana's circles (*HL* 24).

One of the earliest and still most emphatic confirmations of this
judgment comes from Long himself. He begins his autobiography,
Every Man a King, with the implication that there was little in any
way select about his childhood, much of which, he would have us believe, he spent working the family farm. "Rising before the sun," he
lamented, "we toiled until dark"; "the rows were long; the sun was hot;
there was little companionship." Other authorities, however, tell a
much different story. Thomas O. Harris, another early biographer,
counters that "[n]o myth identified with the early life of Huey P. Long
has endured with as much vigor as the overworked farm-boy fable."
His brother Julius found in these complaints nothing but "sob-stuff,"
his sister Charlotte later adding that "Huey never got near a plow un-
less somebody else was using it." One Winn tale even tells of local
farmers having to pay him a flat rate for picking cotton because a
farmer paying him by the pound had once caught him trying to sneak
a watermelon into his bag (*HL* 42). But if, as Long would later write,
he "hated" his work on the farm, he soon found employment both
more enjoyable and far better suited to his particular talents.[6] At fourteen, he secured a job peddling books on consignment from a Texas
book dealer. Though business at first was slow, he quickly discovered

6. Huey P. Long, *Every Man a King* (1933; reprint, Chicago: Quadrangle, 1964), 6;
Thomas O. Harris, *The Kingfish: Huey P. Long, Dictator* (1938; reprint, Baton Rouge:
Claitor's, 1968), 10; Beals, 30.

that he could attract more customers by singing and playing a mando-lin between sales (*HL* 33). He also proved a natural at public speaking. After he successfully carried a polling precinct during the 1908 Louisi-ana gubernatorial race, parish officials asked him to represent them at a debate against a traveling political lecturer (*HL* 43). The following year, his performance at a statewide debate competition earned him a scholarship to Louisiana State University (*HL* 38). It soon seemed that, even if he had wanted to, he could hardly avoid a future in politics: even before his eighteenth birthday, he had learned how to work a crowd and win a debate and was not far away from learning how to carry an election.

Because he never graduated high school (not, as he claims in *Every Man a King*, because the award was not generous enough), Long could not accept the scholarship to LSU. Instead, he took what would prove the fortunate route of leaving Winnfield for a career in traveling sales. His first position was with the N. K. Fairbank Company, a New Orleans concern known mostly for marketing Cottolene, a cotton-seed-oil-based lard substitute (*HL* 48). Required by the company to promote the product by way of bake-offs, Long was to name Rose McConnell, a young stenographer from Shreveport, the winner of one 1910 competition (*HL* 51). Less than three years later, he married her (*HL* 67). After his tenure at Fairbank, Long sold canned goods for the Houston Packing Company (*HL* 55), fruits and vegetables for the Dawson Produce Company (*HL* 58), and household starch for the Faultless Starch Company (*HL* 64). All, it seems, were legitimate concerns. Not so his next employer, the Chattanooga Medicine Com-pany. A manufacturer of what were clearly patent nostrums, the outfit attracted a *Journal of the American Medical Association* charge that its best-selling product, the Wine of Cardui, was a "vicious fraud." Os-tensibly for the relief of gynecological ills, its active ingredient was nothing more than forty-proof alcohol.[7] Though they certainly never made him rich—just barely kept him solvent, in fact—Long's years on the road were far from a waste of his time. In the end, he would earn himself the best training possible for a future in politics. He

7. Long, *Every Man*, 8; William Ivy Hair, *The Kingfish and His Realm: The Life and Times of Huey P. Long* (Baton Rouge: Louisiana State University Press, 1991), 51.

seems to have traveled every inch of Louisiana, to have met its every inhabitant, and, in the process, to have acquired a perhaps unprecedented knowledge of both. As he himself would later comment, he who would become a great statesman needs more than training in just politics and law. He also needs to know the people, what they need, and why they need it (*HL* 69). In addition to offering Long a way off the farm, then, his first four years in traveling sales afforded him something that would prove far more valuable: plenty of time to meet, talk with, and learn about those who, though he knew them at the time as but customers, he would one day be calling his constituents.

Between his stints at Houston Packing and Dawson Produce, Long began what later would become a more permanent vocation, the study of law. First, though, in accordance with his mother's desire that he enter the ministry, he moved to Shawnee, Oklahoma, home of the Oklahoma Baptist University seminary. He most likely never enrolled there (*HL* 57), however, for he almost immediately left for nearby Norman to study law at the University of Oklahoma (*HL* 61). Williams writes that if Long's record in his one year there was hardly stellar, he performed respectably for someone who spent more time on the road and in area gambling dens than in the classroom or law library (*HL* 62). Not for two more years, and only after his stints at Faultless Starch and the Chattanooga Medicine Company, would he begin to study law in earnest, and that would come only when his older brother Julius financed his first and only year at Tulane University Law School (*HL* 72). Thus also began one of the most persistent of the legends surrounding Long, the myth that finds him earning a law degree in record time. Basso, as have many, claims that Long accomplished the near-impossible, fulfilling the requirements of a three-year program in the span of a mere eight months. According to Williams, though, his academic record contradicts this claim and each of the hundreds, if not thousands, like it (*HL* 73). Lacking a high school diploma, Long was not eligible even to register for a degree program and therefore had to follow the path set for every "special" student in the same situation. Auditing the only two semesters allotted him, he supplemented his rare moments in the classroom with months of studying some sixteen to twenty hours a day for the orally administered bar exam available to any aspiring but degreeless lawyer (*HL* 74–75). He passed easily on his first attempt, and on May 15, 1915, was admitted to the Louisiana state bar (*HL* 79). The twenty-one-year-old had in no way completed a three-year law program—had completed no program at all, in fact—but he had achieved the nonetheless noteworthy distinction of winning admission to the state bar with remarkable speed, if not relative ease. As Robert Penn Warren—who would also perpetuate the myth of the eight-month degree—would comment, "*That's* first-class brains."[8]

Within months, though, Long would learn that even so estimable an accomplishment would not guarantee him success as an attorney. His caseload was initially so light and trifling that it left him almost as bored as broke, and he quickly found himself back on the road, this time peddling kerosene containers (*HL* 80–81). Not until he specialized in the relatively new area of workers' compensation law would his practice truly begin to prosper (*HL* 82–83). At the same time, his reputation began to change. No longer known only for traveling sales, he began to gain at least local renown for taking a stand against corporate interests in the name of the common laborer (*HL* 84). In 1916, his concern for such issues took him for the first time to the state legislature. There as the guest of a local senator trying to reform state policy, he found himself so angered by the sight of elected legislators essentially bowing down to corporate representatives that he stood up and, neither invited nor officially recognized, blasted the assembly for its unconscionable subservience. As he would later write, he found it "disgusting." The presumptuous young intruder, as one might imagine, only incensed the starchy legislators, but the exposure his views finally found would later force the legislature to rewrite workers' compensation laws to better favor the laborer (*HL* 111). Several years later, Long would assert that he had never taken a case against a poor man—his efforts as an attorney, he wrote, were always "on the side of the small man . . . the under-dog"[9]—and for the entirety of his career in the courtroom, he never did. He occasionally represented a corporation in one of the ever-present disputes over Louisiana oil and timber rights, but he never took their side against a poor man, in the end ar-

8. Basso, "Legend," 107; Ken Burns and Richard Kilberg, *Huey Long* (RKB/Florentine Films, 1987).

9. Long, *Every Man*, 25–28, 37.

guing far more cases for the underdog, more commonly drawing lines between himself and the corporations (*HL* 87–90).

Within a sentence or two of relating Long's first impressions of the legislature, Williams casts doubt on the details of his supposed reaction to it. Except for a matter of months, after all, Long had lived his entire life in Louisiana and therefore knew, as did all who could say the same, exactly who controlled state politics (*HL* 109). V. O. Key implies a similar assessment in *Southern Politics in State and Nation*. He writes that, at the time, state legislators were widely known to be puppets of an industrial oligarchy that, in conjunction with the New Orleans Old Regulars—the South's only political machine of note—had maintained open control of Louisiana politics since just after the Civil War. The root cause of Long's reaction, then, had been not discovering, but for the first time witnessing in person the machinations by which business and industry controlled—or, as Long was later to put it, had "brow-beaten, bulldozed, and intimidated"—the legislature to a degree unmatched in any other southern state. What made the Louisiana machine so uncommonly powerful, Key explains, is the fact that the state's geography left it prey to an unusually large combination of industrial interests. Most states have to contend with natural gas and electricity providers, for instance, but Louisiana also has to contend with the shipping, the sugar, the cotton, the lumber, and—largest and most powerful of all—the oil industry. In the end, the sheer strength of these corporations created a record of domination more unequivocal than that found anywhere else in the South.[10] Worse still is the fact that the combination of so much industrial power and the oligarchy's arrogant resistance to strengthening anything other than its own privilege left early-twentieth-century Louisiana stricken with poverty and plagued with a social system that, compared to those of other states, was "almost primitive." Louisiana ranked thirty-ninth out of the forty-eight states in average gross income, its 87,000 gainfully employed accounting for less than 2 percent of its total population. It claimed no one with an income exceeding $1 million a year, only one with an income exceeding $500,000, barely fifty with incomes eclipsing

10. V. O. Key, Jr., *Southern Politics in State and Nation* (New York: Vintage, 1949), 158–59; Long, *Every Man*, 57–58.

$100,000. On average, Louisianians grossed a mere $1,270 a year. The state ranked forty-seventh in literacy, with nearly 16 percent of its adult population classified illiterate. More than 14 percent of its rural white males had never completed the first grade, and 40 percent had never completed the fourth (*HL* 186–87). When Huey Long, then, less than two years after his brash attack on the state legislature, made a bid to enter the Louisiana political arena, he clearly knew not only the conditions he would have to improve, but whom his fight to do so would earn him as enemies.

That fight began in early 1918, when Long declared for the office of third-district railroad commissioner. By no means a high-profile position at the time, it was nonetheless what Williams describes as the perfect place for such a headstrong young newcomer (*HL* 120). Because former commissioners had concentrated more on ingratiating themselves with public utilities and transportation providers than on actually regulating them, the Railroad Commission, as William Ivy Hair describes it in *The Kingfish and His Realm,* was anything but an efficient or aggressive agency. The time was right, therefore, for Long to turn it into one. First, though, he would vitalize the way candidates campaigned for such positions. Instead of concentrating on larger cities, which he already knew would support his more urban-based opponent, he blanketed smaller towns and surrounding rural areas with letters and posted circulars (*HL* 122). He perfected what he called the "art" of driving close to the tallest trees and standing on top of his car to hammer campaign posters as far as possible beyond the reach of antagonistic hands.[11] He then applied his experience in traveling sales to a seemingly endless number of door-to-door calls, many of which came late at night, some even during the earliest hours of the morning. These visits, Williams writes, only sound counterproductive. The farmers who received them were not infuriated but flattered, inevitably went back to bed thinking more of themselves than they had when they had risen to answer Long's knock. Important politicians, after all, did not call on just anybody at such hours. As a result of what Williams calls "as imaginative a campaign as Louisiana had ever seen," the

11. Hair, 86; Long, *Every Man,* 75.

twenty-five-year-old Long, in November 1918, won election to his first public office (*HL* 123–25).

Once in that office, it seems he could hardly wait to strike out against the oil interests. Even as early as his third commission meeting, he introduced legislation to bring pipeline companies more firmly under commission control (*HL* 126). Shortly thereafter, he attempted to increase the tax for extracting natural resources from the ground or water (*HL* 144). Though more modest than some of his later attempts, these proposals marked the beginning of perhaps the most far-ranging war Long would ever wage, one that, during his tenure as commissioner alone, would earn him the ire of oil industry executives, fellow commissioners, several of Louisiana's more conservative legislators, even two successive governors (*HL* 127–39)—one of whom would charge him with two counts of criminal libel for alleging that Standard Oil pulled the strings of his administration (*HL* 150). Yet oil interests bore only the brunt of these proposals. Long also fought a telephone rate increase all the way to the U.S. Supreme Court (*HL* 168–71), in the process earning Chief Justice William Howard Taft's praise as perhaps the greatest legal mind he had ever encountered (*HL* 105). But in 1924, after he had lost his first bid for the Louisiana governorship, his reelection to the Public Service Commission—the Railroad Commission had been renamed in the interim—was to prove anticlimactic. For though he would occasionally fight such battles as the one to have the Lake Pontchartrain Causeway built without, rather than with, a toll (*HL* 227), his efforts more often addressed his future than his present. Nevertheless, in something less than a decade, he had reanimated the once-complacent commission and, more importantly, returned to Louisiana and Louisianians at least a portion of the resources they had for years been handing over to large corporations. At the same time, though, he had also given many the impression that he was doing so to further his interests more than theirs (*HL* 242), for in the process of so publicly reining in the corporations, he had also turned his name into a household word (*HL* 162)—one whose definition statewide increasingly read, a "courageous young reformer battling the forces of corporate greed" (*HL* 230). The "impertinent, smilingly reckless rough-neck," Davis writes, was beginning to emerge a "raw, sweaty St. George."[12]

Though ten years might amount to more time than he meant to spend in the position, his tenure as commissioner ultimately proved the stepping-stone to the governor's mansion he had all along intended (*HL* 120). But before he could begin the trip to Baton Rouge, he would have to attempt it twice. As noted above, Long lost his first bid for the governor's mansion in 1924, just before the end of his first term as commissioner. The weather, he explained, was one factor that had cost him the victory. Election-night rain had so thoroughly muddied un-paved country roads that his rural supporters had been unable to make it in to the polls. Williams, however, counters that this story is no more veracious than that surrounding his eight-month law degree. The rain did reduce his vote, but not decisively (*HL* 212). Williams explains that the loss was more likely Long's own fault, the result of his reluctance to take a stand on the campaign's most divisive issue, proposed legislation that would all but outlaw the Louisiana Ku Klux Klan (*HL* 208). Since Long considered all racial and religious issues distractions that only claimed time better spent solving economic problems and working to increase his now-burgeoning personal power, he had attempted to avoid the Klan issue altogether and in the end had sacrificed both the votes of those who took a firm stand on it and the gubernatorial race as a whole. In the state democratic primary—which, at that time, may as well have been the election itself—he placed third out of three candidates (*HL* 209–11).

Since interest in the issue had subsided when he entered the 1928 race (*HL* 246), Long's second campaign for governor looked much like his first. Beginning with printed circulars (*HL* 264), he followed with public speeches, delivering even more in 1928 than he had in 1924. Attempting to speak, it seems, to every potential voter on a tour unprecedented in scope, he traveled more than 15,000 miles to deliver some 600 speeches to an estimated 300,000 Louisianians (*HL* 265). His platform had changed little in the intervening years. At his campaign opener, he began with his now-familiar charge that the New Orleans

12. F. Davis, 64.

Old Regulars, in conjunction with a corrupt state legislature, were keeping Louisianians as poor, hungry, and illiterate as their ancestors had been. He then promised to wrench the state clear of their short-sighted, self-interested control and put it on par with the rest of the country. Among the measures this transformation would require, he explained, were free bridges, paved roads, and better hospitals, as well as free textbooks for school children, improved aid for farmers, and vocational training for the disabled (*HL* 262). Long expressed these concerns most memorably in what would become the most oft-quoted speech of the campaign, if not his entire career. Standing under the oak where Henry Wadsworth Longfellow's Evangeline waits in vain for the return of her lover Gabriel, Long intoned emotionally that "Evangeline is not the only one who has waited here in disappointment. Where are the schools that you have waited for your children to have, that have never come? Where are the roads and the highways that you send your money to build, that are no nearer now than ever before? Where are the institutions to care for the sick and disabled? Evangeline wept bitter tears in her disappointment, but it lasted through only one lifetime. Your tears in this country, around this oak, have lasted for generations. Give me the chance to dry the eyes of those who still weep here!"[13]

Voters did just that, and in unprecedented numbers. Though early returns overwhelmingly favored his urban-based opponents (*HL* 275), later tallies, upon their arrival from more distant rural areas, told a different story. In the end, Long would command the largest lead of any gubernatorial candidate in Louisiana history, carrying six of the state's eight congressional districts, forty-seven of its sixty-four parishes (*HL* 276). To the observant, the victory was hardly a surprise; it was, indeed, only the most recent indication of a movement that had begun as many as ten years earlier, when, during Long's first term as railroad commissioner, the long-dispossessed Louisiana masses had begun to awaken. They had moved slowly at first, and unsurely, Williams insists, but they were, at last, awakening—for "suddenly a champion had appeared to them, one who promised to lead them to a better life, one who, even if he did nothing else, would give them vicariously the exciting

13. Long, *Every Man*, 99.

satisfaction of insulting the great ones who ignored them." Long, in short, was "a man for the masses to follow" (*HL* 152). And follow him they did, first to the polls, then, by special invitation, to his inaugural celebration in Baton Rouge. Even amid the pomp and pageantry of inauguration day in the capital city, Long made sure his rural supporters there by special invitation did not feel out of place. Davis, who seems to have witnessed the scene first-hand, offers us the most detailed description of it:

> The inauguration was not genteel. Huey had invited the people. They came by special train, by motor car, by mule wagon and afoot. Fifteen thousand of them swarmed through the streets of horrified Baton Rouge; backwoodsmen, in to see one of their own elevated to the seats of the mighty. The men wore galluses, over their Sunday shirts, and black felt hats in the May heat; the women sunbonnets. They were quietly arrogant, impressed by the magnificence of the occasion to which they had been bidden as honored participants. Huey, with backwoods aforethought, saw that there were frequent water buckets around the Capitol—with tin dippers. He had a large, outdoor dance pavilion with country musicians as well as the jazz band he preferred. He wanted them to feel at home. The Governor's reception was reminiscent of that March day in 1829 when the people climbed on the damask chairs, carried mud into the formal chambers and drank whiskey out of barrels at the White House to rejoice with their champion, Andy Jackson.

As Harnett T. Kane, another contemporary authority, was to put it, Long's victory marked the beginning of nothing less than a revolution for the state's previously disinherited lower classes, those who, more than any other demographic, could claim credit for his trip to Baton Rouge. Harris put it more poetically: "Like the setting sun, the Old Order had vanished from view; the New Order, the rising sun, was shining in the political firmament. No Governor of Louisiana ever began his term more strongly fortified with public confidence, or with greater auguries of success, than Huey Pierce Long."[14] The meek may not have inherited the earth, but in 1928 they had at least inherited Louisiana.

14. F. Davis, 96; Kane, 59; Harris, 34.

As much as his enemies would hate to admit it, Long's accomplishments as governor would be undeniably impressive. His social programs expanded and improved charity hospitals in Shreveport and New Orleans to such an extent that the latter could increase its daily patient load from 1,600 to 3,800 and at the same time reduce its death rate by 30 percent (*HL* 546–47). He accomplished even more for education. In addition to fulfilling his campaign promise to provide free textbooks to school children, Long wrought nothing short of a renaissance at LSU, expanding its physical plant, enlarging its faculty, and financing its new medical school, in the end turning a regional institution with a C accreditation rating into a national institution with an A rating (*HL* 513–19). In response to Louisiana's literacy problem, Long established night schools for adults of all races, and as more than 100,000 enrolled during the first year alone, the state illiteracy rate dropped from 10 to 7 percent among whites and from 38 to 23 percent among African Americans (*HL* 523). He strengthened the state's infrastructure still more tangibly. Baton Rouge received a new capitol building, a thirty-four-story skyscraper to replace the capitol Mark Twain once derided as "the monstrosity on the Mississippi," and New Orleans received natural gas service (*HL* 302), a refurbished waterfront (*HL* 425), and one of the largest airports in the country (*HL* 546). The achievement for which Long most remains known benefited the state's outlying areas as well. According to what Williams asserts are the most generous estimates, Louisiana had only 296 miles of concrete roads, 35 miles of asphalt roads, and 5,728 miles of gravel roads when Long took office in 1928 (*HL* 303). Just four years later, as a result of the largest road construction program in the South, the state could boast an additional 1,583 miles of concrete roads, 718 miles of asphalt roads, and 2,816 miles of gravel roads—as well as 111 new bridges. Long's work crew was the largest in America (*HL* 546), employing some 10 percent of the men involved in such projects nationwide (*HL* 547). Somewhat less tangibly, Long's projects brought far more widespread benefits to Louisiana as a whole, for when one recognizes that his term as governor fell during the worst years of the Great Depression, one also realizes that, were it not for Huey Long, Louisiana would likely have had to go without more than just improved educational programs, a new capitol building, and new roads and bridges. "[E]xcept for [its] being a part of the United States," Long once crowed, Louisiana "would never have known a depression."[15]

Yet even while involved in such a dramatic transformation of the state and its leadership, Long often made sure to remind his rural supporters that, regardless of the name he might make for himself for pulling Louisiana out of the mud, he was not far removed from that mud himself, was still in fact what he always had been. His nickname, "the Kingfish," appropriated from a character on the blackface radio show *Amos 'n' Andy* (*HL* 312), went a long way toward that end, but his most successful effort to identify himself with the poor was his promotion of "potlikker," the rural southern staple he found not only "the noblest dish the mind of man has yet conceived" but just what Depression-shriveled stomachs and pocketbooks needed, a dish as nutritious as it is inexpensive. The *Atlanta Constitution* was one of the loudest to agree, and in a lead editorial published his personal recipe for the dish. Editors took issue, however, with his advice as to how one should eat one particular side dish with it. Long stipulated that true connoisseurs dunk their corn pone—their corn bread—in potlikker; editors asserted that they crumble it. Thus began the so-called corn pone–potlikker controversy, which, after an increasingly outlandish debate between Long and *Constitution* editors, first assumed national, then international proportions. So many Americans divided themselves into separate dunkers and crumblers camps that New York governor Franklin Delano Roosevelt—a crumbler, of course—suggested settling the debate by way of the platform committee at the 1932 Democratic National Convention (*HL* 438–39). News of the clash even reached France, where readers followed "*la controverse cornpone*" in Paris newspapers.[16] All, of course, was in fun, but in addition to promoting affordable nutrition at a time when America most needed it, Long garnered a good deal of valuable publicity. To the nation—indeed, to the world—he had become, as Williams put it, "a likeable fellow, a little comic perhaps, but kindly, interested in people's welfare, and extremely entertaining" (*HL* 439).

15. David Zinman, *The Day Huey Long Was Shot: September 8, 1935,* rev. ed. (Jackson: University Press of Mississippi), 6; Long, *Every Man,* 334.

16. Kane, 141; Hair, 212.

Long attracted similar attention, though in no way so lighthearted or positive, for his 1930 reception of Lothar von Arnauld de la Periere, commander of the visiting German cruiser *Emden*. He received the dignified official much as he received many visitors: not at the capitol or governor's mansion, but in his suite at the Roosevelt Hotel in New Orleans, where, in fact, he conducted a good deal of state business. As was also common, he was hardly attired for the occasion. Not only not dressed formally but clad in green pajamas, a red and blue bathrobe, and blue bedroom slippers, Long, in the words of one reporter present, looked like "an explosion in a paint factory" (*HL* 430). What followed would fall just short of becoming an international incident, one prevented only when Long agreed to appease the German consul in New Orleans—who had stormed into state offices shouting, "My country has been insulted. . . . I demand an apology"—by dressing more appropriately and paying a reciprocal visit on board the *Emden* as soon as he could assemble the proper wardrobe (*HL* 431). The incident would supply Long's more conservative observers with considerable ammunition, but as Williams writes, his rural followers loved the mere thought of their champion insulting such a proper German official. Knowing exactly what their reaction would be, Long even joked that he no longer had a future in Winn Parish—not because of the way he had received the commander, but because he had revealed to people back home that he slept in pajamas, an affectation, no doubt, to his pine-hill loyal. Indeed, Long had been known to receive the occasional visitor while wearing nothing at all (*HL* 432). Temperamentally, if no longer geographically, he was still the rural Louisianian he always had been, and he was more than willing to draw the further fire of critics to make sure his rural supporters hadn't forgotten it.

In the eyes of his detractors, such gaffes were only the most innocuous of the black marks Long's record as governor would accumulate. One of the earliest had come when, less than a year after inauguration, he had begun grumbling about the condition of the governor's mansion. To conservatives a fabled symbol of a still more fabled past, the mansion was to Long little more than a termite-infested eyesore. When outraged antagonists argued that governor after governor had lived there in perfect comfort, Long compared them to the boarding-house matron who, after listening to a roomer's grousing about a dirty towel, had replied, "Why, there's been a hundred men used that towel before you, and not one of them has complained." Listening less and less patiently to requests to have it restored, he soon called in a crew from the state penitentiary to raze the beloved structure. "The upper classes were horrified," Williams writes; "the old house that had harbored great governors was gone," and "great traditions were gone with it, torn down by jailbirds" (*HL* 335). The mansion had earlier been the scene of yet another scandal, this one surrounding Alice Lee Grosjean, the attractive young secretary twelve years Long's junior who had signed on with his gubernatorial campaign staff in 1923 (*HL* 254–55). Over the next several years, rumors would take her to be much more than just his secretary (*HL* 317), and the quarters he set up for her in the mansion itself would do little to discourage such talk. Neither would his wife Rose's reaction: According to Hair, when Alice Lee moved in, Rose moved out, returning only when Long moved Alice Lee into the nearby Heidelberg Hotel. Yet when Long too began spending most of his nights at the Heidelberg, Rose left again, this time to return only on ceremonial occasions.[17] Regardless of the fact that, as Williams concludes, an affair between Long and Grosjean— whom he would later install as his secretary of state—is all but impossible to substantiate (*HL* 318), there was evidence enough in the eyes of many to brand their new governor an adulterer.

The charge Long would face still more frequently concerned his specifically political indiscretions. When power was the issue, all other considerations were beginning to go by the wayside. Little else seemed to matter. According to Williams, it would soon become clear that Long's primary objective, in almost every act, had been amassing as much power as possible (*HL* 293). In order to ensure himself not just ascendancy, but absolute supremacy in Louisiana, he had engaged in everything from the merely questionable to the egregiously illegal. He had forced appointees to sign undated resignations (*HL* 294); he had pried into private lives to fuel future blackmail (*HL* 351); he had bullied state lawmakers during legislative sessions supposedly closed to him. Defending the latter, he had once growled, "I'd rather violate every one of the damn conventions and see my bills passed than sit back in my

17. Beals, 156; Hair, 168.

office, all nice and proper, and watch 'em die" (*HL* 298). Harris uses LSU as a metaphor to illustrate the stranglehold these practices soon wrought on the commonwealth. Long's record at LSU, he writes, parallels his record in the state. He resurrected both, but not without tyrannizing them. At LSU, he intervened in the hiring and firing of faculty, dictated to the university president, adapted academic policy to fit his own objectives, stifled university journals, and distributed jobs and contracts according to his own agenda. Allan P. Sindler, in *Huey Long's Louisiana: State Politics, 1920–1952*, corroborates Harris's assessment, concluding that while Long initiated programs to solve an array of problems, he saw only one through to full execution: his effort to establish and maintain what many have called an American dictatorship. And Long's own words only corroborate the assessment. A state senator, enraged by losing an argument to him, once heaved a book at him after a debate. "Maybe you've heard of this book," he foamed. "It's the Constitution of the State of Louisiana." Long, unfazed, replied, "I'm the Constitution around here now."[18]

In 1929, responding to just such power-mad displays, an anti-Long faction of the Louisiana legislature attempted to impeach him. Though he had been governor only a year, hardly enough time, it would seem, to commit so many offenses, that one year had been enough for him to create at least the suspicion of "high crimes and misdemeanors in office," of "incompetency, corruption, favoritism, oppression," and of "gross misconduct." Specifically, the initial resolution accused him of tampering with the state judiciary; attempting to bribe state legislators; forcing appointees to sign undated resignations; illegally dispersing state funds; firing and intimidating school officials; pillaging private property via the state militia; carrying concealed weapons; using abusive language to state officials and private citizens; engaging in immoral behavior at a New Orleans night club; intimidating a political rival; demolishing the former governor's mansion; interfering with the state legislature; and ordering a rival's murder (*HL* 361–62). After nearly a month of testimony (*HL* 371), prosecutors unearthed evidence enough to try him on eight somewhat modified

18. Harris, 157; Allan P. Sindler, *Huey Long's Louisiana: State Politics, 1920–1952* (Baltimore: Johns Hopkins University Press, 1956), 107; F. Davis, 98.

charges: attempting to intimidate a political rival; attempting to bribe state legislators; interfering with the firing of state officials; paying a construction company for work known to be defective; and three counts of misusing state funds. In addition, legislators tacked on a "catch-all" addressing charges that he had required signed, undated resignations of appointees; verbally abused private citizens; illegally fired a college president; knowingly appointed corrupt officials; and demonstrated that he was generally incompetent and psychologically unsuitable for the office (*HL* 380). In the estimation of the accused, however, the charges were about as creditable as those of "highly intelligent animals temporarily bereft of reason and milling about." Even the "most trivial and untoward incident," he scoffed, would have made them "run amuck." Be that as it may, the House, by a tally of fifty-eight to forty, voted to impeach him (*HL* 382). But in taking a full month to do so, prosecutors gave Long more than enough time to make sure the Senate would not do the same. When away from the hearings, he and his lieutenants had often been working to secure the support of fifteen senators—one more than the fourteen needed to quash the indictment—all of whom would affirm that, because of unspecified irregularities and the fact that many of the charges failed to address impeachable offenses, they would not vote to impeach (*HL* 396–97). Upon revelation of what came to be called the Round Robin—the document bearing the resolution and the signatures—during the latter half of the trial, the Senate had no choice but to adjourn *sine die*, leaving Long free to resume his term as governor. The final irony, of course, lies in the fact that, to enlist the fifteen senators' support, Long had had to engage in some of the very crimes their signatures would assert he had never committed. According to Hair, he had used both patronage and, if that did not work, outright threats, to make sure the fifteen senators signed.[19]

Within three years of winning and less than a year and a half of reasserting his rights to the gubernatorial throne, Long announced plans to leave it for the U.S. Senate, third of his four planned stops between Winnfield and the White House. There was, however, something of a catch. Because he refused to leave Louisiana in the hands

19. Beals, 117; Hair, 180–86.

of his lieutenant governor (*HL* 460), he would not be able to assume senatorial duties until four months into the next session. Critics asked if he would not be denying Louisiana its full representation; Long shot back that the seat would not be any emptier than it had been for the previous thirty-two years (*HL* 461). Despite the fact that he was campaigning for a federal rather than a state office, his platform remained essentially what it had been, as he summarized it in a speech during yet another statewide stump tour: "if you believe that Louisiana is to be ruled by the people, that the poor man is as good as the rich man, that the people have a right to pass on issues themselves; if you believe that this is a state where every man is a king but no man wears a crown, then I want you to vote for Huey Long for the United States Senate. That is the platform I am running on" (*HL* 467). Though this is hardly a platform at all, the vote it generated looked much like that of its predecessors. Yet in addition to the strong rural response Long always inspired, the urban response was stronger than it had ever been before (*HL* 480), so strong, in fact, that the Old Regulars, watching as Long encroached upon what had traditionally been their territory, saw no other option but to join forces with him (*HL* 481–83). In addition to confirming his control over the governor's mansion, then, Long's election to the U.S. Senate brought with it both the customary seat on Capitol Hill and control over what for decades had been Louisiana's most powerful political ring. Just sixteen months after dodging impeachment, Huey Long had become, in Hair's assessment, "the virtually unquestioned boss of Louisiana."[20]

Thus his senatorial debut some three months later: on January 25, 1932, when he strutted into the U.S. Senate to take the oath of office, he did so with an air less befitting a U.S. senator-elect than an underworld politico. Despite long-standing rules to the contrary, he puffed on a huge cigar that, just before he took the oath, he deposited on the desk of the Democratic minority leader. As the *New York Times* lamented, "the Terror of the Bayous" had not been in Senate chambers even an hour before he had broken its every rule of storied decorum. At first, however, his fellow senators would not have to endure many such performances, for he would miss 81 of the 137 days in his first

20. Hair, 207.

legislative session. And Williams implies that even on the fifty-six days he was actually on the floor, his colleagues more than likely wished him elsewhere. Because the Senate, to Long, was little more than a platform from which he could pitch his pet concerns—and, of course, promote himself—as far as possible beyond the borders of Louisiana (*HL* 560), he took little interest in any business other than his own (*HL* 556). As he would later assert in *Every Man a King*, "I had come to the United States Senate with only one project in mind, which was that by every means of action and persuasion I might do something to spread the wealth of the land among all of the people."[21] During an otherwise unrelated debate just after his arrival, in fact, he had seized control of the Senate floor to declare the Great Depression the result of only a single cause: the fact that so few Americans controlled so much of the country's wealth (*HL* 557). His colleagues, as would increasingly become the case, showed nothing even approximating interest. Even when he began formulating a concrete plan to redistribute the nation's wealth, the Senate summarily defeated its consideration, needing nothing more formal than a voice vote to do so. According to Williams, however, Long was more than satisfied with the effort. It may have met with decisive defeat on Capitol Hill, but he had augmented more than ever before his increasingly national reputation as the champion of the underdog, the enemy of the privileged (*HL* 560–62).

Since the American masses would welcome his ideas more warmly than their representatives had, Long would become, during his years as U.S. senator, one of the most powerful elected officials in the country. Not even the outcry of August 1933—when an intoxicated Long was roughed up at Long Island's Sands Point Bath and Country Club for allegedly urinating on a patron instead of in the urinal in front of him (*HL* 649–51)—would fully diminish the public's enthusiasm for what came to be called Share Our Wealth. Influenced by everything from the ancient Hebrew practice of periodically forgiving debts to the populist and socialist leanings of 1900s Winn Parish (*HL* 76–77, 116–17), his plans finally found their true audience when, on February 23, 1934, he launched his Share Our Wealth Society in a coast-to-coast

---

21. Hair, 234; Long, *Every Man*, 290.

radio broadcast. Taking the William Jennings Bryan phrase "Every Man a King" as its slogan (*HL* 692), the program was composed primarily of ideas Long had been injecting into Senate debates for the previous two years. Its central provisions called for a plan by which the federal government—because, as Long saw it, no American family should own or earn more than three hundred times the average— would tax any family owning more than five million, or earning more than one million, dollars a year. The government would then so evenly distribute the revenue generated that every American family could own a home, an automobile, and "ordinary conveniences" worth no less than five thousand dollars combined and would earn no less than two thousand dollars per year, one-third of the national average (*HL* 693). America's response to the program was unprecedented. Between the night of the inaugural radio address and the end of the following month, the Share Our Wealth Society enlisted more than 200,000 members; by the end of the next year, it would claim more than 3,000,000 (*HL* 700). And America nearly buried Long in letters: an average of 60,000 a week by April 1935, more than 30,000 a day for each of the twenty-four days following one particular speech (*HL* 698). By Hair's accounting, however, these numbers are something less than surprising, for in an era when nearly half the nation's families had to subsist on less than $1,250 a year, who wouldn't support a program that promised nearly twice that sum? To put these figures in perspective, he calculates that if Long had introduced Share Our Wealth in 1990, the home allowance alone, to match his 1934 proposal of $5,000, would have been set as high as $50,000. If introduced in 2004, the figure would probably have climbed beyond $60,000. In light of these figures, perhaps the most surprising fact is that the program failed to create more of a sensation than it did. In the end, though, Long's proposals may well have been little more than cheap appeals to public need. Recent researchers have calculated that the plan could not have generated the sums promised, and Hair doubts that Long even proposed it in earnest. As one of his closest associates would later divulge, Share Our Wealth was little more than a scheme "to get attention"— was, in short, nothing more than "a lot of bullshit." Even the most generous observer has to admit that Long's figures never quite assumed final form and that the project as a whole was grossly lacking in detail.

Earnestly proposed or not, the plan attracted considerable attention both at home and abroad. According to an April 1935 tally, the 27,431 Share Our Wealth clubs in the United States and Canada could boast a combined membership of more than 7,682,000—a force Long planned to muster, of course, to spearhead his next move, that from Capitol Hill to the White House.[22]

More than those from any other chapter in his life, the physical characteristics Long exhibited as senator are those posterity continues to attribute to him. When we hear the name Huey Long today, we think less frequently of the thirty-year-old than the forty-year-old, less frequently of the 160-pound "gangling young hick" of a gubernatorial candidate than the 200-pound "all-wool-and-a-yard-wide Kingfish" (*HL* 200, 267). After being ushered into Long's Capitol Hill offices in the mid-1930s, Davis recorded the following first impressions:

> His skin was ruddy, speckled with tiny spots of pigment. I got an impression of jowls which a closer observation did not confirm. His nose stands out, a comic feature broadened into a slight bulb, long and tilted at the tip. . . . Huey's nose is neither so great as Cyrano's as represented by Walter Hampden, nor is it hooked in the Durante pattern. It is, nevertheless, a considerable nose, which, quite likely, embarrassed Huey as a child and may, although I have consulted no psychiatrist on the point, account for his well-known aversion to trading punches with exasperated opponents. The nose would make a conspicuous target.
>
> With another nose, the Senator would be what is known as a handsome man. His hair is chestnut colored, crisply curly, and the forelock that he shakes at opponents in debate and audiences on the stump has a decided wave. His eyes are round, large, dark, eager and comprehending. The irregular contour of his face, his cheek muscles having been enlarged by oratory, might pass for rugged- ness. He has the orator's wide, loose mouth. . . . In caricature, he resembles Babe Ruth.

Recent Hollywood casting directors would seem to have agreed: the same actor, John Goodman, played Babe Ruth in the 1992 feature *The*

22. Hair, 270–72.

Babe and Huey Long in the 1995 made-for-cable movie *Kingfish: A Story of Huey P. Long*. Long's wardrobe was even more distinctive. Though a white linen suit was something of a trademark for him at one point (*HL* 267), he often tried to tastefully combine something beyond a white jacket, white shirt, and white slacks—and usually failed. To those who knew him well, the green pajamas, red and blue bathrobe, and blue bedroom slippers that greeted the commander of the *Emden* were anything but out of character. Long, it seems, often looked like "an explosion in a paint factory." Invited to dine with the Franklin Delano Roosevelts after the 1932 Democratic National Convention, he showed up in an outfit that Williams describes as atrocious even by Long's standards: a patterned sports jacket, an orchid shirt, and a pink tie. So stunned was Roosevelt's mother that, at one point during the meal, she whispered to those seated near her, "Who is that *awful* man sitting on my son's right?" (*HL* 602). By all contemporary accounts, though, Long hardly needed to dress so shockingly to attract attention. He had what one observer termed the "kindlin' power," the magnetism to mesmerize and, simply by stepping into view, to translate to all those around him his seemingly boundless energy (*HL* 417). He never seemed to stand completely still, Williams writes. "Some part of him was always in motion." Even when more or less at rest, he would gesticulate with his hands and shoulders, rock back and forth on the balls of his feet, scratch after some fugitive itch (*HL* 200). Another observer wrote that "everything about [him] is exaggerated; his voice is too loud . . . his gestures too sweeping, his sudden movements of earnestness too fanatical, his commands too noisy." Still another commented that on the stump he had a "freewheeling" body. His head, his hair, his arms—"everything would move in a different direction" (*HL* 266). His performances on Capitol Hill were no more restrained. Davis writes that on the Senate floor he "quiver[ed] with energy, creating a pool of restlessness about himself." Arms "a-flail" and face "contorted," he cast a "frenzied figure" during debates. He had an "animal quality." For all he knew, Davis confesses, Huey Long might have had the devil in him.[23]

---

23. F. Davis, 24–26; Raymond Gram Swing, "Forerunner of American Fascism," in *Huey Long*, ed. Hugh Davis Graham, Great Lives Observed (Englewood Cliffs: Prentice-Hall, 1970), 92.

Of all the charges Long drew during his tenure in the Senate, one of the most incessant found him expending too much of that energy in Baton Rouge, not enough of it in Washington. In response to one such complaint—a fellow senator's charge that missing 81 of one's first 137 legislative days was "indefensible"—Long maintained that he had been away on "very important business" of state as well as nation. In truth, however, the business that so often called him away was less important to either than to the senator himself. More often than not, it concerned his efforts to make sure that, while its chief engineer was away in Washington, his political machine continued both to gain ground and gather speed. Before leaving for Capitol Hill, he had secured the election of O. K. Allen, his hand-picked successor, as governor, as well as those of his preferred legislative candidates in an unprecedented fifty-four of Louisiana's sixty-four parishes (*HL* 539). That did not mean, however, that he was ready to leave the state in their hands. As Hair writes, even though Long occupied a federal rather than a state office, he continued to command so much control over Louisiana that even the title "governor" became meaningless. Indeed, one of the most oft-repeated pieces of Long lore has it that while he was away in Washington, Long browbeat his puppet governor into such submission that when a leaf blew across Allen's desk one day, he signed it. He treated the legislature no less dictatorially. He called special sessions whenever he pleased and, invading at whim and bullying both House and Senate, he suspended the rules and simply rammed bills through to passage, often without letting legislators even read them (*HL* 727). Raymond Gram Swing, author of *Forerunners of American Fascism* (1935), described one 1934 session as follows:

> Huey Long is ubiquitous. Now at the Speaker's chair for whispered consultation, now on the floor, he speaks to this man and that, then in the aisles, laughing, shouting, gesticulating. His loud voice is easily heard over the din. He is in a boisterous humor. As United States Senator he had no business there, no official status. The technicality occurs to no one. Why should it? This is Huey's Statehouse, Huey's legislature, Huey's state, his and his alone. The business proceeds; Long answers a question from the floor, he grins and waves his arms, he struts and grimaces with eyes protruding,

face flushed. He is like a young father on a romp in the nursery. Anyone can see how much fun it is being dictator. Six years ago a Louisiana legislature nearly impeached him. Now see where he is: he has more power in one state than ever a man in American history; he is stronger than a king.

In seven of these sessions between August 1934 and September 1935, the state legislature passed more than 225 bills, 44 of them during a single five-day session (*HL* 6). While many proposed taxes to support Long's ever-expanding slate of social programs (*HL* 661), many were not so ostensibly altruistic. Several, in fact, were what Williams asserts were blatantly shameless power grabs. One in particular granted the governor all authority to call out the state militia whenever he deemed necessary—not just in cases of widespread crisis—and at the same time denied state courts all power to challenge that authority (*HL* 726). Long framed these bills for one reason only, Williams asserts: to increase the state's power over localities and the administration's power over what few foes were left standing—or, in other words, to still further augment the personal power of Huey P. Long (*HL* 738). As he himself once boasted, "I control the legislature like a deck of cards, and I will deal it to suit myself."[24]

According to three writers who watched him at work, Long dealt still more—the whole state, in fact—to suit himself. Kane writes that by the time of his tenure in the U.S. Senate, Long directly controlled more people than, and had amassed as much power as, any other single figure in American history:

> He possessed the state government, the Governor, the university, all commissions and departments; the Legislature, the public schools, the treasury, the buildings, and the Louisianians inside them. The courts were his, except in isolated instances, and he had the highest judges. He had a secret police which did anything he asked: kidnapped men, held them incommunicado, inquired without check into private matters of opponents. He ran the elections. He counted the votes. He disqualified any man or woman whom he wanted disqualified. He could order the addition to the rolls of

24. Hair, 234, 240–41; Swing, 91–92; Beals, 94.

any number of voters that his judgment dictated. He was becoming local government in Louisiana. The officials of no town or city were secure. Let a brother or an uncle offend, and Huey would have a mayor or an alderman out of a job and his own man appointed in his place. He was reaching into local police affairs; he was controlling municipal finances by new boards. He could ruin a community by cutting off its taxes, preventing it from adopting substitutes, and then forcing new obligations to break its back. He was moving in upon the parish district attorneys. . . .

Hodding Carter corroborates Kane's claim, its latter half in particular. "It should be repeated," he writes, "that no public officeholder, no teacher, no fire chief or fireman, no police chief or policeman, no day laborer on state projects held his job except in fee simple to the machine." In the end, as Harris puts it, Senator Long was nothing less than the "owner of Louisiana in fee simple, with all reversionary rights and hereditaments, in full trust and benefit, to have and to hold, in paramount estate and freehold, for the balance of his days."[25]

Long was never to bluster or manipulate his way to such dominance on the national level, though, for outside Louisiana he had to contend not only with a Senate whose members mostly found him a nuisance, but with the only politician he considered his equal (*HL* 7), Franklin Delano Roosevelt. Though Long had fought hard to win Roosevelt the White House, had played a pivotal role in securing him the nomination, later even campaigning for him in a number of midwestern states (*HL* 603), Roosevelt was no sooner in office than Long began to bait him, and neither quietly nor just in private. His primary charge was that the new president had reneged on campaign promises (*HL* 631), particularly those concerning his ostensible support of Long's plan to redistribute national wealth. Roosevelt, however, was no O. K. Allen, and instead of acquiescing to Long's harassment and demands, countered by rerouting all Louisiana-bound federal patronage out of Long's hands and into those of his remaining enemies (*HL* 636–38). But as the Long machine was self-supporting and could easily survive without federal funds, Long's vilification of Roosevelt only in-

25. Kane, 128–29; Hodding Carter, "American Dictator," in Graham, 109; Harris, 166.

tensified, eventually winning him an unexpected visit from more than fifty Treasury agents sent to investigate his and his cronies' tax returns (*HL* 797). Illegalities uncovered among even his lesser lieutenants' calculations drew a handful of federal grand jury indictments (*HL* 798), and according to Elmer Irey, head of the Internal Revenue Service at the time, a case against Long himself—"the greatest 'confidence' man [of] the century," as Irey saw it—would soon be forthcoming. At the same time, however, the 1936 presidential election was drawing near, and Roosevelt was growing more concerned about national battles than personal skirmishes. Threatened by Long's ever-expanding power base, even seeing him as a burgeoning fascist who, if the New Deal did not soon take flight, might rise to still further incite the nation's poor and unemployed (*HL* 795), the president conducted an impromptu poll to gauge his rival's potential. What he found was that Long, whom he had come to consider "one of the two most dangerous men in America"—Douglas MacArthur, incidentally, was the other—could very likely accomplish what he had so often threatened (*HL* 845). Long's plan, in short, was to found a separate Share Our Wealth party, nominate an expendable candidate to represent it—which, in splitting the Democratic vote, would throw the election to the Republican candidate, effectively ousting Roosevelt—and then, in 1940, after America had fallen victim to what he reasoned would be an inevitably deeper depression, attempt to secure himself the White House (*HL* 843–44). And "when I get in," Long told Davis, "I'm going to abolish the Electoral College [and institute] universal suffrage, and I defy any sonofabitch to get me out [in] under four terms."[26] The sitting president, as one might imagine, found the possibility more than just a little unsettling (*HL* 845).

The battle between Long and Roosevelt would end there, however, as would all of Long's battles save one—for on September 8, 1935, at the beginning of yet another hastily called legislative session, Long engaged his final opponent. Before the session, Judge Benjamin Pavy had presided over Louisiana's thirteenth judicial district for more than two and a half decades, a term toward the end of which he had emerged one of Long's fiercest adversaries. After the session, Pavy's career was

26. Graham, 60, 110; Sindler, 106; F. Davis, 23–24.

all but over, the victim of a gerrymander Long had set in motion only a couple of hours before (*HL* 861–62). Just what happened afterward, as Long made his way out of the state capitol, remains a matter of more debate. In *The Day Huey Long Was Shot*, David Zinman explains that after Long left Allen's first-floor offices, he encountered a man later identified as twenty-nine-year-old Carl Austin Weiss, a Baton Rouge ear, nose, and throat surgeon and, more significantly, Judge Pavy's son-in-law. During the inquest that followed, one eyewitness testified that it first looked as if Weiss intended only to shake the senator's hand. Long's bodyguards, however, saw the pistol—but not in time to keep Weiss from firing it. While Long made his exit, with a bullet wound some six inches above his waistline, his bodyguards, in the space of a mere six seconds, fired more than sixty shots into his assailant. The young doctor, of course, was dead before he hit the floor. Soon thereafter, Long underwent surgery to repair entry and exit wounds to his colon. But a few hours later he began showing signs of internal hemorrhaging, and subsequent tests revealed a kidney wound overlooked during surgery. Considering his declining condition, doctors decided that any attempt to repair it would be too risky, and Long died a short time later, in the early morning hours of September 10.[27]

When his body was driven back to capitol grounds the next day, it was for the last time. It would never leave them again. His casket was placed atop a black-draped platform in the capitol building's Memorial Hall, just footsteps from the spot where, three days earlier, the fatal shot had been fired. His body was to lie in state there for more than twenty-four hours while an unbroken line of followers filed by to pay their last respects. As Zinman describes the scene, "Lines stretched for blocks. Hour by hour, the vast multitude filed by. . . . Negro and white, rich and poor, men and women, and everywhere Huey's loyal Unwashed that poured out of the hills and bayous. Red necks from north Louisiana and Cajuns from the south. They showed up in dusty overalls, ill-fitting Sunday clothes, rubbing shoulders with city folk in tailored suits. . . . They passed in a never-ending stream." In the end, more than 22,000 people would view the body. They would adorn Memorial Hall with so many flowers that it would take a deputized con-

27. Zinman, 4–5, 9, 115–18, 152–72.

tingent of sixty men more than an hour to remove them. The funeral that followed on September 12 was the biggest and best-attended Louisiana had ever seen, better attended even than those of Jefferson Davis and P. G. T. Beauregard. In his eulogy, delivered by the open grave in the capitol's sunken garden, the Reverend Gerald L. K. Smith addressed a crowd estimated at more than 175,000. The former Share Our Wealth strategist told mourners that "[t]his place marks not the resting place of Huey Long" but "only the burial place for his body." The spirit of Huey Long "shall never rest," Smith intoned, "as long as hungry bodies cry for food, as long as human frames stand naked, as long as homeless wretches haunt this land of plenty."[28]

Less than two months later, Sinclair Lewis inadvertently proved Smith correct: Long's spirit, indeed, was still among the living. Finding Berzelius Windrip something less than completely original, early readers of *It Can't Happen Here* charged Lewis with casting a thinly veiled version of Long as his novel's primary antagonist. Similar assertions followed, so many, it seems, that authors casting the Kingfish in later roles learned not only to expect such charges but to try to circumvent them before their readers could even issue them. The first sentences one finds in Langley's *A Lion Is in the Streets*, for instance, assert that "[t]his novel is fiction and intended as such. It does not refer to real characters or to actual events. Any likeness to characters either living or dead is purely coincidental." As Hamilton Basso sees it, though, all such disclaimers are disingenuous at best, all such likenesses something more than coincidental. The most forthright of the authors examined here, Basso forgoes all disclaimers in *Cinnamon Seed* and *Sun in Capricorn* and, in "The Huey Long Legend"—the *Life* magazine article that would so anger Russell Long—openly places "my own *Sun in Capricorn*" among the four most recent works to take up "what has come to be called the Huey Long story." Dos Passos, Langley, and Warren, authors of the only other novels he cites, may as well admit the same, he implies, for though all three deny that they adopted elements from the same story, it is "hard to see" how they could have done anything else. "To burlesque the point," Basso continues, "it is as if a group of

28. Zinman, 185–90; Hair, 325.

authors wrote about a small, dark man (or a large, fair one) who lived at a place called Montebello (or Cellograndi), founded an institution of learning known as the Academy of Charlottesville (or the College of Albemarle) and composed a document known as the 'Invitation to Independence' (or 'The Declaration of Freedom'), but who was not Thomas Jefferson." A rose of any other size, shape, or color—or by any other name, of course—would still smell like Huey Long, he implies. A few pages later, Basso turns his attention to *All the King's Men* in particular and introduces a more delicately shaded argument. He writes that while Warren's frequent assertions that Willie Stark was never intended to represent Huey Long may be true, it is also true that "once a writer begins to write about these Hueys-who-aren't-Hueys, the real Huey jumps up and clings to his back like the old man of the sea." Authorial intent, he implies, is irrelevant in this regard, for though the fiction that results may truly be "more than a disguised rendering of the known facts of Long's life," the facts inevitably assume such a central role in the fiction that even those "Hueys-who-aren't-Hueys" become, as much as anything else, Hueys. Whether they intended it beforehand or admitted it afterward, the authors of *Number One*, *A Lion Is in the Streets*, and *All the King's Men*, Basso contends, could have begun nowhere else but with the biography of Huey Pierce Long.[29]

Even though all six of the novels considered here—both the four Basso mentions and the two he either omits or overlooks—cast the same factual figure in often similar fictional roles, herding them all into the same generic pen is a bit more difficult than it may seem it should be. Critics have argued for decades now over what, beyond "novel," to call *All the King's Men*—a "morass" of an issue, as one of them put it, only further exacerbated by the presence of its predecessors. If, for instance, we try to call them all political novels, "political novel" is the first designation we have to discard. In *The Modern American Political Novel, 1900–1960*, Joseph Blotner writes that such works address—and "primarily," he stresses—"the overt, institutionalized politics of the office holder, the candidate, the party official, or the individual who per-

---

29. Adria Locke Langley, *A Lion Is in the Streets* (New York: Whittlesey House, 1945), n.p.; Basso, "Legend," 106, 108, 110, 116.

forms political acts as they are conventionally understood." He specifies that the designation not extend to sociological novels—Upton Sinclair's *The Jungle* (1906), for example—or proletarian novels—John Steinbeck's *The Grapes of Wrath* (1939), for instance—or any other novel that focuses less on political action than on "the conditions out of which political action may eventually arise." As Blotner defines it, then, the political novel addresses specific platforms and policies more than general causes and conditions, focusing above all else on the political process and those intimately involved with it. We might easily apply this designation to *It Can't Happen Here, Number One, A Lion Is in the Streets,* and *All the King's Men*—as, indeed, Blotner does himself—but we should stop before trying to apply it to either of the Basso novels. Each is less about politics than its other narrative concerns, *Cinnamon Seed* its panoramic survey of social change in the American South, *Sun in Capricorn*—though Blotner includes it in his study as well—its melodramatic intersection of thriller and romance. Nor does either address what Gordon Milne, author of *The American Political Novel*, considers the defining characteristics of the political novels of the period, works like T. S. Stribling's *The Sound Wagon* (1935): "castigating various abuses on the American political front, carping at the boss, the lobbyist, and the weak-kneed congressman, and bemoaning the worship of the gospel of the 'larger good.'"[30] Each certainly engages in open criticism of a public official, but neither truly concentrates on it, for each boss's political abuses, substantial though they may be, are always subordinate to his personal or more broadly social abuses. Harry Brand and Gilgo Slade are antagonists first, politicians only second. The designation "political novel," therefore—though it is the closest fit we'll find—applies to only four of these six works.

One of the next to venture into this "morass" was Joseph W. Turner, who in his oft-cited *Genre* article "The Kinds of Historical Fiction: An Essay in Definition and Methodology," proposes that, be-

---

30. Joseph W. Turner, "The Kinds of Historical Fiction: An Essay in Definition and Methodology," *Genre* 12 (1979): 333; Joseph Blotner, *The Modern American Political Novel, 1900–1960* (Austin: University of Texas Press, 1966), 8; Gordon Milne, *The American Political Novel* (Norman: University of Oklahoma Press, 1966), 104.

cause of their attempts both to incorporate and to camouflage the recorded past, we refer to these works as disguised historical novels. He reasons that, even though *All the King's Men* references "no actual characters or events"—he seems to have forgotten that Cass Mastern's elder brother Gilbert is a friend and neighbor of Jefferson Davis and that much of Mastern's inset narrative takes place during the American Civil War—parallels between the careers of Willie Stark and Huey Long "are so close that we find ourselves reading the novel as a disguised account of a documented past," something that "stands somewhere between documented history and conventional fiction." No matter how fitting these particular comments, however, Turner's use of the term "historical novel" is a bit troubling. First, and most generally, the works to which he applies it have little in common with the historical romances often popularly associated with the term. More specifically, neither the works he addresses nor those examined here are in the least concerned with what the seminal work on the subject, György Lukács's *The Historical Novel*, describes as the defining characteristic of such a work: its attempt to convince the reader that "historical circumstances and characters existed in precisely such and such a way." Nor do the works examined here take as their central task the representation of a historical figure "in such a way that it neglects none of the complex, capillary factors of development in the whole society of the time." Robert Penn Warren not only denied time and again that his fictional governor is anything like Huey Long but wrote that Willie Stark—far from an embodiment of an entire era—is "only himself, whatever that self turned out to be." Each of these works, moreover, adopts an agenda other than the dramatization of the romantic class struggle Lukács found in the novels of Sir Walter Scott and his disciples and therefore is not, according to the term as critically defined, a historical novel. Avrom Fleishman would approach the issue from a different perspective, but would come to much the same conclusion, for according to the criteria he set forth in *The English Historical Novel*, works that are set so close to the year of their composition—*It Can't Happen Here*, in fact, is set *after* its composition—and works that are almost entirely devoid of historical figures and events, simply should not be considered historical novels.[31] Turner may accurately describe the novels examined here, but because of the terminology he employs, he ultimately offers us no better a classification for them than Blotner does with "political novel."

Nor do two more recent attempts. In *Telling the Truth: The Theory and Practice of Documentary Fiction*, Barbara Foley characterizes *All the King's Men* as a documentary novel, a work that, as she defines it, "is distinguished by its insistence that it contains some kind of specific and verifiable link to the historical world." The documentary novel, she continues, "implicitly claims to replicate certain features of actuality in a relatively direct and unmediated fashion; it invokes familiar novelistic conventions, but it requires the reader to accept certain textual elements—characters, incidents, or actual documents—as possessing referents in the world of the reader." Lewis most likely hoped readers of *It Can't Happen Here* would recognize these referents, as, no doubt, Basso, perhaps even Dos Passos, hoped their readers would do the same, but Langley and Warren, to greater and lesser degrees, tried to deny their very existence. All six of the novels examined here certainly take on an added dimension if readers *choose* to connect them with the extratextual world, but none, in the end, actually *depend upon* their doing so. Historiographic metafiction, as Linda Hutcheon describes it in *A Poetics of Postmodernism*, is a similar hybrid of history and fiction, but one that more self-consciously problematizes generic distinctions between the two. *All the King's Men* is the only Long novel to earn mention in Hutcheon's study, but its predecessors just as certainly "rethink and rework . . . the forms and contents of the past." For the most part, though, each does so for reasons far less cerebral than the foregrounding of what she calls the "theoretical self-awareness of history and fiction as human constructs."[32] Lewis, for instance, admitted

31. Turner, 335, 338; György Lukács, *The Historical Novel* (1937; reprint, trans. Hannah and Stanley Mitchell, Lincoln: University of Nebraska Press, 1983), 43, 127; Robert Penn Warren, introduction to *All the King's Men* (1946; reprint, New York: Modern Library, 1953), v; Avrom Fleishman, *The English Historical Novel: Walter Scott to Virginia Woolf* (Baltimore: Johns Hopkins University Press, 1971), 3.

32. Barbara Foley, *Telling the Truth: The Theory and Practice of Documentary Fiction* (Ithaca: Cornell University Press, 1986), 26; Linda Hutcheon, *A Poetics of Postmodernism: History, Theory, Fiction* (New York: Routledge, 1988), 5.

to writing primarily to deny Long the White House, and Langley, at least according to the most cynical of her critics, was writing primarily with an eye on the Hollywood movie contract she signed soon after publication. All six of the Long novels undeniably have a good deal in common with both the documentary novel and historiographic metafiction, but, again, none is completely enough an example of either to refer to it by that designation.

A more recent attempt, one to return such works to an older classification, comes closer but still doesn't offer us a perfect fit. The centuries-old French designation *roman à clef*, as Jue Chen defines it in "Poetics of Historical Referentiality: Roman à Clef and Beyond," denotes "a kind of fiction in which actual people are presented under fictitious names in [such] a systematic way [that] a comprehensive key is necessary to understand the hidden references of a given text." This key (or *clef*), he explains, assures readers "that the correspondences between fictional and historical versions of the story are not random but consistent and comprehensive." As one example of a *roman à clef*, Chen offers *All the King's Men*—for Willie Stark, as he sees it, simply "is" the "historical Huey Pierce Long."[33] What follows from this oversimplification is a whole series of attendant contentions, each as indefensible as the next: first, that the only difference between Huey Long and Willie Stark is their names; second, that *All the King's Men* is not a fictional text but a veiled biography or history of 1930s Louisiana; third, that correspondences between Long and Stark, once noted, can lead us to others between further fictional elements inside, and further historical elements outside, the text. If these arguments were in any way valid, *All the King's Men* would not be itself, but *Every Man a King* with the names changed. Much the same can be said of certain chapters from *Cinnamon Seed*, for instance, or of *Number One*. The *roman à clef* has afforded a variety of American authors a potent means to covert political commentary—one of the most recent examples is Joe Klein's anonymously published *Primary Colors* (1996), which fictionalizes much of Bill Clinton's 1992 presidential campaign—but the authors examined here should not be counted among them. Each novel

---

33. Jue Chen, "Poetics of Historical Referentiality: Roman à Clef and Beyond" (Ph.D. diss., Princeton University, 1997), 5–6, 22.

might incorporate, to a greater or lesser degree, the biography of Huey P. Long, but because none does so wholesale, and because each truncates or augments it in ways dictated only by independent authorial intent, each is far more fiction than veiled fact. Each clothes an at least somewhat historical skeleton in fictional flesh and clothes, but no novel examined here is such a "systematic" or "comprehensive" one-to-one fictionalization of history to justify our application of Chen's designation either.

Referring to all six of these works by any one designation would therefore be hasty, if not inexcusably procrustean. Only four might comfortably be called political novels, and, even though all six incorporate history, not one is a historical novel or, by extension, a disguised historical novel. Nor are they documentary novels, metafictional novels, or *romans à clef*, even though each displays characteristics of all three. In the end, then, our time might be better spent classifying characters rather than novels. One would not, after all, refer to Herman Melville's *Mardi* (1849) as a political novel simply because it transforms U.S. senator and nullification proponent John C. Calhoun into a slave trader named Nulli. Nor would one classify Henry Adams's *Democracy* (1882) as a disguised historical novel simply because it fictionalizes Ulysses S. Grant, Rutherford B. Hayes, and James G. Blaine. Nor would one call F. Scott Fitzgerald's *The Great Gatsby* (1925) a *roman à clef* simply because Gatsby's mentor Meyer Wolfshiem has much in common with Arnold Rothstein, the gambler who allegedly fixed the 1919 World Series. Each, though—as is also true of the six novels examined here—features one or more characters more a composite of both fact and fiction than a pure example of either. According to Turner, again—for, no matter how much we might question his use of the term "historical novel," his general arguments still obtain—the difficulty of analyzing works written around disguised composites is not defining their conventions but addressing their "double articulation," their peculiar nexus of extratextual historical referents and the independent products of authorial autonomy. Indeed, since we approach these works as both "disguised re-creation" and "completely new creation," our central task, as Turner sees it, is "defining the novel's relationship to recorded history and determining what aesthetic significance it might have."[34]

We might quickly test these contentions by way of the 1936 Sax Rohmer novel *President Fu Manchu*. The British export and so-called Yellow Peril thriller might seem strange company for something like *All the King's Men*, but it too, albeit peripherally, takes up the life and career of Huey P. Long. First serialized in *Collier's* under the title *The Invisible President* (1936), the novel is the ninth in Rohmer's once popular but now oft-denounced Dr. Fu Manchu series, each ethnicity-obsessed installment of which details Western government operatives' never-ending efforts against an Asian criminal mastermind variously described as "sinister," as "superhuman," and as a "satanic genius."[35] The story takes place in a nighttime world of secret agents and international crime syndicates where one had always best be on guard against all manner of spy and hired assassin. It is a breathlessly written, superlative-laced work in which Fu Manchu, no ordinary crime lord but "the greatest menace to social order . . . since Attila the Hun" (309), surfaces in mid-1930s America to take devious advantage of popular discontent during the Great Depression. The federal agents out to stop him, Rohmer gushes, are fighting "not for the salvage of the Constitution, not for the peace of the country," but for nothing less than "the future of the world" (120). At the historical center of the novel is the 1936 presidential election. On the right stands the benign and learned Dr. Orwin Prescott, who, after uncovering and attempting to expose the plot by which Fu Manchu plans to take over the country, is quickly drugged and kidnapped. On the left, in the never-explained absence of Franklin Delano Roosevelt, is Harvey Bragg, the "Bluebeard of the Backwoods," the candidate in whose interest Fu Manchu at least seems to have kidnapped Prescott. The "fate of the United States," of course, as one familiar with pulp serials should know to expect, "hung in the balance" (278).

Though we first hear Bragg dismissed as "a small pawn in a big

34. Turner, 338–49, 346.

35. Sax Rohmer, *President Fu Manchu* (Garden City, N.Y.: Doubleday, Doran, 1936), 191, 276, 283.

game" (13), we soon see federal agents taking him far more seriously than this early assessment would allow. Many, in fact, fear his potential as a dictator. His campaign slogan, "America for every man—every man for America," is just what Depression-era audiences want to hear, and his promise of employment for all who join his League of Good Americans—still more what those audiences crave—earns him fifteen million followers faster than his opponents can count them. There is also the implication, always present but never detailed, that his political accomplishments back home had approached the miraculous. Rohmer, never naming Bragg's home state, gives him only vague ties to the South, and never specifies what office he currently holds there. Roughly a third of the way through the novel, however, we quickly assume our way to answers to both questions. Upon Bragg's first appearance, we see that he is muscular, of medium height, and has straight black hair. His actions, though, seem those of someone larger, with lighter, curlier hair: "He wore a sky-blue bathrobe, and apart from a pair of red slippers, apparently nothing else. But he was Harvey Bragg—Bluebeard; the man who threatened the Constitution, the coming Hitler of the United States. . . . His circus showman's voice shouted down all opposition. No normal personality could live near him. He was Harvey Bragg. He was 'It.' He was the omnipresent potential Dictator of America" (117). Or so he thinks. Behind Bragg, secretly responsible for his every word and action, is Fu Manchu—who, once the one-time "petty local potentate" becomes a "national force" (146), impassively and, precisely according to plan, orders his assassination. Bragg's half brother is the gunman. Slave to Fu Manchu's legendary powers of hypnosis, he unwittingly fires two shots into Bragg only to die immediately at the hands of his bodyguard. Paul Salvaletti, Bragg's confidential secretary and Fu Manchu's true straw man, steps in to assume Bragg's role, both rescuing his legions of distraught followers and promoting even his most "chimerical" promises (286), among them those concerning the national redistribution of wealth. For the second half of the novel, though, Bragg is little more than a half-remembered name as Rohmer turns his attention to the unmasking of Salvaletti and, of course, Fu Manchu himself. One of the last opinions aired of Bragg thus echoes one of the first: in the end, he truly had been "little more than a cog in a wheel" (179).

As Turner sees it, again, the critical difficulty in analyzing such a novel inheres primarily in its "double articulation," its particular combination of "disguised re-creation"—fact camouflaged as fiction—and "completely new creation"—fiction independent of fact. Much of what Rohmer writes of Bragg is clearly the former. Though we know little of his home state and still less of the office he holds there, we can see in his campaign slogan a disguised version of "Every Man a King," can see in his League of Good Americans a disguised Share Our Wealth Society, and can see in his blue bathrobe and red bedroom slippers the garish ensemble Long wore to greet the commander of the *Emden*. On the other hand, much of the novel's relevant material is also "completely new creation." Long was more pudgy at the time than muscular, had curly brown instead of straight black hair, and met his death at the hands of a young surgeon seemingly bent on defending his family name, not a half brother hypnotized by an Asian criminal mastermind determined to take over the country. But for Turner, distinguishing fact from fiction is only the beginning. There is also the business of "determining what aesthetic significance" the relationship between history and fiction might have. Why, Turner would have us ask, would an author incorporate certain facts as documented, incorporate others only beneath a disguise, and ignore others altogether—and what, in the end, does this tell us about the fact, the fiction, and the intersections between them? Rohmer makes these questions easier on us than any other novelist examined here. We might strain *President Fu Manchu* to derive from it a commentary about 1930s America, about how the sociopolitical turmoil of the Great Depression left the masses prey to the hypnotic powers of all manner of alien demagogue, but the sheer outlandishness of a hypnotized half brother's assassination of a Huey Long figure undercuts whatever true "aesthetic significance" the novel's combination of history and fiction might have had. In *President Fu Manchu*, documented history is a means, not an end, little more than a colorfully familiar backdrop for frenetic confrontations between government agents and international crime lords. All is in the name of intrigue, of suspense, and in the end what is important is not so much the sociopolitical implications of the time and place in which the heroes and villains find themselves but the simple fact that they chase each other through them on their way to the final page and, of course,

yet another cliffhanger. The novel ultimately says little about Huey
Long, still less about the 1930s, and the material Rohmer borrows from
Long's biography plays more to the sensationalized interests of those
attracted to the day's banner headlines than any kind of authentic "aesthetic significance."

The six American novels examined here present us with far more
complicated cases. The study that follows, therefore, compares the life
of Huey Long to those of the "Hueys-who-aren't-Hueys" in *It Can't
Happen Here, Cinnamon Seed, Sun in Capricorn, Number One, A Lion
Is in the Streets,* and *All the King's Men* in an attempt to determine
the more substantial "aesthetic significance" of the convergences and
divergences between them. Even though all access the same fund of
factual material, no two do so for the same reason. Individual novels
address everything from the threat of international fascism to social
change in the American South, from the potentially exploitative nature
of the politician-constituent contract to the conflict between professional and familial responsibilities to the metaphysical interdepen-
dence of good and evil. Drawing on the same historical fund Sinclair
Lewis uses to create a Long figure who embodies an American version
of European totalitarianism, Hamilton Basso creates two Long figures
who pose social more than political threats, trample tradition more
than threaten democracy. Drawing on the same historical data John
Dos Passos uses to create a Huey Long figure who, though ostensibly
a public servant, only exploits belief in his public pronouncements to
increase his personal power, Adria Locke Langley creates a Long figure who, though initially an inspiring leader and devoted husband, is
so tempted by gain and corrupted by power that he soon becomes morally repugnant, particularly to those who first supported him. Drawing
on still the same historical data, Robert Penn Warren creates a Huey
Long figure more interested in the philosophical relationship between
ends and means than illustrative of any particular political or social
point of view. Yet all, ultimately, are "Hueys-who-aren't-Hueys," disguised composites who often live the life of Huey Long but, because
of their creators' unique personal and political perspectives, also live
lives unquestionably their own. As they do so, moreover, their authors
increasingly stifle the urge to derive a moral from history, to force on
fictionalized fact the kind of instructive closure fact rarely has on its

own, and fact, by way of fiction, begins to give rise to still further myth—that frustratingly nebulous middle ground of ever-diminishing log cabins, eight-month law degrees, and signature-bearing leaves that, in the words of Hayden White, "is under no obligation to keep the two orders of events, real and imaginary, distinct from one another."[36]

36. Hayden White, "The Value of Narrativity in the Representation of Reality," in *The Content of the Form: Narrative Discourse and Historical Representation* (Baltimore: Johns Hopkins University Press, 1987), 3–4.

1 American Hitler: Sinclair Lewis's Berzelius Windrip

THE YOUNG SINCLAIR LEWIS SEEMS TO HAVE SEEN HIMSELF as something of a radical, and as an undergraduate at Yale in the early 1900s, he was a convincing-enough campus agitator to earn the nickname "Red" for reasons that, for perhaps the first time in his life, had little to do with the color of his hair. Finding life in New Haven increasingly, ultimately impossibly bourgeois, he would drop out during his junior year to take up residence at Helicon Hall, a cooperative Upton Sinclair had established on the outskirts of nearby Englewood, New Jersey. Its inhabitants, according to Sinclair's *The Industrial Republic* (1907), were to live according to two principles: "Communism in material production, anarchism in intellectual." Lewis, however, found his furnace, laundry, maintenance, and janitorial duties a bit less than romantic, and less than two months after moving in, he moved out. Such, it seems, was the measure of his early dedication: as would often prove the case, his politics were more a matter of thought than of anything truly approximating action. In 1911, just after relocating to New York City, he would go so far as to formally join the Socialist Party, but less than a year and a half later, he stopped paying dues and let his membership lapse. He would end up spending five years in Greenwich Village among the likes of John Reed, Floyd Dell, and Randolph Bourne, but he never once protested alongside them, never once contributed to *The Masses* or even the *New Republic*. Indeed, in *Writers on the Left: Episodes in American Literary Communism*, Daniel Aaron numbers Lewis not among the Village bohemians, but among the "hard-working professional people" who lived quietly in their midst. Later, there would be the occasional speech, march, or pamphlet, but Lewis's activism seems almost as halfhearted as it was short-lived. Those who knew him later in life would often question even his bedrock beliefs, ultimately characterizing him as "essentially apolitical," as someone who "could be a liberal, a radical, and a reactionary on three successive days."[1] Whichever of the three we might find more fitting, he was hardly the radical he once wanted to seem.

No radical wrote his novels, to be sure, no communist, no socialist, no extremist of any stripe. Carol Kennicott never advocates the overthrow of capitalism, George Babbitt never endorses municipal ownership of the means of production, and Martin Arrowsmith never so much as entertains the idea that wealth just might be more equitably distributed. Upton Sinclair, in *Money Writes!* assures us that his onetime protégé received a "complete education" in "every aspect of the radical movement" during his stay at Helicon Hall, but at the same time—even on the same page—he is quick to take him to task for not making as much use of it "as the good of his country requires." We can say, though, that while the politics of Lewis's maturity were in no way as ostensibly radical as those of his youth, they did settle down a good bit left of center, a fact readily evident in his best-known novels. Though most frequently approached as satires of middle-class middle-American mores of the 1920s and 1930s, they often also comment upon the American political spectrum of the day. On the far left, for instance, we find communists like Karl Pascal of *It Can't Happen Here,* an auto mechanic who spends more time arguing Marx than working on cars, and Eugene Silga of *The Prodigal Parents* (1938), a would-be editor and fledgling agitator who exits the novel long before its conclusion, pursued by police. Lewis's thoughts on their real-world counterparts—he once characterized American communists as "doctrinaire and foolish"—apply equally as well to either. Much less doctrinaire and a good bit closer to center are Seneca Doane, Zenith's radical lawyer and labor-aligned mayoral candidate, and Miles Bjornstam, Gopher Prairie's lone democrat and, consequently, a suspected anarchist. Both draw little but scorn from their respective communities, a distinction that in both *Babbitt* and *Main Street* is the surest sign of Lewis's

1. Mark Schorer, *Sinclair Lewis: An American Life* (New York: McGraw-Hill, 1969), 92, 112–14, 177–78, 218; Daniel Aaron, *Writers on the Left: Episodes in American Literary Communism* (1961; reprint, New York: Columbia University Press, 1992), 11; Richard R. Lingeman, *Sinclair Lewis: Rebel from Main Street* (New York: Random House, 2002), 378, 411.

sympathy and ultimate sanction. Representatives of the right, finally, comprise the largest, least attractive contingent. Members of an occasionally nameless and faceless but almost always mindless mob, they are, as Lewis describes them in *Main Street*, a "savorless people, gulping tasteless food . . . listening to mechanical music, saying mechanical things . . . and viewing themselves as the greatest race in the world."[2] Initially just victims of a willful blindness toward anything beyond their most immediate horizons, they turn political over the course of Lewis's career, and as 1920 gives way to 1935, as *Main Street* gives way to *It Can't Happen Here*, their self-satisfied cultural myopia gives way to an increasingly threatening conservatism, one that more and more nakedly demands conformity, more and more brazenly punishes those brave enough to defy them. Those who merely shun books in *Main Street*, in short, burn them in *It Can't Happen Here*—and, even before the ashes stop smoldering, go stomping off in search of their owners.

Censors, after all, do not thoroughly enough "safeguard" books—at least as far as *Main Street*'s Raymie Wutherspoon sees it. What he wants in a book is a "wholesome, really improving story," for everyday life "is so full of temptations that in literature one wants only that which is pure and uplifting." Gopher Prairie, Minnesota, is a virtual chorus of such sentiment. The town values respectability above all else, and its inhabitants are gleefully eager to sacrifice whatever knowledge or experience might be necessary to maintain it. To take an interest in anything other than what interests one's neighbors is to risk exposure as a highbrow, a term locally employed as an epithet denoting someone "priggish" and "of dubious virtue." Carol Kennicott's dream of bringing something different to the town, of filling its formidable cultural void with poetry, modern architecture, and community theater, is thus ultimately as good as stillborn. At first, her neighbors' disdain for her dream is essentially harmless. Their closed-mindedness might stifle that rare alien idea, but Gopher Prairie's conservatism is at this point more a general attitude than a political stance per se. Its residents are not without their political opinions, and those opinions rest, except in

2. Upton Sinclair, *Money Writes!* (London: Laurie, 1931), 163; Schorer, 586; Sinclair Lewis, *Main Street* (1920; reprint, New York: Harcourt Brace Jovanovich, 1948), 258.

the rarest of occasions, more than just a little right of center, but no one in town has yet banded together to impose them on anyone else. No one has yet had to: except for Carol and Miles Bjornstam, they may as well be of one mind. When Jackson Elder, owner of the local planing-mill, explains why he has no fear of labor unrest—"They like what I pay 'em, or they get out! That's all there is to it!"—the reaction is uniform. Carol looks on, increasingly ill at ease, while all within earshot nod "solemnly and in tune, like a shop-window of flexible toys, comic mandarins and judges and ducks and clowns, set quivering by a breeze from the open door."[3] Toward the end of the novel, when a more fully united Gopher Prairie rises up against a recently imported high school teacher falsely accused of seducing a student, we watch as these attitudes turn more tangibly threatening. The judges and clowns are not satisfied until they have removed Fern Mullins from her job, run her out of town, and warned all employers to whom she might later apply of what the townspeople, at least, consider her crime. What at first had been a fairly benign closed-mindedness has grown malignant by the end of the novel. It turns active, swiftly organizes, and, even as early as *Main Street,* we watch as representatives of the right apply a force that at least approximates political pressure.

As Lewis's next novel, *Babbitt,* makes clear, this conservatism lurks no less in the city. Zenith may be several times the size of Gopher Prairie—a midsize midwestern metropolis of some 360,000, to be exact—but broader streets don't necessarily lead to broader minds. Middle-class middle-brow businessmen all but saturate the novel with reactionary political views, with talk of how they need to remind "the black man" and "the yellow man" of "his place." The only way to respond to local strikers—who are, of course, nothing but "bomb-throwing socialists and thugs"—as they see it, is "with a club." The central face in this crowd sees things no differently. According to George F. Babbitt of the Babbitt-Thompson Realty Company, "the ideal of American manhood and culture isn't a lot of cranks sitting around chewing the rag about their Rights and their Wrongs, but a God-fearing, hustling, successful, two-fisted Regular guy." Toward the end of the novel, Babbitt uncharacteristically begins wavering between

3. Lewis, *Main Street,* 56, 259, 47.

these same two poles. Increasingly unfaithful to both wife and political party, he begins to wonder if he himself just might be a liberal, even begins defending such so-called radicals as Seneca Doane and the local strikers. To his colleagues in the athletic club and Booster set, this is cause for immediate mobilization. By way of the Good Citizens' League, an organization formed to "put the kibosh on cranks" and make them "conform to decent standards," they subject him to a kind of pressure Fern Mullins never has the time to get to know. Gopher Prairie merely runs the new teacher out of town; Zenith, because Babbitt is an integral part of its business and political identity, demands immediate compliance. A contingent of upper-class businessmen—"high lords in the land of Zenith," we are to understand—descends upon Babbitt with a terse ultimatum: conformity or ruin, social as well as financial. As proof of their word, Babbitt loses his largest account within the following week. He does regain it in the end, but only after concluding his career as a "crank," conforming to "decent standards," and joining the Good Citizens' League.[4] When mustered in *Main Street*, the forces of conservatism amount to little more than a small town's worth of angry parents; in *Babbitt*, they grow a bit more menacing, wielding enough power in the community not only to demand compliance but to exact punishment for deviation from locally prescribed standards.

Conservatives demand still more in *Elmer Gantry*, even threatening something of a moral dictatorship. In the role for which he remains best known, the Reverend Dr. Gantry is a hypocritical but basically harmless clergyman, a man who preaches against alcohol while privately imbibing and against adultery while leering at female parishioners. In his often forgotten but far more menacing role, he is a political rather than a clerical animal, despite his ostensible call to the ministry. His chief asset is his voice. As an undergraduate enrolled in a public speaking course, he had discovered "the intoxication of holding an audience with his voice as with his closed hand, holding it, shaking it, lifting it." The image is instructive, for as Gantry later progresses from smaller to larger pulpits, we watch as he locks his hands over the once-open eyes of larger and larger congregations. He might push little

4. Sinclair Lewis, *Babbitt* (1922; reprint, New York: Harcourt Brace Jovanovich, 1950), 119, 269, 156, 295, 315.

more than Liberty Bonds on his earlier, smaller churches, but by the time he achieves the pulpit of Zenith's Wellspring Methodist, he forces on parishioners an all-out crusade against vice, one in which he has himself appointed a temporary police lieutenant so he can lead raids on the local red-light district. Using radio to transform himself from a local to a regional figure, he next allies himself with the National Association for the Purification of Art and the Press (NAPAP) and begins plotting to crown himself "super-president of the United States" and, someday, "dictator of the world." Planning to consolidate all Protestant political action groups—among them all antialcohol, antievolution, and procensorship organizations—he aims to bring the voting power of its thirty million members to bear on local, state, and national legislatures. Gantry's goal, of course, is to set himself atop this monolithic conglomerate and, as the single most powerful figure in the world, "dictate what [the] whole nation should wear and eat and say and think." But Lewis ultimately denies him this position: at the end of the novel he may grant Gantry both a still larger pulpit and the directorship of NAPAP, but the minister's goal of reigning over—if not reining in—America as its "chief moral dictator" remains for him little more than a dream.[5] Lewis, it seems, was content at the time with the mere threat inherent in such an autocrat, almost as if leaving Gantry's only dreamed-of dictatorship for a character he had yet to create—or, perhaps, one history had yet to provide him.

Except for an isolated incident in *Elmer Gantry*, a mostly peripheral moment in which a preacher-turned-lecturer is beaten and whipped for publicly taking up the subject of evolution, the violence inherent in these increasingly conservative threats does not become physical until *Ann Vickers*. By the time Lewis's heroine, as a prison reformer, enters Copperhead Gap Penitentiary, she has already battled the forces of conservatism as a suffragette and a social worker. These forces are at their worst, though, in the moral dictators of Copperhead Gap, one of whom attempts to justify the facility's execrable conditions by arguing that prisons, after all, are not supposed to be picnics. After fifteen months of looking on in suppressed horror while inmates endure

5. Sinclair Lewis, *Elmer Gantry* (1927; reprint, United States of America: Signet, 1967), 12, 393, 394, 398.

roaches and rats, maggot-infested food, days in a sweatshop and nights on a bare concrete floor, Ann finds herself sneaking into an off-limits basement to uncover the fate of four women who had incited a riot while protesting the severity of their treatment. What she finds them suffering is the fate of Lewis's previous liberals made more overtly physical. For the crime of asserting their rights, for daring to question the status quo, they find themselves subjected to days of almost Torquemadan torture. In a damp, dark, windowless room in the bowels of the penitentiary, Ann stumbles across a blood-spattered whipping post and, nearby, its most recent victims. "They whipped us," one of them cries. "Stripped us to the waist—the men guards. Tied us to the post, with our arms out, and licked us with a strap with holes in it."[6] Every day since, the guards had returned to chain them to their doors for some six hours at a time, stretching their hands so high above their heads that they have to stand on tiptoe to keep their arms in their sockets. The violence latent in the archconservatism of Gopher Prairie, of Zenith's Good Citizens' League, of Elmer Gantry's moral dictatorship—community morality made compulsory upon growing threats of retribution—thus becomes concretely physical. Yet, even as brutal as this punishment is, it occurs only locally. The punishment exacted is more physically violent in *Ann Vickers* than in previous novels, but its immediate victims number only four. In *It Can't Happen Here,* reactionary violence will become still more physical and will range over the whole of the American citizenry. The impulse that first caused a handful of parents to run Fern Mullins out of Gopher Prairie will give rise to a totalitarian regime overrunning all America.

It Can't Happen Here takes the dictatorship from *Elmer Gantry,* adds the physical brutality of *Ann Vickers,* and dramatizes the result on a national scale. Published in 1935, but beginning in 1936—and thereby illustrating what Lewis wanted to make sure America would defeat in the upcoming presidential election—the novel embodies this everincreasing dictatorial threat in the forms of the Reverend Paul Peter Prang, a radio evangelist, and the Honorable Berzelius "Buzz" Windrip, a U.S. senator and Democratic presidential candidate. Lewis's central character, a sixty-year-old small-town newspaper editor named

6. Sinclair Lewis, *Ann Vickers* (1933; reprint, New York: Collier, n.d.), 366.

Doremus Jessup, is one of the few who recognize these men for what they are. More often than not, though, his warnings are dismissed as the standard rant of the local liberal, the politically eccentric pariah of his tiny Vermont town. Jessup's predictions of a native dictatorship often inspire such comments as, "That couldn't happen here in America, not possibly!" After hearing these responses just one time too many, Jessup launches into what soon becomes a tirade: "The answer to that," he begins, "is 'the hell it can't!' Why, there's no country in the world that can get more hysterical—yes, or more obsequious!—than America. Look how Huey Long became absolute monarch over Louisiana, and how the Right Honorable Mr. Senator Berzelius Windrip owns *his* state. Listen to Bishop Prang and Father Coughlin on the radio—divine oracles, to millions. Remember how casually most Americans have accepted Tammany grafting and Chicago gangs and the crookedness of so many of President Harding's appointees? Could Hitler's bunch, or Windrip's, be worse?" After cataloguing figures that still further prove his point—Billy Sunday, Aimee Semple McPherson, William Jennings Bryan, the Ku Klux Klan, and the Kentucky nightriders, among others—Jessup concludes with a question: "Not happen here? . . . Why, where in all history has there ever been a people so ripe for a dictatorship as ours! We're ready to start on a Children's Crusade—only of adults—right now, and the Right Reverend Abbots Windrip and Prang are all ready to lead it!"[7] And lead it they do. With the strength of Prang's followers united behind him, Windrip wins the White House and, to the surprise of seemingly all but Jessup, immediately establishes the American Corporate State and Patriotic Party, more commonly known as the Corporate, or Corpo, regime. Just as Jessup had prophesied, the fascist dictatorship had indeed come to America.

Windrip begins building his regime overnight. Within hours of his inauguration, he declares the Minute Men, his private troops, an official auxiliary of the U.S. Army—but one answerable only to him—and quickly issues them automatic weapons. The next morning, he calls for the immediate passage of a bill granting him complete control of the federal government. When a hundred congressmen revolt, he declares

7. Sinclair Lewis, *It Can't Happen Here* (New York: Doubleday, Doran, 1935), 21, 22.

martial law and orders their arrests. When citizens protest, he has the Minute Men take aim and open fire. He then fills the empty congressional seats with Minute Men, strong-arms Congress into passing his original bill, and dispatches troops to the houses of Supreme Court justices to keep them from challenging the new law. Finally, he forbids access to the airwaves and arrests any journalist in any way critical of his actions. Within the year, he outlaws all political organizations unaffiliated with the American Corporate State and Patriotic Party and effectively replaces all labor organizations with the National Council of Corporations. In the name of ending unemployment, he inters the nation's poor in hastily constructed labor camps. In the name of ending crime, he arrests all known or suspected criminals. In the name of suppressing popular opposition, he orders that anyone acting or speaking against the state be confined in one of several new concentration camps—or that they simply be executed. As the Minute Men who staff these camps begin reaching for the iron rods and the castor oil, Americans effectively lose their right to free speech. As extreme as these tactics are, however, Windrip's Corpo regime is but the next natural step in the archconservative campaign Lewis had been tracking since 1920. What Gopher Prairie thinks, Berzelius Windrip executes; what Elmer Gantry dreams, Berzelius Windrip realizes; what Copperhead Gap initiates, Berzelius Windrip intensifies.

This scenario might sound absurd today, and Lewis might seem more than a little alarmist for even conceiving it, but according to several authorities on the era, 1935 was precisely the "mighty serious hour" one of his characters claims it is (20). Roosevelt's New Deal, then entering its third year, had been far more successful in its first, and though it had unquestionably checked the devastation of the Great Depression, it had not come close to ending it. Explaining that the 1934 national income of $48.6 billion was substantially higher than that of 1933, Arthur M. Schlesinger, Jr., writes that it was still nearly $40 billion, or more than 80 percent, lower than it had been in 1929. Urban workers earned 13 percent less in January 1935 than in January 1929, farmers nearly 30 percent. Far more Americans worked in 1934 than in 1933, but almost ten million of them, some 20 percent of the national workforce, were still unemployed. Schlesinger writes that the economy had recovered enough to curb despair but not enough to actually inspire promise. What made the hour still more serious, he continues, was the rise on both left and right of a new breed of American extremist, demagogues and rabble-rousers set to turn the era's socioeconomic turmoil to their own radical advantage. One of the most prominent of those on the left, according to William Manchester, was Upton Sinclair, who campaigned for the governorship of California on a platform proposing a statewide network of communes like Helicon Hall—though Helicon Hall failed, as would Sinclair's campaign. For the most part, however, this "threat from the left," as Manchester puts it, was "absurd." The threat from the right, on the other hand, was potentially far more troublesome. As Schlesinger explains, the "primary political fact" of 1935 was the rise not on European but American soil of an entirely new band of "political prophets," popular leaders who sought a solution to the Great Depression in nothing less than an American incarnation of European fascism. Schlesinger numbers among the more radical of these figures "General" Art J. Smith, a professional soldier whose militant Khaki Shirts advocated the dissolution of Congress and the extermination of America's Jewish population, and William Dudley Pelley, a former screenwriter who founded his own militant group, the Silver Shirts, upon Adolph Hitler's 1933 ascension to the German chancellorship. The threat such leaders posed was in no way as comical as it might seem today. Fascism, as journalist George Seldes wrote in 1935, "not only exists in America," but "has become formidable." It "needs only a Duce, a Fuehrer, an organizer, and a loosening of the purse strings of those who gain materially by its victory, to become the most powerful force threatening the Republic." Americans "who cannot see the growth of Fascism" or, worse, see it and "deny its existence," he concluded, "are either the many who do not know what Fascism really is" or "the few who prefer euphemism—a patriotic American name for a distinctly European product."[8]

8. Arthur M. Schlesinger, Jr., *The Politics of Upheaval*, vol. 3 of *The Age of Roosevelt* (Boston: Houghton Mifflin, 1960), 2–3; William Manchester, *The Glory and the Dream: A Narrative History of America, 1932–1972*, vol. 1 (Boston: Little, Brown, 1974), 120–23; Schlesinger, 16, 70, 79–80; George Seldes, "To Americans Facing Fascism," in *Sawdust Caesar: The Untold History of Mussolini and Fascism* (New York: Harper, 1935), xiii.

It Can't Happen Here, published the same year as Seldes's warning, was thus understandably greeted less as a literary than a political work. Writing in *The Nation,* R. P. Blackmur found it "a weapon of the intellect rather than a novel," not "a seizure and showing forth of life" but "a declaration of things to come sprung from a faith of which the substance is things hated[,] not hoped for." Writing on the front page of the *New York Times Book Review,* J. Donald Adams concurred with Blackmur, finding its merits as a novel negligible, but adding that, "as prophecy of what could happen," it would certainly inspire debate. Granville Hicks, writing in *The New Masses,* attempted to squelch any talk of artistry altogether, for the novel should not be judged as a work of art, but as a "political tract." It makes two things "perfectly clear," he wrote: that "fascism is entirely possible in the United States" and "that it would be damned unpleasant." More than anything artistic and, presumably, frivolous, *It Can't Happen Here* was to Hicks a "tremendously useful book" that was "likely to raise the issue of fascism more sharply than it has ever been raised in America before." It may not be a "great" book, he conceded, but it is a "significant" one in which Lewis addresses "the great issue of his day." Clifton Fadiman's praise in the *New Yorker* was still more unqualified. *It Can't Happen Here* was not only the most important book of Lewis's career, Fadiman exclaimed, but "one of the most important books ever produced in this country," one that "should take its place with 'Uncle Tom's Cabin' and with the writings of Tom Paine and Thomas Jefferson." Though "I do not believe I have ever before recommended the reading of any book as a public duty," he wrote, "I do now so recommend 'It Can't Happen Here.'"[9]

Another oft-sounded note in reviews of the novel held that, far from being unique, Windrip's Corpo regime is a mere translation into American terms of the dictatorships established in western and central

9. R. P. Blackmur, "Utopia, or Uncle Tom's Cabin," review of *It Can't Happen Here,* by Sinclair Lewis, *The Nation,* 30 October 1935, 516; J. Donald Adams, "America under the Iron Heel: A Novel by Sinclair Lewis Pictures a Fascist Dictatorship," review of *It Can't Happen Here,* by Sinclair Lewis, *New York Times Book Review,* 20 October 1935, 1; Granville Hicks, "Sinclair Lewis: Anti-Fascist," review of *It Can't Happen Here,* by Sinclair Lewis, *New Masses,* 29 October 1935, 22–23; Clifton Fadiman, "Red Lewis," review of *It Can't Happen Here,* by Sinclair Lewis, *New Yorker,* 26 October 1935, 83.

Europe during the decade and a half prior to the novel's publication. Adams wrote that what happens to Windrip's enemies is "pretty much what has happened to all those who have not bent the knee before the dictatorships of Russia, Germany and Italy." Herschel Brickell, writing in the *North American Review*, found that Lewis's descriptions of Corpo concentration camps "parallel exactly similar descriptions of such institutions in Germany" and that various other Corpo practices are the result of Lewis's following "an established pattern." Writing in the *New Republic*, Robert Morss Lovett took these arguments still farther, insisting on one-to-one correspondences between various factual and fictional elements. In *It Can't Happen Here*, he wrote, Hermann Goring and Joseph Goebbels "become" Lee Sarason, Windrip's chief lieutenant; Hitler's Storm Troops "become" the Minute Men, Windrip's private army; and Hitler's *Mein Kampf* becomes *Zero Hour— Over the Top*, Windrip's campaign biography. Lewis, it seems, had reasoned that if readers could connect the factual and the fictional, could see similarities between what had taken place in Europe and what takes place in the America of his novel, they might more readily apprehend the severity of the threat Schlesinger's "political prophets" posed to their own America. What Lewis had hoped, it seems, is that readers might hear in Jessup's implication that never "in all history has there ever been a people so ripe for a dictatorship"[10] a warning not just for fictional characters but for the Americans reading about them as well.

Americans already knew it could happen *there*, for they had seen Mussolini seize control of Italy, Stalin seize control of the U.S.S.R., and Hitler seize control of Germany. Lewis wanted to show them that it could also happen here, that Americans were just as capable as Europeans of right-wing thought so extreme it could result in dictatorship. To help his readers make the jump from foreign to domestic totalitarians, he therefore translates not just factual Europeans but factual Americans into ostensibly fictional fascists. The most benign of the pair at the heart of *It Can't Happen Here* is Bishop Paul Peter Prang,

10. Adams, 1; Herschell Brickell, review of *It Can't Happen Here*, by Sinclair Lewis, *North American Review* 240 (1935), 543; Robert Morss Lovett, "Mr. Lewis Says It Can," review of *It Can't Happen Here*, by Sinclair Lewis, *New Republic*, 6 November 1935, 366.

a radio evangelist and founder of the 27,000,000-member League of Forgotten Men, a leader whose potential for power, as Lewis puts it, could be matched by no man in history. His weekly radio addresses, "to millions the very oracle of God" (39), peddle religion as well as politics, Prang deftly maneuvering between Old Testament–era scenes of turmoil and dispossession and Depression-era scenes of the same. So compelling is this concoction that when Prang instructs his flock to vote, his followers do so, and "in His name" (40). Lewis, as we have seen, at one point compares the fictional Bishop Prang to the factual Father Charles E. Coughlin of Detroit—but the fact that Prang is but a fictional Coughlin would have escaped the notice of few contemporary readers. Indeed, Coughlin was such a pervasive presence at the time that, a year after the publication of *It Can't Happen Here*, he would find himself fictionalized again, this time in Rohmer's *President Fu Manchu*. Alan Brinkley, one of the foremost authorities on Depression-era demagoguery, explains in *Voices of Protest* that by 1935 Coughlin had built a following "of bewildering proportions." Broadcast nationally on dozens of stations, his radio program attracted an audience estimated at more than forty million listeners, and he received more mail at the time than any other American, Franklin Delano Roosevelt included. To these considerable multitudes Coughlin had once pitched religion alone, but as America sank farther into the Great Depression, his message became almost exclusively political, eventually resulting in the National Union for Social Justice,[11] the political action group that clearly inspired Prang's League of Forgotten Men—which, not coincidentally, shares its initials with Coughlin's Little Flower Ministry. Lewis, in short, wanted readers to realize that the dictatorial impulse flourished almost as openly in America as in Europe—and in figures far less openly radical, far more openly accepted, far more frighteningly persuasive than Art J. Smith and William Dudley Pelley.

It Can't Happen Here was not the first novel in which Lewis had turned factual figures into fictional characters. According to Mark Schorer, his first and still most influential biographer, Lewis wrote most of his novels only after months of research. *Babbitt*, for instance,

---

11. Alan Brinkley, *Voices of Protest: Huey Long, Father Coughlin, and the Great Depression* (New York: Knopf, 1982), 83.

was not truly underway until he had devoured half a library shelf of books on advertising and real estate. Such material routinely afforded him the detail to flesh out characters' lives, but in the case of *Arrowsmith* (1925), a book almost as much fact as fiction, it provided him nothing less than his central characters. Since Lewis's knowledge of the medical profession extended little beyond his memories of growing up the son of a small-town doctor—which seem to inform the novel's first chapter, but could afford him little more—he turned to an established authority on the subject. Without biologist Paul de Kruif, in Schorer's estimation, *Arrowsmith* would probably not exist. De Kruif devoted months to the novel's planning, not only tutoring Lewis in the bacteriology and epidemiology that pervade its almost every page, but even suggesting its central characters and storyline. Most of the novel's characters, Schorer explains, are composites of scientists de Kruif had known—Jacques Loeb among them—or, more simply, representations of scientists he had known, with their names and attributes rearranged. Acknowledging his debt to de Kruif in a 1923 letter to H. L. Mencken, Lewis wrote that *Arrowsmith* would be "my best book"—but one that "isn't just *mine* by a long shot." Indeed, as Lewis's most recent biographer, Richard R. Lingeman, notes, de Kruif was originally to have received a quarter of the novel's royalties, coauthor's credit on its cover, and a $12,000 advance for the time he put into planning it. At one point Lewis even wondered whether in the end de Kruif "won't have contributed more than I have." His initial work on *Elmer Gantry* required even more collaboration. Beginning with Kansas City clergymen William L. Stidger and L. M. Birkhead, Lewis eventually traveled America interviewing and occasionally even assuming the pulpits of dozens of different ministers. The novel is far from the *roman à clef* that *Arrowsmith* is, but even so, Lewis's claim that "No character in this book is the portrait of any actual person" is more than a little misleading. Those who aided in its planning contend that, while Gantry may not represent any one of them in particular, his almost every thought and action was first one of their own.[12] One might justly paraphrase Schorer to the effect that, without figures like de Kruif, Stidger, and Birkhead, a good deal of Lewis's corpus would not exist.

---

12. Schorer, 314, 364–66, 418; Lingeman, 219, 250; Schorer, 441–50; Lewis, *Elmer Gantry*, 7.

Lewis spent far less time on research—if it can even be called that—for *It Can't Happen Here*. Schorer reports that, as soon as he decided to write a novel about the rise of American fascism, Lewis threw himself into what for him was an unprecedented effort. Three and a half straight months of nine-hour workdays later, he had another finished novel on his hands. So "serious" did he consider the "hour," it seems, that he took no time to conduct the kind of research he had put into works like *Babbitt, Arrowsmith,* and *Elmer Gantry*. That work would have been largely unnecessary anyway, for Lewis was then married to international news correspondent Dorothy Thompson. As he often told reporters asking his opinion of current events, she, not he, was "the political expert." According to Schorer, the two met in Germany in 1927. An eight-year observer of the central European political scene, Thompson served as the Berlin correspondent for the *Philadelphia Public Ledger* and the *New York Evening Post* and had recently been named Berlin bureau chief of the Central European News Service. Four years later, in 1931, she secured an interview with an increasingly powerful German official not yet well known in America, National-Socialist Party leader Adolph Hitler. The syndicated articles and book that followed, *I Saw Hitler!* (1932), were all well-enough respected in their day, but when Hitler ordered her expulsion from Germany in 1934—an all but unprecedented act at the time—she instantly became an international celebrity. Overnight, it seemed, Thompson became "an American oracle, one of those very few who have the corporate, general permission to tell people what to think." By 1935, when Lewis was at work on *It Can't Happen Here*, she was what her most recent biographer calls "the leading American voice in the war against fascism." By all accounts, however, her husband was less than elated about the fact, especially when her professional career began to intrude upon his personal life. Vincent Sheean, a family friend and, later, biographer of the Lewis-Thompson marriage, recalls that "this was all very hard on Red," for he had

> betrayed a dislike for political argument, abstract discussion, journalistic excitement and table-pounding from the earliest days; now this dislike was not only betrayed but asseverated, enforced as a rule. Many is the time I have heard him say "No more *situations* or

I will go to bed." Ultimatum. Generally he pronounced it *sityashuns* in order to make it seem more contemptible. *Sityashuns* referred to events on the continent of Europe, in general, and in particular to events in Central or Eastern Europe or to anything connected with Adolph Hitler. Neither Dorothy nor I could possibly avoid talking of such things at the time. Most of her friends were, roughly speaking, in the same frame of mind. If Red could get through an evening with Dorothy and me, or Dorothy and [various other friends], he did so by imposing his own will and forbidding the discussion of that which most dominated our minds.

So inundated would Lewis become with talk of the sort that, as Sheean reports, he eventually began joking, "If I ever divorce Dorothy I'll name Adolph Hitler as co-respondent." Nothing approximating a Lewis–de Kruif collaboration seems to have taken place between Lewis and Thompson—recent critics warn against crediting Thompson with a "substantial" amount of influence over the novel—but Schorer concludes that, even so, *It Can't Happen Here* would not exist were the two not married at the time.[13]

One of the most apparent outcomes of Lewis's frustration with the situation—the one in his home no less than that in Europe—is the inconsistent tone of *It Can't Happen Here*. He seems to have become so irritated with the *sityashun's* incursions into life with his wife and friends that at times he simply could not treat his material with the seriousness the novel would need if readers were to receive it as the earnest warning he supposedly intended. This attitude announces itself no later than the third paragraph, when we are introduced to Brigadier General Herbert Y. Edgeways, a retired U.S. Army officer whose address to the Fort Beulah, Vermont, Rotary Club is "nothing funny"— or, we are told, "at least not obviously funny" (1). Over the course of the next several pages, Edgeways will espouse ideas that the success of the novel will depend on readers' finding not just "not obviously funny" but not funny at all. Stemming from his belief that in the decade and

13. Schorer, 608; Peter Kurth, *American Cassandra: The Life of Dorothy Thompson* (Boston: Little, Brown, 1990), 210; Schorer, 487; Vincent Sheean, *Dorothy and Red* (Boston: Houghton Mifflin, 1963), 249, 207, 254; Kurth, 218; Sheean, 263; Stephen L. Tanner, "Sinclair Lewis and Fascism," *Studies in the Novel* 22 (1990), 60; Schorer, 608.

a half since World War I Americans had shamelessly lost their sense of purpose, Edgeways proposes that, to restore this failing sense of national character, those in command should provoke a second world war. All arguments to the contrary are irrelevant, he claims, for the American armed forces "have power, and power is its own excuse!" Germany and Italy, after all, had lately demonstrated similar philosophies and are to be praised for their successes. "We've got strength and will," he says they have implied, "and for whomever has those divine qualities it's not only a right, it's a *duty,* to use 'em!" (9). In a satire, such sentiment would be "obviously funny," for readers would recognize it as parodic instead of mimetic. In that *It Can't Happen Here* will later ask us to condemn Buzz Windrip for not just espousing but practicing similar philosophies, its tone on far too many occasions contradicts its ultimately didactic intent. In a realistic novel, which is what *It Can't Happen Here* tries to be, sentiments like these, if we are to take them seriously, should be frightening—and indeed they will be later in the book—but, in that they are not always frightening, in that Lewis expects us to laugh at them in Chapter 1 but shrink from them in Chapter 20, the inconsistency undermines the otherwise serious, even fearful, attitude he needed his readers to take toward the subject. Works like *Arrowsmith* and *Dodsworth* (1929) prove that Lewis could set satire aside when necessary, an attempt he also should have made in *It Can't Happen Here,* for it is difficult to fear what we are also asked to find funny.

Just as Lewis's life with Thompson seems to have colored his narrator's tone (and may also help explain why the Corpo regime seems more European than American), it also seems to have influenced his physical characterization of Windrip. Surprisingly, perhaps, the dictator cuts a far from menacing figure. From descriptions of press photos, we learn that he is nearly a dwarf, that he has straight black hair, an "enormous" head, "pendulous" cheeks, "mournful" eyes, and a "luminous, ungrudging smile which . . . he turned on and off deliberately, like an electric light" (85). Later, at the Madison Square Garden rally that offers us our best glimpse of him on the stump, he looks "stooped and tired," enters "prosaically," and "awkwardly . . . lumber[s]" onto the stage (118). Though far from terrifying, these statements sound suspiciously like the component parts of particular descriptions of a figure who, by 1935, had become terrifying to millions around the world. While Windrip is almost a dwarf, Thompson's subject, from the beginning to the end of *I Saw Hitler!* is the "Little Man." He is "formless, almost faceless, a man whose countenance is a caricature, a man whose framework seems cartilaginous, without bones." He is "inconsequent and voluble, ill-poised, insecure," a man whose movements are "awkward, almost undignified and most un-martial." Just as Windrip can turn his smile on or off, depending on his audience, Hitler's is "an actor's face," one "[c]apable of being pushed out or in, expanded or contracted at will." The wolf, it seems clear, is Adolph Hitler. The sheep's clothing, however, is that of a different figure, one sometimes—and not just in *President Fu Manchu*—referred to as the American Hitler. Lewis writes that the clothes Windrip wears on Capitol Hill look like those of an insurance salesman, but, when farther away from the public, he might easily be found in a camel's hair overcoat, a yellow silk shirt, a red tie, and a checked cap. On one occasion he changes out of formal attire and into, among other articles, red slippers, red suspenders, and blue sleeve garters—an outfit that recalls, of course, the "explosion in a paint factory" that greeted the commander of the *Emden* in New Orleans. Lewis's most imminent threat to American democracy may look like Adolph Hitler, but he dresses—and, as we shall see, thinks and acts—more like another burgeoning tyrant Thompson interviewed, a certain Louisianian she found "shrewd, fantastic," and, unsurprisingly, "not altogether unlikeable."[14]

Just as Lewis occasionally compares Father Coughlin to Bishop Prang, he occasionally casts Huey Long as a factual foil to the fictional Windrip. *It Can't Happen Here* thus became the first and was to remain the only such novel to invoke the Kingfish by name. As we have already seen, Jessup at one point equates how Long had become "absolute monarch" of Louisiana with how Windrip had seized control of his state, which carries no name in the novel. Later, in a description of the Long that clearly clashes with the Hitler in Windrip, Lewis writes that during his career on Capitol Hill Windrip's "only rival as the most

14. Marion K. Sanders, *Dorothy Thompson: A Legend in Her Time* (Boston: Houghton Mifflin, 1973), 204; Dorothy Thompson, *I Saw Hitler!* (New York: Farrar and Rinehart, 1932), 13, 14.

bouncing and feverish man in the Senate had been the late Huey Long of Louisiana" (37).[15] These red herrings, however, do little to convince readers that Windrip is not a fictional embodiment of Long. Long's name appears time and again in the novel's reviews, many critics asserting, as did R. P. Blackmur, that Windrip is directly "modeled on" Long. One later critic would even assert that Lewis's "half-hearted attempt to affirm the fictionality of his characters" falls farther than short, for though he names the figures who inspired them just after introducing "thinly disguised versions" of them, their "real-life models remain easily recognizable." Where such critics err, however, is in thinking Lewis even attempted to hide the facts behind his fiction, even tried to create "thinly disguised versions" of Long and Coughlin that are anything other than "easily recognizable." In an interview conducted several years after the novel's publication, Lewis revealed at least part of his motivation for writing It Can't Happen Here. Though the wording of his responses is somewhat suspect—the interviewer took notes on the conversation, but did not record it on tape—Lewis admitted, in so many words, that "I based my story on Huey Long. It's men like that who start dictatorships." Clearly, then, he would affirm reviewers' assertions that It Can't Happen Here is more political tract than novel. Indeed, what one scholar referred to as an overt "attempt at influencing American politics" is even more deliberately that than he may have imagined. In another late interview, one with his friend Luther Stearns Mansfield of the Swarthmore Department of English, Lewis went so far as to admit that It Can't Happen Here is the result of his entrance, alongside unnamed associates who also feared Long's potential, into a February 1935 pact to make "some positive effort to thwart Long's political ambitions." One might hypothesize that his wife was one of this group, that their neighbor Seldes was another, that their family friend and future biographer Sheean was perhaps an-

15. Direct references to Long in It Can't Happen Here are most often, but not always, to "the late" Huey Long. According to Schorer, Lewis forwarded the novel to publishers in early August 1935, then sailed for Europe—from which, after learning of Long's assassination some two weeks later, he cabled editors, asking them to insert "the late" in front of all such references. The fact that the finished novel, published October 21, 1935, contains references to both a living and a "late" Huey Long is therefore the result of last-minute editorial work (609).

other, but Mansfield offers no further details. Lingeman, summarizing a letter Thompson wrote Schorer in 1959, adds that the group once gathered to discuss the agreement in New York City's Algonquin Hotel, but he too tells us nothing about its particular makeup.[16] More than just a fictional politician, then, Windrip is a character created to cripple the political future of a factual figure who, at the time of the novel's composition, was threatening to do to all of America what he had already done to one state in particular. In creating him, however, Lewis was careful, for Windrip is enough like Long for readers to recognize him as a clear fictional counterpart but not so completely akin to him that their similarity robs Lewis of the license the novel as a genre affords him. Writing fiction rather than fact, he was free to ignore the earlier, more liberal components of Long's record to emphasize his later, more conservative tendencies, to transform him into the most extreme embodiment of right-wing radicalism since Copperhead Gap started whipping its prisoners. Protected behind Windrip's disguise, Lewis was free to insert near the center of *It Can't Happen Here* not just a conservatively slanted version of Long's biography, but a worst-case scenario of what he would later admit he was fiercely fighting to prevent: a 1936 Huey Long presidency.

Since material from Long's childhood could hardly harm Windrip—and, by association, Long himself—even if cast as slanderously as imaginable, the largest part of it in *It Can't Happen Here* is unrecognizable as such. Long was born in 1893, Windrip in 1888; Long was raised the son of a southern farmer, Windrip the son of a western pharmacist. The more Long matures, though, the more Lewis attacks him. When writing of Windrip's college career, he tells us that, unlike Long, who never actually enrolled at Oklahoma Baptist University, Windrip both attended and graduated from a Southern Baptist institution with all the academic standards of a Jersey City business college. Lewis then

16. Blackmur, 516; Tanner, 58; Allen Austin, "An Interview with Sinclair Lewis," *University of Kansas City Review* 24 (1958), 199, 203; James Lundquist, *The Merrill Guide to Sinclair Lewis* (Columbus: Merrill, 1970), 41; Luther Stearns Mansfield, "History and the Historical Process in *All the King's Men*," *Centennial Review* 22 (1978), 215–16; Lingeman, 398.

translates Long's years as a traveling salesman to still more damaging effect. Ignoring all the more reputable firms for which Long worked, he bestows upon Windrip a version only of Long's stint peddling products like the Wine of Cardui. In Lewis's hands, the material takes on an almost nefarious character, one whose relevance to Windrip's political career quickly becomes clear—even in spite of the overly and perhaps fatally glib tone. Lewis writes that, just as a much younger Long had played the mandolin to draw customers to his book sales, Windrip once played the banjo and performed card tricks to attract passersby to Old Dr. Alagash's Traveling Laboratory, a concern that specialized in such patent nostrums as the Choctaw Cancer Cure, the Chinook Consumption Soother, and the Oriental Remedy for Piles and Rheumatism. As if Windrip's defrauding the gullible and infirm were not enough, Lewis adds that, in doing so, he inevitably hastened the demise of many who otherwise would have sought a doctor's expertise. "But since then," Lewis concludes, "Windrip had redeemed himself, no doubt, by ascending from the vulgar fraud of selling bogus medicine, standing in front of a megaphone, to the dignity of selling bogus economics, standing . . . in front of a microphone" (85–86). When he sees no chance to inflict political harm, Lewis merely alters information benignly; ample opportunity to do greater damage, he seems to realize, will soon follow. The license the former affords, in short, is precisely the license the latter requires.

Though Lewis approaches Long's career as a lawyer in much the same way, he also seizes upon opportunities to withhold from Windrip, or to handicap him with adulterated versions of, Long's more celebrated courtroom triumphs. After law school, when Long was winning acclaim for his efforts in workers' compensation, Windrip was merely running a standard practice, earning himself no distinction whatever. No matter what one says of Long's later career, one must admit that, initially, at least, he accomplished a great deal for many who without him would likely have become casualties of somewhat piratical concerns. The same cannot be said of Buzz Windrip. Though not yet the archconservative he will become, he is far from a public servant, and even when Lewis grants him some small measure of Long's early success, he does so only to show him vindictively, egomaniacally gloating over it. In *Zero Hour,* excerpts from which, in the manner of those from "Pudd'nhead Wilson's Calendar," preface chapters at the center of the novel, Windrip at one point addresses a conflation of Long's storied war against the utilities and various other interests. Before recounting his decade-long battle against the Sangfrey River Light, Power, and Fuel Corporation, Windrip openly blasts its owners as "the meanest, lowest, cowardliest gang of yellow-livered, back slapping, hypocritical gun-toters, bomb-throwers, ballot stealers, ledger-fakers, givers of bribes, suborners of perjury, scab-hirers, and general lowdown crooks, liars, and swindlers that ever tried to do an honest servant of the People out of an election." In that he always defeated them in the courtroom, though, he assures us that his outburst is professional rather than personal, "entirely on behalf of the general public" (156). In this instance, at least, Lewis's satire is appropriate to his purpose. Never mind the fact that no such passage appears in *Every Man a King*—though Long does once refer to Standard Oil as "nefarious" and once refers to its policies as "plunder-grabbing."[17] More importantly, what Lewis achieves by way of the passage is the denigration of one of Long's most celebrated civic-minded triumphs into little more than a cheap personal victory. The implication, of course, is that Long engaged in such battles, as Windrip does, only for his own good, not, as he claimed, for the good of the people.

Lewis makes use of similar ammunition when addressing Windrip's tenure as a state politician. The fictional character and the factual figure may have served in only similar capacities, but their acts of office were at times identical. Windrip never sat on a state utilities/transportation board, and he progressed, somehow, from an unspecified state position other than governor to a U.S. Senate seat, but his winning his most unqualified acclaim for road construction and education reform leaves his story something less than fictional. The very presence of such material in *It Can't Happen Here* also proves Lewis not entirely averse to incorporating untarnished versions of at least a few of Long's more celebrated accomplishments. What we soon realize, though, is that he includes this material only to increase his reader's recognition of the Long in Windrip. Consequently, in each

17. Huey P. Long, *Every Man a King* (1933; reprint, Chicago: Quadrangle, 1964), 152, 64.

subsequent instance in which Lewis portrays Windrip unfavorably, the damage to Long's reputation is intensified. Consider, as perhaps the clearest case in this point, the fact that when Windrip realized he should not run for governor, he goaded another official into running in his stead, later making sure the people knew it was he, not the governor himself, who had done so much for the state. The reader, of course, is meant to see Long's treatment of O. K. Allen in Windrip's treatment of his own puppet governor—and the fact that the man to whom Windrip issues orders was, at the time, at least nominally his superior only makes Windrip, and, by association, Long, seem that much more of a tyrant. What Lewis tells us about U.S. Senator Long by way of state politician Windrip is much what he had implied about Long as a young attorney: that even though he accomplished a great deal for his supporters, he accomplished far more for himself, a reading that, as Williams suggests, was prevalent in Louisiana in the early 1930s. Lewis implies that as a senator Long may have continued his campaign for the underdog, but he did so mainly to augment his own personal power.

What Lewis shows us of Windrip's employing that power suggests less the local bully than the burgeoning totalitarian. If his Stalinesque campaign to buy tractors to lend the state's farmers does not imply enough, we soon read that, because he saw the United States soon seeking closer ties with the Soviet Union, Windrip used his Long-like clout at the state university to establish there the first course in Russian ever taught in that part of the country. He then quadrupled the size of the state militia and watched proudly as its members rose worshipfully to his side when, shortly thereafter, the state tried to indict him for embezzling $200,000 of tax revenue. Occupying legislative chambers and state offices, they established machine-gun posts on streets near the capitol and simply ushered Windrip's accusers out of town. The episode alludes to some of the most scandalous incidents in Long's career, including his alleged grafting of state funds, his impeachment, and his impending prosecution by the Internal Revenue Service, among others. Yet it also alludes to two less infamous, but still more power-mad moments: his alleged kidnapping of two political opponents during his U.S. senatorial campaign and his ruthless attempt to ensure the election of his hand-picked candidate during the 1934 New

Orleans mayoral race (*HL* 471–76). To bring about the latter, he ordered the national guard to seize the New Orleans offices of the registrar of voters, even to install machine guns in office windows, to "protect" the books from his opponent's supposed henchmen (*HL* 722–23). Some incidents, it seems, are so openly tyrannical, so nakedly totalitarian, that Lewis needed not embellish them whatsoever. So too his assertion that during his term as senator Windrip was "as absolute a ruler of his state as ever a sultan was of Turkey" (34). If the facts themselves are not ignominious enough, Lewis alters them accordingly; if ignominious enough on their face, as are many that make up Long's record as governor and senator, all Lewis needed do was transcribe them.

His portrait of the candidate holding court in his hotel room also exhibits little if any embellishment. The scene could have been almost directly transposed from any of Long's frequent stays at the Heidelberg in Baton Rouge or the Roosevelt in New Orleans. To one observer—and, again, Lewis's tone undercuts the true danger inherent in such brazen manipulations of power—the scene embodied all the commotion of a tabloid newspaper office's trying to cover a story about Bishop James Cannon setting fire to St. Patrick's Cathedral, kidnapping the Dionne quintuplets, and eloping with Greta Garbo in a commandeered tank. Everyone from stockbrokers to bootleggers, labor leaders to oil lobbyists, seeks him there, and he routinely promises support to politicians of any stripe if they will only promise him theirs. Lewis writes that Windrip "grinned and knee-patted and back-slapped; and few of his visitors, once they had talked with him, failed to look upon him as their Little Father and to support him forever" (90). As was Long (*HL* 320), Windrip is too busy to sleep more than a few hours a night. When not meeting with his legions of visitors, he can usually be found shouting into the phone, often all day and all night long. In a single twenty-seven-minute period, Windrip calls Palo Alto, California; Washington, D.C.; Buenos Aires; Wilmette, Illinois; and Oklahoma City. On another occasion he receives sixteen calls from clergymen requesting that he condemn a burlesque show and seven from promoters asking that he praise it. He makes sincere promises to each but does nothing whatsoever for any. Long's method of conducting daily business promised such colorful translation into fiction that it would eventually inspire a handful of similar scenes in the novels that followed. More than just verisimilitude and color, though, it afforded Lewis a way to illustrate the difference between the public and the private politician, to expose the fact that, no matter what Windrip—and, by implication, Long—seems in public, in private he is a crass manipulator of power, a tyrannical puller of strings local, national, even global, and, most unforgivably, an unblinking hypocrite who shamelessly reneges on apparent promises. He makes equally fervent pledges to representatives of opposing parties and then quietly denies in private what he most fervently asserts in public.

Lewis, it seems, found that any attempt to sabotage Long's run for the White House had to first substitute a portrait like the preceding for the public portrait his followers knew so well. For no matter how deviously Windrip wields power behind the closed doors of his hotel suite, most of these performances are hidden from all but his closest associates. What most observers see is not the guileful manipulator but what Lewis dubs the "Professional Common Man," who, though running for the nation's highest elected office, has nonetheless convinced millions that he is essentially no different than they. Publicly, at least, Windrip professes faith in the everyday nobility of dogs, in thick pancakes smothered in artificial syrup, in waitresses working small-town restaurants, in the simple persistence of Henry Ford, in the almost mystical superiority of anyone who somehow amasses a million dollars. Spats, on the other hand, and walking sticks, caviar, hereditary titles, tea, and poetry not syndicated in daily newspapers are "degenerate" (88). Lewis's illustrations of Windrip's dramatizing this commonness are but thinly veiled versions of Long's doing the same. Just as Long drew figures as high-ranking as then-governor Roosevelt into the corn pone–potlikker debate, Windrip regales the U.S. Senate with lessons on how to catch catfish and challenges the Chief Justice of the Supreme Court to a sling-shot duel. Just as Long insulted Germany but amused Louisiana by wearing green pajamas to greet the commander of the *Emden,* Windrip insults Britain's Duke of York by skipping an embassy dinner in his honor but later pacifies him with a personal visit and a bouquet of geraniums that, even if it does not quite quell the British outcry, does win him among American mothers the kind of support his earlier antics had won him among their husbands. In that it becomes one of his most constant targets, it follows that Lewis found the American dictator's talent for concealing his true character behind the mask of a commoner one of the most dangerous weapons in his arsenal, and precisely because it was so disarming. Long biographer Thomas O. Harris points to the chief benefit of the guise: anyone who thinks Long was "a vulgarian" simply because "vulgarity was inherent in his make-up is only reaching half the truth." Long "was a vulgarian on the political rostrum because he found that it paid dividends in votes."[18]

Both Windrip and Long are also cunning enough orators to occasionally drop the Common Man facade just long enough to lift themselves above, but not expose themselves as anyone wholly superior to, their truly common followers. For if Windrip is the Common Man, he is also, as Lewis puts it, the Common Man "twenty-times-magnified by his oratory." So while his followers see him as one of their own, they see him at the same time as a man "towering among them" (88)—but not, it should be noted, *above* them—and therefore they all but bow down to him in praise. His platform is almost entirely illusory, his ideas are almost "idiotic," and Windrip himself is "a public liar easily detected" (86), but he captivates his audiences just the same, for he is—as Thompson found Hitler, as many found Long—"an actor of genius," a born performer with a tremendous range. Lewis writes that there was no more talented actor than Windrip on stage or on screen. "He would whirl arms, bang tables, glare from mad eyes, vomit Biblical wrath from a gaping mouth: but he would also coo like a nursing mother, beseech like an aching lover," and in between acts would so artfully animate dead facts and figures that, even when they were inaccurate or just plain incorrect, he could continue to manipulate his audience as craftily as Elmer Gantry ever had his. Still more frighteningly, Windrip could also claim so convincingly that he was "neither a Nazi nor a Fascist but a . . . homespun Jeffersonian-Lincolnian-Clevelandian-Wilsonian Democrat" that listeners would visualize him "veritably defending the Capitol against barbarian hordes" even as he "innocently presented as his own warm-hearted Democratic inven-

18. Thomas O. Harris, *The Kingfish: Huey P. Long, Dictator* (1938; reprint, Baton Rouge: Claitor's, 1968), 94.

tions" all the "anti-libertarian, anti-Semitic madness of Europe" (87). And Windrip's skills only grow more menacing when Lewis lets him showcase them all over the country. Just as Long, engaged in any number of campaigns, traveled to parts of Louisiana previously untouched by either predecessor or opponent, Windrip, during his campaign for president, logs some 27,000 miles on a train trip through all forty-eight states. In just forty days he delivers more than six hundred speeches, reaching some two million Americans in the process. In this respect, Windrip is little more than a better-traveled version of Long. Besides granting him greater geographical range, Lewis does little to modify this material—for such powerful talents of persuasion, it seems, are more than threatening enough in themselves.

Further magnifying this threat is the abject desperation of the two million Americans who attend Windrip's rallies and of several million more who do not. Their search is not as much for *the* solution as it is for *a* solution, any solution at all. Except for the fact that those we meet are for the most part urbanized, Windrip's faithful are much like those who, as Long biographer Forrest Davis described them, employed almost every means necessary to make the trip to Baton Rouge for Long's inauguration. On the night of Windrip's Madison Square Garden rally, Jessup too finds a ragged assemblage who, though high on hope at that moment, at any other moment would have been downtrodden and distraught. Most are blue-collar workers who, if lucky enough to still hold a job, spend long days just trying to thread another needle, prepare another tray of food, or answer another maintenance call, long nights worrying about dirty diapers, dull razor blades, and the ever-rising cost of rump steak. Even those few who can afford suits of clothes wear transparently inexpensive ones inevitably stitched by what were probably palsied fingers. Still, just as Jonathan Swift's Brobdingnagian dwarf puffs himself up around the relatively diminutive Gulliver, they pathetically look down on those who cannot afford what they find finery, commenting, "I don't know why all these bums go on relief. I may not be such a wiz, but let me tell you, even since 1929, I've never made less than *two thousand dollars a year!*" For the most part, though, Windrip's hopeful are "[k]ind people, industrious people, generous to their aged, eager to find any desperate cure for the sickness of worry over losing the job"—in short, the "[m]ost facile material for any rabble-rouser" (116). In addition to this contingent there is also a slightly less desperate group that does not attend the rally, for its members are victims less of hunger than of "congested idealism." Among them Lewis is quick to include a number of intellectuals and individualists who somehow find in Windrip, even despite his "clownish swindlerism" (95), a reinvigoration of the nation's increasingly hobbled economy. Lewis thus adds to those history portrays as Long's supporters a slightly more prosperous group seeking an unorthodox solution to the Depression, and by associating them with such a duped gathering of the "facile," he attempts to dissuade them as well—his own readers, perhaps—from supporting Huey Long.

Unlike Long, Windrip lives to win the presidency—and, in writing of his doing so, Lewis moves from what had been to what he hoped would never be, frustrating in the process all further attempts to compare factual figure and fictional character. Or so it might seem: for though Long did not live to enter a presidential race, he left behind a book detailing what he claimed he would do once he won one. Published in September 1935, the very month of his assassination, *My First Days in the White House* is a so-called prophecy in which Long essentially fictionalizes himself and the presidency he never lived to attain. Curiously, considering that *It Can't Happen Here* did not appear for more than a month after his assassination, *My First Days*, almost as if alluding to Lewis's title before Long could have known of it, begins with the sentence, "It had happened." America, his second sentence explains, "had endorsed my plan for the redistribution of wealth," and "I was President of the United States." More significant than this apparent coincidence between first sentence and title is the fact that, though both books were written at roughly the same time (*HL* 845)[19] and examine, in a sense, the same subject, *My First Days in the White House* takes an understandably utopian stance toward the assured certainty of a Long presidency, whereas *It Can't Happen Here* takes an understandably dystopian stance toward the mere possibility of the same. Long, after all, was trying to enlist readers' aid in making It happen, Lewis to enlist their aid in making sure It did not. What happens

19. Huey P. Long, *My First Days in the White House* (Harrisburg: Telegraph, 1935), 3; Schorer, 608.

in Lewis's America, therefore, in direct contrast to what happens in Long's, is the ultimate unmasking of a democrat as not just demagogue, but dictator—precisely what Lewis warned would happen if America elected Long to Windrip's position.

In *My First Days,* Long explains that one of his first acts of office would concern the philosophy, or perhaps scheme, for which he was best known. In a congressional address on the second day of his term, he calls for the creation of an enormous federal agency to assess the distribution of national wealth. Details come not from the president himself, but from figures including J. P. Morgan, Jr., who, in a letter more transparently, even comically expository than truly inflammatory, objects to Long's "effort to decentralize wealth through the confiscation of individual fortunes in excess of five million dollars, gradually to be reduced even below that to something less than two million dollars." The next figure to address the issue is John D. Rockefeller, Jr., who, ironically, has agreed to chair the National Share Our Wealth Committee. Rockefeller explains that, after the confiscation of so-called surplus income, the Federal Share Our Wealth Corporation will divide and distribute it in the form of stock to the American people. Final details come from President Long himself, who in another congressional address specifies that, since no American family should earn less than one-third of what the average family earns, all shall receive a yearly income of at least $2,500 and own no less than $5,000 to $6,000 worth of household "comforts and conveniences."[20] In *It Can't Happen Here,* Windrip's plans for the seizure and distribution of "excess" wealth—plans derived not from *My First Days,* of course, but from any number of Long's pronouncements dating back to Share Our Wealth's February 1934 debut—differ only in detail. The fifth of his Fifteen Points of Victory for the Forgotten Man, the platform that wins him the White House, stipulates that yearly incomes be limited to $500,000, lifetime inheritances to $2,000,000, personal fortunes to $3,000,000. All wealth in excess of these sums will be seized and either distributed among the populace or retained to cover the costs of administration. In that he not only builds Windrip's program upon the outline of Long's own but specifies that it will seize more—and not

20. Long, *My First Days,* 69, 109–11.

just for distribution to the citizenry, but for suspiciously vague admin-
istrative expenses—glossing over all detail as to how it will be divided
and distributed, Lewis makes Share Our Wealth seem that much more
illusory, that much more suspect, that much less ostensibly benevolent
than Long purported.

Long explains that another early act would initiate widespread
banking reform. Because the nation's banks, according to his unnamed
secretary of the treasury, had seized control of American industry and
commerce only by way of the masses' hard-won capital, Long proposes
that his administration establish a federal bank to be overseen by popularly elected directors. Specifics are scarce, as is often the case in *My
First Days*, as had often been the case since Long first proposed such
notions, but his secretary approves of the plan, commenting that, in
addition to more equitably distributing the financial power bankers
had all but appropriated from the people, the plan would create a safer
system that the citizenry itself would administrate. The first of Windrip's Fifteen Points, on the other hand, in no way sounds so reasonable. It begins by stipulating that all fiscal matters—all banking,
investment, finance, and insurance—be subject to the "absolute control" of a Federal Central Bank, a concern to be administered not by a
popularly elected, but by a presidentially appointed, board that, completely independent of Congress, would regulate finance as only it sees
fit. Windrip also charges this board—"for the Profit of the Whole People," of course (75)—with the eventual government seizure of all natural resources and public utilities. Lewis thus takes another issue
associated with Long, one potentially totalitarian enough on its own,
and makes it all the more so by affiliating it in the reader's mind with
the phrase "absolute control," then by listing among its specifics an almost immediate shift of power away from the people and their elected
representatives and toward the president alone. And while natural resources and public utilities are essentially irrelevant to Long's plans for
banking reform, Lewis expands what had been only a general idea to
such an extent that we watch as Windrip plots to commandeer them
as well. In that his power-mad proposition is similar to but far more
acquisitive than Long's original initiative, it makes the latter, by association, seem that much more rapacious.

In the name of a far more malicious form of character assassination,

Lewis burdens Windrip with particularly odious racial views that Long was never known to espouse. Historians and scholars have often praised Long for his attitude toward, and work for, races other than his own. In *The Mind of the South*, for instance, W. J. Cash commends him for being the first southern demagogue "largely to leave aside" race, a view that Williams often corroborates, adding that while the privileges he wanted to extend African Americans might not seem significant now, they were at the time "large, almost revolutionary, far more than any other Southern politician was willing to give" (*HL* 705). Consider as a contrast the image of Windrip that Lewis paints by way of Point 10: African Americans, he decrees, shall not vote, hold public office, practice law or medicine, or teach beyond grammar school, nor shall an African American family earn or inherit more than $10,000 a year. To make sure he fittingly assists African Americans who understand their "proper and valuable place in society," though, he proposes that those who serve more than forty-five years as domestics or common laborers be allowed at age sixty-five to petition a board of white officials for a yearly pension of up to $700 per family—but only upon proving all absences from work the result of sickness alone. Long may not exactly have fought to enfranchise African Americans—Williams insists that, at the time, it would have alienated his constituency and effectively ended his career (*HL* 705)—but he in no way hindered the cause, either. Nor did he try to circumscribe them to the lives of menials or propose for them more restrictive Share Our Wealth regulations. Instead, he was known for establishing night schools to fight illiteracy among all races, and for arguing that, "Black and white, they all gotta have a chance. They gotta have a home, a job and a decent education for their children."[21] In this instance, instead of merely exaggerating one of Long's own views, Lewis denies it outright, handicapping Windrip with something far worse than a simply more extreme version of a view Long in fact espoused. Windrip here, in short, seems more Hitler than Huey Long, more a potential proponent of genocide than anything even approximating racial equality.

21. W. J. Cash, *The Mind of the South* (1941; reprint, Garden City: Doubleday, 1954), 291; Roy Wilkins, "The Irrelevance of Race," in *Huey Long*, ed. Hugh Davis Graham, Great Lives Observed (Englewood Cliffs, N.J.: Prentice-Hall, 1970), 78.

Long returns, however, to help Windrip write Point 15. More than just the central plank in his platform, Windrip's most urgent imperative, Point 15 seems the very inspiration behind *It Can't Happen Here,* the embodiment of what Lewis was most writing to prevent. What he feared, it seems clear, is that Long, once admitted to the White House, would seize control of the United States just as he had eventually seized control of Louisiana. What Long took years to win, however, Windrip demands upon entrance:

> Congress shall, immediately upon our inauguration, initiate amendments to the Constitution providing (a), that the President shall have the authority to institute and execute all necessary measures for the conduct of the government during this critical epoch (b), that Congress serve only in an advisory capacity, calling to the attention of the President and his aides and Cabinet any needed legislation, but not acting upon same until authorized by the President so to act; and (c), that the Supreme Court shall immediately have removed from its jurisdiction the power to negate, by ruling them to be unconstitutional or by any other judicial action, any or all acts of the President, his duly appointed aides, or Congress.

An addendum to the Fifteen Points, moreover, states that the League of Forgotten Men and the Democratic Party consider none but Point 15 "obligatory and unmodifiable" (78–79). Power thus trumps even money, for not even Windrip's plans to confiscate wealth and centralize national finance attain the status of absolute imperatives. Long would have trouble answering charges that he had approached government—albeit state instead of national—in much the same way. Descriptions of him as a U.S. senator demanding the passage of forty-four bills in a single session of the state legislature are little more than localized illustrations of Windrip's demand that Congress serve in only an advisory capacity, and Long's disregard for Louisiana law in forging a stranglehold on his state Supreme Court is but a similar realization of Windrip's demand that the U.S. Supreme Court be divested of all power to counteract the president (*HL* 736). In sum, Windrip's demands on the national level are little but fictionalized projections of Long's actual acquisitions on the state level. Windrip thus realizes the dictatorship Elmer Gantry only dreamed of, thereby becoming the sin-

gle most formidably powerful figure in Lewis's corpus, the one character who most clearly embodies his greatest political fears.

On the closing pages of *My First Days*, Long imagines for us an
America that, as a direct result of his initiatives, has blossomed into
the very Utopia he envisioned. America's most trying problems have
been solved. Educational reform has revitalized the nation's schools;
updated machinery has increased production and simultaneously
earned workers more leisure time; the homelessness, hunger, and unemployment of the Great Depression have been all but completely
vanquished. So successful is the Long presidency that, on a trip he
takes to examine firsthand his modern American renaissance, he hears
but one lone complaint—that he had not run for president sooner. On
the closing pages of *It Can't Happen Here*, no one voices such praise
for Windrip, for what follows from his initiatives—which are, in many
cases, but exaggerated versions of Long's own—is not Utopia, but
Pandemonium. As Lewis imagines them, the results of such a presidency are not the sunny scenes Long describes, but the dark, violent
days Doremus Jessup has to struggle to survive. Once the new president assumes absolute power, the novel proceeds as follows: One of
Windrip's henchmen kills two pacifist college professors, and Jessup,
after restraining himself for nearly a year, revolts by way of an editorial
column. For criticizing the Corpo regime in print, he finds himself
summarily imprisoned on charges of everything from criminal libel to
high treason, and a perhaps worse fate follows his parole. Released to
assist the Corpo takeover of his newspaper, he is instructed to write
only what they dictate and to serialize the complete text of Windrip's
Zero Hour. For Jessup, however, "the prostitute days" of *The Daily In-
former* do not last long (241), for he boldly resigns to write covert
propaganda for the New Underground, a counterrevolutionary organization founded by Walt Trowbridge, the former U.S. senator who had
escaped over the border into Canada after losing the 1936 presidential
race to Windrip. However, Jessup's stint editing *Vermont Vigilance*
proves almost as short as his previous assignment, for when marauding
Corpos uncover an antiadministration article in progress during a raid
on his home, they arrest him yet again. This time they take him to a
concentration camp, beat him with a steel rod, force a quart of castor
oil down his throat, and sentence him to seventeen years' confinement.

Six months later, though, he escapes, and he is soon smuggled into Canada by way of the reopened Underground Railroad. There, he works more closely with Trowbridge and his men, who, at the end of the novel, assign him a new identity and send him back over the border to disseminate anti-Windrip propaganda. "And still Doremus goes on in the red sunrise," the novel's last sentence reads, "for a Doremus Jessup can never die" (458).

It Can't Happen Here is thus a warning—one fully intended, widely accepted, and often even acclaimed as such—written that Americans might be spared the same journey, that they might not have to agitate, much less crusade, to save the country. The reader for whom Lewis writes is one who would argue, along with Jessup's more unwitting associates, that a dictatorial regime could never overrun the United States. Dramatizing such foolhardy thinking in contexts national ("Country's too big for a revolution. . . . Couldn't happen here" [54]), regional ("things like that couldn't ever happen here in New England" [171]), even personal ("nothing bad can happen here, in this solid household" [213]), Lewis works to remedy such blindness by illustrating that, as all but Jessup realize only after the fact, "It *can* happen here" (294). Yet the novel is also directed at all optimists, relativists, and true-blue Americans who would argue that even if it did happen here, our fabled native humor and independent spirit would save us from the specific fate of so many million Europeans. Within months of Windrip's inauguration, many who had reasoned the same discover that handcuffs, horsewhips, and steel rods have the exact effect here as there. Despite all its differences, America, as Lewis saw it, could spawn just as restrictive a regime as Europe had. According to what Jessup designates his "biology of dictatorships" (344), all such regimes, no matter where their capitol, derive from the same mind-set, thrive upon the same oppression, violence, and terror. It was almost as if Mussolini, Stalin, Hitler, and Windrip had all read the same "manual of sadistic etiquette." So, too, even in the "humorous, friendly, happy-go-lucky land of Mark Twain," we watch as "the homicidal maniacs [have] just as good a time as they had had in central Europe" (345). It not only could happen here, Lewis argues, but it could happen here with the same inhumane devastation as it happened there.

At the same time, Lewis also warns readers of at least one distinct difference between European and American incarnations of these regimes. Whereas those who led them in Europe openly claim their Fascist, Communist, and National Socialist labels, those who will lead them in America will deny them for just that reason. Long himself, after all, was widely credited with saying that, when fascism comes to America, it will do so as antifascism (*HL* 760). Ideology aside, the word fascism is, as one of Jessup's associates puts it, only that: "Just a word—just a word" (22). Fittingly, what Lewis calls Windrip's "master stroke" is that, just as he convinces Americans that they can get rich simply by voting themselves rich, he so adamantly denounces fascism that both Republicans who fear democratic fascism and Democrats who fear republican fascism readily pledge him their support. Jessup is one of the few who look below the semantics of the situation to realize that the true threat to freedom and equality is not any one totalitarian movement in particular but the masses' placid tolerance of the rabid intolerance that is so much a part of them all—a fact obscured in America by the presence of fascists who preach against fascism in the name of traditional American constitutional democracy. The leader Lewis most hopes to expose in *It Can't Happen Here* is an American who, at least on the surface, "seem[s] so different from the fervent Hitlers and gesticulating Fascists and the Caesars with laurels round bald domes." That leader employs the same homespun American humor as Artemus Ward, Mark Twain, and Will Rogers but, examined more closely, also employs the tactics of Mussolini, Stalin, and Hitler, even though he would refuse a place among them. *It Can't Happen Here,* then, is almost as much compliment as condemnation: for in so explicitly warning readers to look for the dictator behind the commoner's mask, the fascism belying the antifascist stance, the stark reality below the humorous surface, Lewis inevitably portrays Long as not just an imminent threat but the single most deviously disarming threat to mid-1930s American democracy. At the very least, it seems, he wanted to make sure America didn't laugh itself to death.

The situation, as Lewis saw it, was far from funny, and to make sure his readers fully grasped that fact, he created a character who looks like Adolph Hitler but thinks and acts like Huey Long. To make still more immediate the possibility he feared enough to fight by way of a sworn pact, he shows Windrip first winning the White House, then erecting from within it a regime that, though more the work of a European fascist than an American democrat, is nonetheless built upon exaggerated versions of Long's own proposals. Lewis's goal, in short, was to assassinate Long's character by associating him with a fictional politician who resembles him just enough for readers to recognize the Long in him but who differs enough from him to earn Lewis the license to freely present by way of fiction what he feared the world of fact would one day see. In general, his method was as follows: If a given biographical incident reflected badly enough upon Long, Lewis incorporated it as documented or rewrote it to reflect still more badly upon him. If the facts were more benign, Lewis simply changed them to earn himself further license. If they reflected well upon Long, Lewis either ignored them altogether, rewrote them for the worse, or, if they were from a particularly celebrated chapter of Long's career, incorporated them more or less as documented to increase readers' recognition of the factual figure in the fictional character. No matter the means, the end is always the same: character assassination. Long and Windrip have their differences, of course, but those differences are more matters of degree than class. Windrip may be something less of a lawyer than Long was, but what stands out is the fact that both fight the big man for the ostensible benefit of the little. They also share the same wardrobe, run governments from hotel suites, bully their political appointees, pitch wealth redistribution schemes to revivify Depression-wracked America, and, most significantly, employ political tactics that, no matter what they might call them, are clearly fascistic. Berzelius Windrip is not, of course, the Huey Long historians tell us was, but he is, despite the external differences, the Huey Long Sinclair Lewis warned us could be.

When his chief lieutenant Lee Sarason suddenly deposes and then deports Windrip at the end of the novel, though, we realize that Long embodied only the most immediate of what Lewis found dictatorial threats to America. As one character had put it earlier, "Windrip's just something nasty that's been vomited up. . . . Buzz isn't important—it's the sickness that made us throw him up that we've got to attend to. . . . Got to cure it!" (132). No matter how distracting they might be, symptoms like Windrip, we are reminded, are ultimately subordinate to the "sickness" itself, the archconservative virus that, even after Lewis diagnosed it in Gopher Prairie, went on to ravage Zenith, Copperhead Gap, and, in *It Can't Happen Here,* all of America. Yet for all his call for a cure, Lewis can offer only treatment: greater personal vigilance against America's tolerance of, if not inherent tendency toward, archconservative interests. One of the few conclusions of which Jessup remains certain is that dictatorships are not as much the fault of dictators themselves as of the millions of "conscientious, respectable, lazy-minded Doremus Jessups" who complacently let them "wriggle in, without fierce enough protest. . . . It's my sort," Jessup realizes, all the so-called responsible citizens, who have invited a dictator into their very homes. He therefore absolves Buzz Windrip and implicates his own "timid soul and drowsy mind," finally asking, "Is it too late?" (224). "No, it is not too late," Lewis wanted all Americans— particularly those sleeping through watch—to answer, for their dedication to defeating the archconservative virus that so ravages Jessup's America was the first step toward preserving their own America as well. Before the novel could be published, though, even before Jessup could pose his question to readers, one American returned what he no doubt would have considered a correct, even if extreme, answer. For the world of fact soon found what the world of fiction lacked, exactly what Jessup himself had sought: that rare physician whose treatment of a single symptom may well have prevented an American epidemic of the "sickness"—Dr. Carl Austin Weiss.

In the end, perhaps, Lewis should have been grateful for the fact: for even as much as *It Can't Happen Here* implicitly endorses acts like Weiss's, it hardly seems capable of inspiring them. Even if Long had lived to see it published, he would likely have had very little to fear, for Lewis only occasionally calls readers to arms. As self-destructive as it might sound, he devotes a good deal of the novel to trying to amuse his audience. Budd Schulberg illustrates the potentially disastrous effects of these contrary intentions in a 1960 *Esquire* article. He writes that, as a Dartmouth undergraduate in the mid-1930s, he invited Lewis to campus to speak on the subject of "Fascism and the Novel." Instead of addressing the politics behind *It Can't Happen Here,* however, Lewis opened with impersonations of Coughlin, moved on to impersonations of Long, concluded with a joke, and then asked if there were questions.

When several followed, all of more serious import than his own offerings, his face grew red, his responses monosyllabic, and he stood up, shouted "You young sons of bitches, you c'n all go to hell!" and promptly stormed out of the room. Such, it seems, is the effect of satire on those expecting something more mimetic: they can turn as easily on the author as on his intended target. Because of just such contradictions, because it attempts to warn us on one page and amuse us on the next, *It Can't Happen Here* is at times more protracted burlesque than what Schulberg says the Dartmouth audience had expected— "something Profound and Significant about fascism."[22] Some seven decades later, what remains most striking about the novel is not its portrayal of archconservatism's absolute conquest of America but Lewis's inability to keep caricature from eroding the earnest attitude his novel needs if it is to sincerely warn its readers. Reviewers wrote that this was not the satire readers had come to expect from Lewis. But if it is not at least something of a satire, how are we to react to a brigadier general's promoting world war as a restorative for the flagging American spirit? How are we to read scenes like that in which U.S. Senator Theodore Bilbo, as Windrip's new ambassador to Russia, reviews a military parade in Moscow? The context alone—though clearly parodic on its face—would seem rife with the potential for commentary about Bilbo's programs in Mississippi and Washington, but Lewis forgoes all such opportunities to turn the scene into even more of a gag. Stalin has to be carried off after reviewing 317,000 Soviet troops, but Bilbo stays on to review 626,000—all of whom mistake him for the Chinese ambassador. Though hardly the radical he once wanted to seem, Lewis at least appears to have taken the threat of American fascism seriously, at least appears to have wanted his readers to do the same, but he simply could not restrain his satirical impulse thoroughly enough to issue a consistently urgent warning. Even in small doses, humor is not the means toward what reportedly was his end. What worked for Long thus works against Lewis—who may have been able to appreciate, but could not begin to duplicate, his subject's masterful talent for manipulating the American masses.

22. Budd Schulberg, "Lewis: Big Wind from Sauk Centre," *Esquire*, December 1960, 114.

2 Snopeses in the Statehouse: Hamilton Basso's Harry Brand and Gilgo Slade

AT FIRST, AT LEAST, HAMILTON BASSO WAS IMPRESSED—so impressed, in fact, that in telling the story of Huey Long's stumping the Pelican State for governor, he spends more time describing his reaction to one particular campaign stop than setting the scene of it for his readers. He almost seems to forget background detail, writing, for instance, that the date of the stop came during the late fall, but leaving it to us to infer that, as Long was elected governor just a few months later, the year had to have been 1927, the campaign itself his second for the office. He then adds that the stop took place in southern Louisiana, but he neither places it more precisely on the map nor hints at whether we should imagine the candidate's haranguing a bustling small-town square, for instance, or perhaps somewhere more characteristically Acadian, maybe the shady threshold of a moss-draped, cypress-clotted bayou. He does tell us, though, that the weather was unseasonably warm that day, and that the men beginning to gather there were all sweating through their shirts as their wives, standing quietly beside them, tried to cool themselves off with palmetto-leaf fans. About the candidate himself, however, Basso—a young reporter then living in his native New Orleans—is a bit more forthcoming. He writes that he soon found himself one of many surrounding a dormant Ford convertible in which a sweat-soaked Long, from a makeshift dais atop its broad backseat, was "pouring acid in their eyes," as Basso tells us they put it in that part of the state. Long's message, of course, included his trademark attacks on corporations, public utilities, and the Old Regulars and his trademark promises for better roads, free schoolbooks, and lower gas and electric rates. Forgoing all pretense toward the journalistic objectivity he had had to observe at the time, Basso would concede in the 1935 *Harper's Monthly* article "Huey Long and His Background" that the overheated locals were not the only ones taken with what they had heard that afternoon. It was easy to believe the young candidate, to find him "earnest and sincere," he wrote, for as public service commissioner Long had been fighting for much of the past decade the same forces he was then so aggressively baiting. He seemed a man of the people as much as of his word, for he spoke to them in their native tongue—"American instead of bombast"—and to such clear effect that, nearly eight years after the fact, Basso would remember joining in the easy laughter at his barnyard and cornfield humor. "They understood and liked him," he wrote, and "I liked him too. I had just become awakened politically, [was just] beginning to take an interest in such things," and, he confessed, "I thought that here was a young and forceful radical it would be well to support."

"So I was glad," Basso continued, when "this wild young mustang from the hills of Winn Parish" won the state a few months later. Dispatched the day of the election to file a story on Long's victory celebration, he found himself that night among the chaos of campaign headquarters. As he approached the governor-elect, then shaking hands amid drifts of campaign paraphernalia, though, what had once been elation suddenly left the young reporter. Long's face, Basso wrote, was flushed an aggressive red. His eyes were bloodshot, his shirt thrown open at the collar, and he looked nothing like the man of the people from that afternoon in the south of the state. The man who would later take on the semblance of Dorothy Thompson's Hitler at that moment looked more like John Milton's Satan as he first musters his fellow demons in the depths of Pandemonium. Gathering his lieutenants around him, Long declared, conspiratorially, "You fellers stick to me. We're just getting started. This is only the beginning. We'll show this New Orleans gang who is boss. From now on I'm the Kingfish. I'm gonna be President someday." Basso went on to write that between that night in early 1928 and the day some seven years later when he described it in "Huey Long and His Background" he had heard assertions of the sort enough times to more fully comprehend Long's unabashed compulsion, if not maniacal drive, for power. At that moment, though, he was hearing them for the first time, and as only a recent initiate into the world of politics, he had not yet realized that what the office-seeker seems in public is not what the officeholder is in private. What left him so angrily disenchanted was the fact that the megalomaniac he was watching jump-start his machine was also the apparent man of the people he had watched charm the rural masses just a few short months before. "I felt"—and "not without a smoldering of rebellion"—Basso confessed, "that I had somehow been betrayed."[1]

What would follow from him over the next few decades bears witness to more than just a "smoldering" of rebellion: *bonfire* might be a better word to describe it. Basso began retaliating almost immediately. Covering events like the governor-elect's victory celebration for the three largest New Orleans newspapers, he spent the early years of his career as a reporter so frequently raising Long's ire that the governor once had him thrown out of his hotel suite and on another occasion had him arrested by the National Guard. Upon promotion to the *New Republic* in the mid-1930s, Basso took what had earlier been only local and statewide retaliation to the much broader national level. Of the shorter articles he wrote for the *New Republic*—where, as something of the resident authority on the subject, he published more than a half-dozen articles on Long—one of the first and most revealing is his 1934 review of *Every Man a King*, "Mr. Senator, Come Clean!" Beginning from the third-person perspective common to such pieces, Basso wrote that "[t]he Senator hides too much." Quickly shifting into the more aggressively direct, if not downright confrontational, second-person, he brashly asked, "[W]hy do you avoid so many points of interest?" Readers want to know, he insisted, more about the impeachment proceedings and "just what you did to erect your dictatorship. We should like to have the low-down on the Long Island affair—not because we are interested in why you did what to a man's trouser leg, but because it was probably the most important act of your political career." The "whole trouble," he concluded, is that "[w]e've never been able to believe you. You've fooled us too many times, and . . . we can't help believing you are holding something back. Come on, Mr. Senator. Tell us all."[2] Despite the shrewd confidence, if not brash cockiness of the

1. Hamilton Basso, "Huey Long and His Background," *Harper's Monthly*, May 1935, 663–64.

2. Inez Hollander Lake, *The Road from Pompey's Head: The Life and Work of Hamilton Basso* (Baton Rouge: Louisiana State University Press, 1999), 13; Hamilton Basso, "Let's

voice and perspective, one still senses here the sting of betrayal the young reporter had felt six years earlier. How else logically explain his charge that the Sands Point Bath and Country Club had been the scene of Long's greatest achievement? The comments, clearly, are more personal than professional: more than that Long had fooled America "too many times," it seems the "whole trouble" may well have been that he had once fooled the reviewer himself.

Yet Basso would not always portray Long in such an injurious light. He applauded him in one article, for instance, as the only politician in Louisiana history even to try to deliver on his promises. For the most part, though, Basso's contributions to the *New Republic* and other national magazines portray him even more negatively than "Mr. Senator, Come Clean!" Turning from the political to the social import of Long's tenure in the governor's mansion, Basso wrote in "Huey Long and His Background" that, even though Louisianians should have known in 1928 that they should brace for an unusual, if not unprecedented term of office, they were in no way prepared for what their new governor would actually unleash upon the state. For

> [w]hat Huey did, in effect, was to stride into the Governor's office, take off his coat, put his feet on the desk, and spit tobacco juice on the walls. The office of Governor until that time had always been considered one of importance, to be accorded at least a show of outward respect, and the antics of the Kingfish (an appellation taken, despite all the fables undertaken to explain it, out of the blackface radio program) left them shocked and aghast. Nor did Huey give them time to recover. He applied shock after shock, adding confoundment to confusion, until they, and his political opponents, were reduced to a state of impotent rage, and the rest of the country was laughing its head off.

Adding that there was not "a tradition or a ceremony he did not violate," Basso went on to catalogue a few of Long's specifically social transgressions. He had run the state from a hotel suite; he had taken part in—and fled—public fistfights; he had worn pajamas to greet a foreign dignitary; he had drawn national press for urinating on a night

---

Look at the Record," *New Republic*, 20 February 1935, 41; Hamilton Basso, "Mr. Senator, Come Clean!" *New Republic*, 21 February 1934, 54.

club patron.[3] There was a Snopes—one comprised, it seems, of two parts Clarence, one part Flem—in the statehouse, and Basso wanted the world to feel his resentment. Yet at the same time, he also knew better than even to whisper the word "eviction." Sinclair Lewis might try to eliminate the problem he feared Long might become, but to Hamilton Basso, Long was not a problem to be solved so much as one of the more blatant indications of a sociohistorical trend that, however lamentable he might find it, he knew he was powerless to halt. Long might violate "tradition" and "ceremony" on an almost daily basis, but such, as Basso saw it, was as much a function of history as the individual actions of any one participant in it.

History—southern history in particular—had long been one of Basso's abiding interests. More than a decade before W. J. Cash would publish *The Mind of the South,* Basso had begun chipping away in both fiction and nonfiction at the almost sacred mythology of the Old South, its stately plantation homes, beneficent gentlemen planters, inviolate ladies, and contented slaves. He had begun his campaign as early as six years before "Huey Long and His Background" when, in his first novel, *Relics and Angels,* he had introduced readers to Helen Montross, a young woman who, taking advantage of the relative anonymity afforded her at a fashionable resort, greets a potential suitor with what the narrator assures us is an aristocratic hand. She is no "ordinary" person, we are told, no "average" young lady we might meet on the street, but the daughter of one of the South's most distinguished families.[4] What her suitor had not seen, however, is that, upon his arrival at her cottage, Helen had shooed her mother out of sight for fear the woman's dirty apron and worn-out slippers would expose her family's true socioeconomic standing. Hoping Helen could attract and marry money at the resort, they have spent their last dollar on room and board, and her mother has to perform the household chores herself. Helen's lineage is a complete fabrication, her moneyed southern pedigree as fictitious as her tales of attending schools in Paris and strolling

---

3. Hamilton Basso, "The Death and Legacy of Huey Long," *New Republic,* 1 January 1936, 217; Basso, "Long and His Background," 670–71.

4. Hamilton Basso, *Relics and Angels* (New York: Macaulay, 1929), 84.

moonlit, honeysuckle-laden verandas in delicate ballroom gowns. Although a minor character in the novel and in Basso's body of work, Helen is the first of many Basso characters who, facing a present they find far from ideal, retreat into a past that may or may not have actually existed.

The prologue to his next book, *Beauregard: The Great Creole,* finds Basso trying to account for this peculiarly, though not uniquely southern phenomenon. His arguments were not original even at the time, but they illustrate his early thoughts on what would become for him a primary target. The prologue begins in 1865, with Basso writing of defeated and demoralized southerners' attempts to return to life as they had lived it before the Civil War. Everything they had known, every system they had established, every value they had embraced, was in ruin. Bereft of their present and, for all they knew, of their future as well, they retreated into the only thing left them—their past. In their imaginations at least, plantations thus became more stately, planters more beneficent, ladies more inviolate, slaves more contented. It was a "beautiful, wonderful" era, Basso wrote, but one that ultimately had about it "the too-lovely unreality of a magnolia in moonlight." Like Helen Montross's past, the southern past, as he put it, simply "was not like that." Sentiment of the sort had nonetheless given rise to the postbellum South's plantation school, home to such writers as Thomas Nelson Page, author of the overtly sentimentalized *In Ole Virginia* (1887)—deluded peddlers of nothing more than "fables and fancies," as Basso saw them. And Page's twentieth-century successors fared no better in his estimation. Though the contemporary of all but the eldest members of the Fugitive and Agrarian groups, Basso was no more the ideological bedfellow of John Crowe Ransom, Donald Davidson, Allen Tate, and Robert Penn Warren than of Thomas Nelson Page himself. He derided the Twelve Southerners' *I'll Take My Stand* (1930) as a volume positively "afflicted" with nostalgia, a "prose-poem to the past" more than the statement of viable socioeconomic philosophy they intended; he derided the Agrarian agenda in general as little more than a foolish attempt "to lock the barn door after the horse had been stolen." Basso's aim for his own books, understandably, was different. As he announced in an early letter to Maxwell Perkins, his celebrated editor at Scribner's, his own novels would address the "essential reality," not more "fables and fancies," of the American South. As he defined it, his mission was to "get rid of all the old sentimental truck and explain, by using facts instead of poetry, what has happened here . . . and why this romantic conception is so untrue." Long, ironically—though Basso was never to give him credit for it—was on a similar mission. Williams wrote that Long never once "seriously" addressed "the two great Southern legends, the Old South and the Lost Cause. At a time when most politicians attempted to assuage the misery of the masses by spinning tales of past glories—the lovely South before Sumter, Jeb Stuart's dancing plume, the boys in gray plunging up the slopes at Gettysburg—Huey Long talked about economics and the present and the future." On at least this one point, then, Long and Basso agreed. Just as Long "forcibly introduced a large element of realism into Southern politics," Basso's hope was to do the same for Southern letters.[5]

His target, as he termed it in a 1935 *New Republic* essay, was "evasive idealism"—the act of hiding harried modern heads in the only recently pristine sands of the antebellum South. Basso found attempts of the sort not just counterproductive but such a consistent affront that he would often insert diatribes against them into otherwise unrelated works. His third novel offers us a clear case in this point. A tale of haves and have-nots, *In Their Own Image,* though set in South Carolina, is not what most would consider a southern novel. More concerned with escalating economic conflicts than with the cultural peculiarities of any one region, it presents a series of uncomfortable, mostly unsuccessful juxtapositions between blue bloods and blue-collars against backdrops ranging from polo matches to textile strikes. Into the midst of such material—which could truthfully be set anywhere the idle rich flock—strolls a minor character named John Pine, an interloper who at one point makes the seemingly stray comment that corn whiskey is worthy of at least one heroic poem. A discussion of southern heritage ensues—and, some might say, intrudes—and Pine ends up drawing fire for comparing the southern past to an oft-used,

5. Hamilton Basso, prologue to *Beauregard: The Great Creole* (New York: Scribner's, 1933), x–xi; Hamilton Basso, "A Spotlight on the South," *New Republic,* 18 April 1934, 287; Lake, 80, 17; T. Harry Williams, *Romance and Realism in Southern Politics* (Athens: University of Georgia Press, 1961), 135–41.

all but communal crutch. As he so witheringly puts it, native southerners who walk independently of their ancestors, who walk without their heritage "moving like a cyclorama behind [them]," are "damn rare." The average Anglo-Saxon from the South, Pine says,

> can't be just plain Bill Jones of Pickensville, Georgia. He has to be Mr. William deLacey Jones whose maternal grandfather, Colonel Edward Ravanel deLacey, was aide-de-camp to General Lee at Gettysburg and whose paternal grandfather, General Lucius Pringle Jones, commanded the Fourth Division of the Army of Tennessee at the battle of Shiloh. He is further descended, on his mother's side, from Governor Nance Pinckney Polk who entertained Lafayette when he spoke to the people at Beaufort, and on his father's side from Lieutenant Benbow Hastings Monkwell, the second son of Lord Benbow Hastings Monkwell, who fought with Packenham at the Battle of New Orleans.

When confronted with the overwhelming local opinion—that "all that means something!"—Pine responds,

> Of course it does. But what? That's what I want to find out. I know all the usual answers—family pride, historical tradition, a participation in the history of your country. Those answers are valid and important but they finally crystallize into the general meaning implied by the word heritage—and that brings us back to my question. What of it? What does it mean? How does your heritage help you, as a modern man, to contend with the problems of modern life? It seems to me that you Southerners have another heritage you never think of. . . . Your real heritage, unless I am greatly mistaken, is not what your grandfathers did during the Civil War, but the modern South. To hear most Southerners talk, however, the modern South doesn't exist. Your heritage ended in 1865. You have been so busy affirming the past you have forgotten all about the present.

Pine's final point is Basso's own, and in far more works than just *In Their Own Image:* that the modern South, even if it cannot or will not forget its often overglorified past, must focus on the present at least long enough to resolve its more immediate problems—the textile strike threatening a neighboring South Carolina town, for instance.

Yet even as much as Basso attempts to return the scene to the central concerns of the novel, what most stand out are the lengths to which he will go to challenge his southern readers to see that their true heritage did not end, but only began, in 1865. William Faulkner, Basso's friend and fellow contributor to the New Orleans *Double Dealer*, would have Gavin Stevens assert in *Requiem for a Nun* that the past "is never dead," is, in fact, "not even past."[6] Basso not only disagreed, but often issued exhortations arguing much the opposite.

His fourth novel, *Courthouse Square*, takes these arguments still farther, this time putting them into the mouth of a southerner—an insider instead of an outsider—and advocating the absolute abolition, rather than just a momentary setting aside of all things past. Unlike the intrusiveness of the subject matter in his previous novel, the material is integral to, and in many ways comments upon, the novel's central action, much of which surrounds the violence engulfing a mid-1930s southern town as an African American tries to buy the dilapidated home of the town's long-dead white founder. The white community's outrage, as one might imagine, stems more from abstract, outdated, race-based animosity than from anything concrete, contemporary, or personal. The past—at least according to the novel's reactionary white community—is still very much present. Reflecting on these conflicts before they erupt into violence, David Barondess, the novel's narrator and foremost progressive voice, wonders what would happen if the South were suddenly struck with amnesia, if it could no longer remember its sacrosanct past. "Wouldn't it collapse or fly into pieces," he asks, "or whatever it is the earth would do if gravity took a day off?" The question leads him to an awkward but instructive metaphor: "This is what the past is down here: gravity. . . . *The South is a separate planet, held together by the gravity of the past and tending, because of habit and inertia, to continue in the same orbit year after year.*" He then considers, as perhaps the most immediate case in this point, the practice of setting meals around nineteenth-century agricultural routines instead of twentieth-century commercial schedules. Though many had left the

---

6. Hamilton Basso, "Letters in the South," *New Republic*, 19 June 1935, 164; Hamilton Basso, *In Their Own Image* (New York: Scribner's, 1935), 172–74; William Faulkner, *Requiem for a Nun* (1951; reprint, New York: Vintage, 1975), 80.

farm for the factory, they continued to keep what Barondess calls plantation hours. In and of itself, he realizes, this one fact is not significant, but "it does illustrate the time-lag characteristic of the whole South: the retention of symbols and concepts of a culture when, actually, that culture no longer exists." It was "absurd" to "live in memory," he continues a few pages later, for "Memory was only a deception, the tricky rewinding of a film . . . giving an illusion of immediacy and permanence to things perishable and long since gone. . . . If only there was no such thing as memory. If only you could end the past—drown it as you drown unwanted puppies in a stream. Not to remember. Not ever to remember again. . . ." Barondess at this point speaks directly for Basso, who had once proposed to Perkins a book to be entitled "Death over Dixie." As he argued in his abstract, it was "high time" to "say goodbye to Dixie," for even if the region remains, "latitude and longitude fixed," it is no longer the place to which the name once applied. To survive the twentieth century, he wrote, the South will have to progress, alongside the rest of the country, toward "a changed order." Its inhabitants will probably never stop talking, much less thinking, about the supposed glories of the past, but they must come to realize that Dixie, in short, simply is no more.[7] Henry W. Grady had made much the same point some fifty years earlier, calling for a New South to replace the Old, but as Hamilton Basso saw it, not enough southerners seem to have heard him.

A more succinct distillation of this argument appears in Basso's 1939 *New Republic* article "The Future of the South." The piece begins with a narrative of three figures intended to represent Dixie, one of whom, Colonel Robert Cartledge of South Carolina, stands surveying his six hundred acres of slave-worked rice fields. The year is 1850, and the Colonel's world seems safe, he secure within it, surrounded as he is by an array of the props Basso derided when he found them in modern fiction, everything from moss-draped oaks to a white-columned plantation house. A few pages later, though, the Civil War has intervened, past has become present, and the Cartledges have been forced into town, their former plantation house now the winter home of

7. Hamilton Basso, *Courthouse Square* (New York: Scribner's, 1936), 198, 200, 205; Lake, 77–78.

wealthy strangers. Rice still grows in rare spots, but only to lure ducks to visiting hunters. The Colonel's grandson, now on public subsistence, often passes the property, but a No Trespassing sign forbids his setting foot upon it. Appomattox, Basso writes, was the difference: "there the present began," he asserts, there the past "ended," and attempting to deny either is as foolish as it is futile. "The tradition of the Old South," he concludes, "is lost in the past: part of the mist, part of Appomattox, part of our state of mind. To pretend otherwise is to indulge in a masquerade not unlike the annual garden-club festival in Natchez." What "we cannot do," he warns his readers, is "waste time and strength in defense of theories and systems, however valued in their day, which have been swept down by the moving avalanche of actual events."[8] Huey Pierce Long, as Basso had made clear in earlier essays, was just such an avalanche—a force that swept down many theories and systems valued in the day of his predecessors. Any attempt to stop him, however, would only be a waste of time and strength, an impossible attempt to return the South to the days before Appomattox, to redirect, as Basso saw it, nothing less than the course of history. As alternatives, moreover, the dilemma left Louisianians only abject loss or the deluded futility of trying to resurrect the past—a no-win proposition Basso found so troubling that he could not help but examine it in two further novels, *Cinnamon Seed* and *Sun in Capricorn*. Each has a fictionalized Long embody the lamentable but inevitable regression Basso found in Long himself, but both books tell us that, at the same time, the only alternative to him and the sociohistorical decline he heralded was the "evasive idealism" Basso ceaselessly derided. No matter how odious the present, he reiterated, hiding in the past is only more so.

More an ensemble piece than the story of any one particular character, *Cinnamon Seed* is a novel that focuses less on Dekker Blackheath, the character some call its protagonist, than on escalating social tensions between the rising New South and declining Old. Like Faulkner's *Sartoris* (1929), *Cinnamon Seed* introduces a panorama of characters both

8. Hamilton Basso, "The Future of the South," *New Republic,* 8 November 1939, 71, 74.

young and old, both black and white, all of whom struggle to find new footing in an era of unprecedented social upheaval. Set mostly at the Louisiana plantation Willswood during the decade and a half between 1917 and the early 1930s (with occasional flashbacks to the early 1840s), the novel centers on the aristocratic Blackheath family, most of whose members value the past far more than the present. To the patriarch Langley, for instance, "there was nothing but the past." It was a "tragic" past, one "filled with death and dishonor," but only in his memories of it does he find "the essential meaning of himself, the source-spring of his unyielding pride."[9] To his young grandson Dekker, on the other hand, the past is almost entirely irrelevant, as it has less to do with him than with his grandfather, his great-grandfather, and other long-dead forbears. To Dekker, easily the most progressive member of the modern Blackheaths, all the old stories of these men seem "a little impossible" (297). The conflict splits the novel's African American characters as well. Horace, the old retainer, may consider himself an "[o]le plantashun nigger" (274), but the much younger Sam, though also raised at Willswood, eventually leaves Louisiana for the North to seek an identity independent of race—"to be not a Negro," as he puts it, "but a man" (281). Most central to this perhaps overly schematic novel is not any one of these characters in particular but, again, the sociohistorical forces that increasingly upset them all as the New South increasingly displaces the Old.

The most prominent embodiment of this conflict concerns Carter Blackheath, the firstborn of Langley's two sons. Upon the suicide of his younger brother, Kinloch, Carter is charged with the task of filling his former seat in the family law practice. Harry Brand, the local lawyer Carter finds Kinloch's worthiest replacement, however, has been since birth *persona non grata* around the Blackheath hearth: decades earlier, Peter Brand, Harry's grandfather, had committed a dereliction for which most Blackheaths still hold all Brands accountable. An overseer at Willswood in the years before and just after the Civil War, Brand had exposed what until that time had been the Blackheaths'

9. Dorothy Scarborough, "A Louisiana Senator," review of *Cinnamon Seed,* by Hamilton Basso, *New York Times Book Review,* 25 February 1934, 8; Hamilton Basso, *Cinnamon Seed* (New York: Scribner's, 1934), 15.

only private shame. In no less public a setting than a courtroom, he had testified that Langley's father, Robert, had fathered a child by one of his slaves and that that slave's murderer, some seventeen years later, was not the accused, Langley himself, but his mother, for whom he had tried to take the blame. Because of this antiquated fact—not because of any question as to the professional qualifications of Brand's grandson Harry—Carter, more than fifty years later, still finds his staffing decision difficult. It takes him days of deliberation, but he finally comes to the agonized conclusion that his reservations are irrational and based on "ancient prejudice" alone; he vows therefore not to be "hamstrung by the past. That was part of a very special kind of philosophy that died in the [eighteen] sixties . . . and this is nineteen-seventeen" (31). We can perhaps imagine Basso, some five years before he would write "The Future of the South," thinking—though not, of course, in the same words—that we cannot "waste time and strength in defense of theories and systems, however valued in their day, which have been swept down by the moving avalanche of actual events." Carter realizes that he has a law firm to run in the twentieth, not the nineteenth century, and therefore agrees. "Times had changed," he reasons; "men thought and acted differently" (31).

Or at least some do: upon learning that Carter had indeed asked Brand to join the family practice, his older sister, Olivia, despite her brother's lecture on the injustice of holding a man accountable for his ancestor's sins, turns from disbelief to rage. Responding to the news by letter, she writes that "if anybody told me that a Blackheath and a Brand were going to be partners I would have told them they were crazy. . . . I'm so mad at you, I could slap your face" (78). An even more dramatic reaction follows from her father, Langley, the only living character who witnessed the original offense. His condemnation applies not just to Carter but to his siblings as well, for all band together to keep from him news of the impending partnership: *"Damn him! Damn them all! Disgracing [me] and then uniting to keep it from [me]. . . . Blackheath and Brand . . . rascal and fool. . . . Brand and Blackheath . . . Blackheath branded"* (162). More dramatically still, these thoughts prove the old man's last, for the accompanying shock brings to an end the life of *Cinnamon Seed*'s foremost representative of the South's old order. Past crimes not only cloud present opinion but divide those who disagree as to their present relevance. Yet the crimes of the Brands, as the Blackheaths perceive them, are in no way limited to Peter's generation. His grandson Harry has a few of his own—many of which Basso borrows from his old friend and, later, nemesis, Huey P. Long. Basso seems to have seen the Kingfish as such a constant affront that turning his likeness into the most blatant fictional embodiment of degenerating southern culture required relatively little alteration. Brand, consequently, emerges the most consistently realistic disguised representation of Long to be found in fiction. *Cinnamon Seed* may not incorporate every significant detail in his biography—Dos Passos's *Number One* will incorporate more of them, many even approaching the obscure—but it does force more of them into a far smaller space than any other novel examined here.

When we first meet Brand, he is thirty-one years old and has just joined a law firm formerly occupied only by Blackheaths. He both looks like Long at the same age—he is of medium height, pug-nosed and potbellied, and has curly red hair—and has lived his life much as Long lived his. The son of a poor sharecropper from a northern Louisiana parish named Gwinn—a thinly veiled allusion to Long's Winn Parish distinguished only by the tacked-on *G*—he had been a boy picking cotton beside his father when he realized the farming life was not for him. At fourteen, the same age at which Long left Winnfield for a career in sales, Brand ran away to Baton Rouge to divide his time between high school and a part-time job in a hardware store. In his spare time, he read: Scott, Dickens, and especially the Bible. Four years later, upon graduation from high school, he had grown into a "gangly, loud-mouthed youth" with a pronounced fondness for flashy ties (116). After a three-year stint in traveling sales—a period during which he learned to sell himself, as much as his suspect products, with a combination of jokes, cheap giveaways, and Biblical quotations—Brand began studying law at the state university. As Basso so clearly bought into the myth of Long's having completed a three-year law program in a mere eight months,[10] Brand finished a similar course in a single term, earning the highest score on the bar exam as well. For the next three years, he practiced law in his native Gwinn Parish and then, again like

---

10. Hamilton Basso, "The Huey Long Legend," *Life,* 9 December 1946, 107.

Long, turned contacts from his days in traveling sales into support for his first attempt at public office. In a slight variation from Long's career, the election earned him a seat not on the railroad commission but in the state senate. Yet even if such discrepancies keep the young politicians' early resumes from reading like carbon copies of one another, they are, in the end, fewer and far less substantial than their much more apparent similarities.

Brand's title is well-nigh irrelevant anyway: for no matter the status of the office he attains, he is incapable of acting in it as anything more refined than the thin-soled salesman he once was. Just as Long once joked that a *Saturday Evening Post* editorial was at least partially responsible for Share Our Wealth (*HL* 117), Brand derives much of his governing philosophy from the sales manual he studied while representing a crushed oyster-shell company. He found in its slogan, "*To sell shell sell yourself*," a "philosophy with which a man could remake the world. If a man sold himself," he reasoned, "all things could be his. The great men of the world . . . Napoleon, Washington, Jefferson, Lincoln . . . were great because they had sold themselves" (116). We first see this laughably reductive philosophy at work when Brand places in New Orleans newspapers an advertisement announcing his addition to the Blackheath law firm. After summarizing his career, it takes up the lengthy and ostensibly harmonious relationship between the Brands and the Blackheaths. Carter takes immediate issue with the ad, its public reference to his grandfather in particular, and the dispute that erupts quickly illustrates the new partners' conflicting perspectives. After Brand crows, "Pretty good stuff, ain't it?" (118), Carter stiffly responds that, instead of running an ad in the newspaper, he had planned to send something more appropriate to long-standing clients and members of the bar. Brand counters that such formalities only alienate their target demographic, those who have not yet become their clients, not those who already are. Legal services, after all, are "just like a can of beans," he argues. "The only difference is that they don't come wrapped in tin. You've got to sell them both. You've got to advertise!" (119). Just as Long's entrance into the Louisiana governor's mansion signaled to Basso the death of "tradition" and "ceremony," Brand's entrance into the Blackheath law firm signals to Carter the death of the "more dignified" (118). Though a successful lawyer and newly elected state senator, Brand cannot see the world from any other perspective or engage it with any other mind-set than that of a former fertilizer salesman.

His efforts to *"sell shell sell"* himself in the state legislature prove no less jarring—and, even for all the antics it has no choice but to abide, his home state earns much less in return than Long's Louisiana earned abiding his. Brand is easily Long's equal at attracting attention. Some of his more memorable acts of office include sponsoring an egg-laying contest to advertise the oyster shell he had represented, promoting corn pone and pot liquor as the official state dish, and embroiling himself in an assortment of fistfights, most of which he flees in fear. The egg-laying contest exhibits at least a little embellishment, for though Long never staged precisely such an event, he did stage a series of bake-offs to promote Cottolene. The corn pone and pot liquor anecdote comes straight from his biography, of course, as do the fistfights, for Long had incited several even before that night at Sands Point. Later in the novel, an unnamed man in a roadside drugstore alludes to one of the most infamous. Brand, he asserts, is nothing but a coward, for he had once fled Old Man Janders when the outraged elder had threatened to punch him. The real "old man" was Louisiana governor J. Y. Sanders, and the incident, as Basso incorporates it, differs only in that a capital S has become a capital J and that Long's version of the story, which includes his returning to pummel his opponent (*HL* 271), has been omitted altogether. Brand, though, is far less adept than Long at actually serving his constituents, instead of just entertaining them. His initiatives as state senator often mirror Long's as governor but in the end are far less successful. One bill proposes to provide schoolchildren with free textbooks, but Brand cannot win its passage, as Long did. And though he pledges himself publicly "to the cause of the people, for the poor against the rich" (117), he beats a quick retreat when he has to make good on his denunciations of oil companies and public utilities. Rumors eventually abound that his ostensible enemies had paid him to call off his attacks. Basso thus engages in some of the same character assassination Sinclair Lewis would employ a year later in *It Can't Happen Here,* for though he makes Brand every bit the legislative jester Long was, he deprives him of the early successes Long achieved for his constituents, leaving Brand, in the end, little more than a foolish nuisance in an arena far too demanding for him.

Brand's transition from senator to governor is a bit more faithful to the historical record. Basso may show us nothing of the candidate on the campaign trail, but the details he offers us of election day itself look strikingly like those of early 1928. Long's opponent, Riley Joe Wilson, had spent some fourteen years "embalmed"—as Basso put it in his *Harper's* article—in the U.S. House of Representatives.[11] Brand's opponent Tillson had spent only twelve years there but had been so indolent in the position himself that he has to announce his candidacy as a near-unknown. As the first returns arrive, moreover, the comments aired around a drugstore radio sound much like those likely uttered on the night of Long's election. When listeners learn that Tillson has beaten Brand three to one in the first New Orleans precinct to report, one man echoes an opinion many voiced about Long at the time: "[T]hat don't mean nothing," he says. "We all know Harry will get licked in New Orleans. The ring will carry New Orleans for Tillson without any trouble. Harry's strength is in the country" (204). Later that night, when tallies from the state's more rural precincts begin to arrive, the man's prediction proves correct. "There you are!" he exclaims. "I told you so! It'll be like that all over the country parishes. That's where Harry's strength is. He said himself that it was going to be the country people who would elect him" (205). By the next morning, Brand has more than made up for his initial deficit, and later that day a New Orleans newspaper describes a scene that looks suspiciously like the one Basso witnessed the night Long won election to the same office. A photo taken at campaign headquarters shows a rumpled governor-elect propping his feet on a cluttered desk and declaring, "I'm just a boy from the country . . . but I guess the city slickers know who's boss now. If New Orleans wants to get anything from me while I'm governor, the New Orleans crowd will have to fall in line. I'm the kingfrog in this pool. When I say hop, all the little frogs will have to hop. I want to thank all my friends in the country who voted for me. I know who elected me governor and I'll never forget it" (207). Except for the most cosmetic of changes—as Winn became Gwinn and Sanders be-

11. Basso, "Long and His Background," 663.

came Janders, Wilson becomes Tillson, the Kingfish the King-Frog—
Brand's gubernatorial victory and the smug self-portrait he paints for
reporters immediately thereafter might as well be Huey Long's own.
Since Long's most celebrated gubernatorial successes had already
inspired Brand's most conspicuous senatorial failures, Basso turns
Long's most infamous gubernatorial escapades into the only noteworthy events of Brand's entire term of office. His exploits strike his constituents incredulous within only months of his inauguration. Rumors
quickly begin to circulate of official collusion with underworld bosses,
of late-night governor's mansion bacchanals, of "corruption and crookedness and knavery everywhere," and word of these shenanigans soon
spreads far beyond Louisiana. As a result of his loud pronouncements
as the self-proclaimed King-Frog, his brash prediction that he would
win the White House by 1936, and his increasingly widespread promotion of corn pone and pot liquor, the "loud-mouthed lout . . . who had
somehow managed to become governor" soon becomes a national figure (236). Then, sporting a nightshirt in obvious need of repair, Brand
assumes the international stage. The episode is clearly based on that
surrounding the visiting commander of the *Emden,* but Basso not only
changes details—the battleship and its chief are now French, not German—but brings the incident to a more obnoxious conclusion than
even Long himself did. After the nightshirt-clad governor receives the
delegation, after the delegation protests the insult, and after the governor pays a conciliatory visit on board the cruiser, he explains to its
commander that he knows he owes him an apology, but that he had
not been told who his guests were. "If I had known it was you," he
explains, "I wouldn't have worn that old nightshirt. I would have put
on a new one" (240). As would Lewis the following year, Basso turns
his first fictional Long into an even more cunning buffoon than Long
himself, engaging in much the same kind of character assassination as
Lewis—but, again, to comment on, rather than attempt to solve, what
the author considered an insoluble problem.

Claiming he can offer all America the uplift he somehow believes
he brings Louisiana, Brand, like Long before him, soon sets his sights
on the U.S. Senate. His renown has only increased at this point, for
he has foiled a recent impeachment attempt, just as Long foiled one
himself, with the aid of a Round Robin signed by fifteen state senators

who vowed to acquit no matter the evidence. Brand's chief mode of attack during the campaign that follows takes up no particular political issue but, instead, the fact that his opponent, an Old Regulars stooge with four successive terms in the U.S. Senate, wears a goatee: "any man who wore a goat's beard," Brand claims, "must have a goat's mentality" (316). In all but name—he has none in the novel—this opponent is much the same as the one Long faced in his own race for the Senate, Joseph E. Ransdell, a four-time U.S. senator Long dubbed "Old Feather Duster" because of his own goatee (*HL* 464). Basso duplicates several other facts of the sort when setting the scene of Brand's campaign but turns to events both earlier and later than Long's own to heighten the hysteria surrounding the election. Despite the fact that the Old Regulars reversed their long-standing opposition to Long only after his election to the Senate (*HL* 481–83), Basso's version of the New Orleans ring, fearing that nothing short of assassination could prevent a victory for the King-Frog, reverses its support long before election day. Similarly, the ammunition Basso offers Brand's unnamed opponent is the stuff of scandals that surfaced not during but before Long's senatorial campaign. Much of it, in fact, is what fostered the thwarted impeachment attempt. The accusation that Brand hired a professional gunman to murder a political opponent, for instance, as much as duplicates the charge that Long ordered a bodyguard to kill J. Y. Sanders, Jr. (*HL* 355), the son, in a sense, of Basso's Old Man Janders. The opposition's problem, however—just as it seems to have been Basso's own—is that, even after the revelation of these facts, the citizenry remains unmoved. The opposition, therefore, digs on. The next scandal they engineer, though, will have less of an effect on their intended target than on one particular—and completely unsuspecting—private citizen.

What the opposition uncovers is an almost forgotten series of events that had taken place during Brand's second year as governor. In an attempt to replenish empty state coffers, Brand—as had Long before him (*HL* 716)—proposed that the legislature levy an additional tax on chain stores operating in the state. The bill was not well received, but "since Brand was the state Senate and the House of Representatives as well as governor" (317), it almost immediately became law. When, shortly thereafter, the owner of several grocery stores chal-

lenged Brand's definition of a chain, the governor replied that the matter was one for the courts and advised him to seek counsel. Within
weeks, Carter Blackheath had argued and won the case for the plaintiff, not only saving the owner—and simultaneously denying the
state—some $75,000 a year, but earning himself $20,000 in the process. When the opposition uncovers the transaction in the midst of the
senatorial campaign, its newspaper portrays it as a clear case of graft
and corruption, yet another "tentacle of the slimy octopus . . . slowly
choking the state to death" (318–19). Blackheath and Brand had accepted a bribe, the article charges, and if the word "justice" meant anything in Louisiana at the time, they would already be behind bars. To
Carter, who reads the article one morning during breakfast, the
charges are devastating. With a face as drained of color as the napkin
in his lap, he sits staring silently as his hard-won reputation seems to
crumble to dust in front of him. Through her tears, his wife Elizabeth
whimpers, "I'll never be able to hold up my head again. . . . I'll never
be able to look anybody in the face again" (319). What first had tarnished only the Blackheath law firm now tarnishes living, breathing
Blackheaths. Langley and his daughter Olivia, it seems, may well have
been right about the Brands.

An anxious call to the King-Frog at his hotel suite earns Carter the
following advice: "Hell, that ain't nothin' to be scared about. Let them
shoot their mouths off all they want to. What the hell do we care? We
don't have nothing to worry about. . . . Just forget it" (320). Such brash
assurances notwithstanding, the situation remains precarious for Carter. But only for a while: by midday, he begins to see the charges more
from Brand's point of view, begins to see himself as the innocent victim of an underhanded political trick. "I'm a lawyer," he rationalizes.
"When a client comes to me, and asks me to take a case, I have to
protect his interests. That's what he hires me for. No man will condemn me for doing my duty" (321). Later that afternoon, he finds his
earlier reaction increasingly laughable, and when a pair of reporters
calls on him for comment, he not only denounces the charges as absurd, but threatens to sue for libel. The next day, when his rebuttal
appears in the paper, both Carter and Elizabeth find it "the dignified
reply of an upright, honest man"—a man "beyond reproach" (323),
Carter concludes. Carter, then, not only seems to scheme alongside

Brand and against the state but, once caught, instead of confessing or distancing himself from his law partner, seeks his advice on how to weather the consequent scandal. He approaches the situation not as a gentleman with his honor at stake but as a conscious manipulator of public opinion more concerned with escaping unscathed than with protecting the integrity he once esteemed. Carter thus emerges the willing victim of perhaps the worst crime with which he charges Brand—"dragging decent men into the mire" (320)—and, as phrases like his own "beyond reproach" take on meanings entirely different from those they held during his late father's lifetime, the Old South's fabled honor sinks farther into the New South's "mire." Dixie, Basso reiterates, is dead.

As if dragging a Blackheath into this mire were not enough, Brand also aids in the more tangible destruction of a more sacrosanct symbol of the Old South. Except for a few years during and just after the Civil War, the Blackheaths' riverfront plantation had stood undisturbed. Complete with pillars, galleries, and an array of outbuildings, surrounded by inviolate gardens and cane fields, Willswood embodies everything Basso so often reminded readers was more a part of the past than of the present. Brand seems to see things the same way—as did Long, particularly when it came to the old governor's mansion. Five months after a federal flood-control initiative began claiming the land surrounding nearby levees, gone are the lawn, the lower gardens, and at least half the oaks that had led up to the front door. Comparable devastation surrounds the plantation, stretching in some directions for miles. Final plans call for a road to be moved several hundred yards closer to the house, which soon will find itself at the edge of one of Brand's many new highways. Blackheath appeals, both early and late, are in vain. Olivia Blackheath, principal resident of Willswood after her father Langley's death, even stomachs her disgust enough to seek assistance from Governor Brand, who—wearing a light gray suit and a bright orange tie, incidentally—explains that he can do nothing for her. Sacrificing her home to the greater common good will cut four miles out of the trip from New Orleans to Baton Rouge, he tells her, a boon for all industries on the Mississippi. Despite an earlier promise that no Blackheath will have to ask twice for his assistance, Brand does nothing for her, privileges industry over tradition—a most anti-

Agrarian act—and, in the primary instance in which we see him at work, places the future before the past, New South, again, before Old. To Basso, though, lamentable though Olivia's loss may be, she and all those who see the world from her perspective will simply have to adjust. Attempting any other course of action, Basso would later argue, would be anachronistic, if not foolishly counterproductive.

Just how closely his constituents associate Brand with the historical developments Basso has him embody can best be gauged during a conversation between Olivia and her nephew Dekker. The most outspokenly conservative of living Blackheaths, Olivia often refers to Brand as "that trash." In one of her most pointed comments on the subject, she plays Basso to Brand's Long by inserting the politician into the broader context of Louisiana's storied past. "The king-frog!" she rails. "To think that after all the fine men we've had as governors of this state we have to have trash like that!" (207). Dekker's response, in addition to shedding new light on the situation for Olivia, also helps connect some of the novel's more discursive narrative strands:

> "There you go off on a tangent again! Of course he's trash. What did you expect him to be—an aristocrat! If he was he wouldn't have been elected."
> "What kind of crazy talk is that?"
> "I'm talking sense. You don't seem to realize it but the South has changed. The day of the aristocrat is over. . . . It's men like Brand who run the show nowadays."
> "You're talking like a fool."
> "Brand was elected, wasn't he?"
> "Yes! And he was elected because a lot of damn fool people think like you do! He's trash and nothing you can say can convince me he isn't! All I can say is God help the State of Louisiana." (209)

Further deliberation convinces Olivia that her nephew had not been trying to antagonize her but had only been stating the facts as he saw them, not defending Brand. Reflecting on their conversation later that day, she begins to wonder if Dekker's perspective on the South is actually more accurate than her own, tragic though that would be for her to admit:

For a moment it seemed that it was. It had changed, just as he said, all the old things were gone and forgotten. There was a new way of life now, the old strict forms were shattered and broken, people thought and acted differently. If [her father Langley] was alive he would be out of place, outmoded . . . sitting in the shadow of the Confederate flag.

The thought shocked her. She dropped her knitting and looked from the window. She could see the flowing mound of the levee and hear the distant voices of the negroes harrying the mules in the fields. Once all this had stood for something, merged into a rich, congruent, organic design whose significance transcended the material facts of acres and slaves and a big house with trees. But now, if what Dekker said was true, that significance was gone . . . lost. (209–10)

However much Olivia's view of what Brand embodies may change, her opinion of Brand himself does not. When we leave him, just as when we met him, Brand is to Olivia "just trash—the worst kind of trash" (367). What Olivia laments, though, Basso objectively narrates: plantations have given way to factories, descendants of patricians have been forced to petition descendants of their overseers, and what Olivia calls trash has taken the place of what she calls aristocrats. The day of the gentleman statesman is gone, Basso shows us, the day of the salesman-politician arrived, and there is little Olivia or anyone like her can do to change it. No matter how evasive her particular brand of idealism, she simply cannot return the South to what it was or, much less, to what she imagines it was—and neither, Basso argues, could anybody else.

In that *Cinnamon Seed* centers on argument more than character, turns fact into fiction to take up history more than human nature, and spends more time paraphrasing Long's biography than detailing the character of his clone, *Sun in Capricorn,* in at least these respects, is its antithesis. The story of one man rather than several, the novel is free to focus more fully on character. That does not mean, however, that it improves upon *Cinnamon Seed*—or, for that matter, that it even transcends its own exhausted formulas. An often unsuccessful mix of political intrigue and romantic thriller, its central narrative is slight at best, almost, as one reviewer put it, "naïve." As Louis D. Rubin has written, "The novel is neither high drama nor a commentary on the state of man on Louisiana earth during the 1930's. It is simply a thriller."[12] Set in both actual and invented areas of 1930s Louisiana, *Sun in Capricorn* essentially begins when Hazzard, a small-town lawyer on business in New Orleans, meets an attractive young woman named Erin. Although his uncle Thomas has just announced for the U.S. Senate race against nefarious Louisiana governor Gilgo Slade, and though Hazzard is fully aware of the fact that Slade's henchmen are trailing him all over New Orleans, he is no more cautious than to exit Erin's room one morning in full view of whoever might be standing there with a camera. A photo of his departure soon becomes fodder for the smear campaign Slade designs to destroy his uncle Thomas, and after several breathless chapters devoted to Hazzard's attempt to help Erin evade the opposition (who hope to prosecute them both on a morals charge and thus destroy the reputations of all associated with them) Thomas's son Quentin, in an angry attempt to avenge the multiple affront to his family's name, assassinates Slade at a campaign rally. *Sun in Capricorn* thus casts a character much like Long not as just one of several embodiments of its central concern but as something much closer to the heart of the novel, its villainous chief antagonist.

Surprisingly, perhaps, *Sun in Capricorn* does relatively little with Long's political career. Basso spends page after page of *Cinnamon Seed* paralleling the lives of factual figure and fictional character, but he devotes more space in *Sun in Capricorn* to characterizing the despot than detailing the stages of his career. Increased attention to this material, however, does not always produce more subtle shades of character. As one reviewer put it, Long himself may have been a composite of both good and bad characteristics, but Hamilton Basso, in creating a "literary image" of him, dealt somewhat "sparingly" with the good. Rubin has written much the same, commenting that, over the course of the novel, Slade remains little more than "a sinister but shadowy back-

12. Gwen Bristow, "Gilgo Slade of Louisiana," review of *Sun in Capricorn*, by Hamilton Basso, *Saturday Review of Literature*, 19 September 1942, 16; Louis D. Rubin, Jr., "All the King's Meanings," in *The Curious Death of the Novel: Essays in American Literature* (Baton Rouge: Louisiana State University Press, 1967), 224.

ground presence," which leaves little doubt—doubt that may have lent the novel at least some degree of complexity—about his being "a fascist, a menace, a scoundrel, and a despot." Joseph R. Millichap, author of the first full-length study of Basso, makes much the same point. He finds Slade "completely reprehensible," a "figure of almost consummate evil"—which both misses "much of the interest inherent in Huey Long's story" and turns what should have been realism into something more akin to melodrama. But Basso seems to have thought he had written the kind of novel Millichap wanted to read. A few months before its publication, he wrote to Malcolm Cowley that *Sun in Capricorn* would achieve nothing less than the fictional dissection of a dictatorship: "The leader, the group-insignia, the sinister associates, the hollow hanger-ons, the worshipful dispossessed lower-middle class mass—they are all there." The year was 1942, and dictatorships were on the minds of worldwide millions. "I sure [as] hell was not interested in writing a novel just about Huey Long," he declared.[13] Unfortunately, the same one-sidedness that diminishes his dictator diminishes almost everything surrounding him, and what we are left with, even despite characters representing every segment Basso had mentioned in his letter to Cowley, is a novel "just about Huey Long," and an insubstantial one at that. The one-dimensional characterization common to such novels at times works in Basso's favor, though, for, constrained by the dictates of neither historicity nor verisimilitude, he found himself free to concoct some of the most extravagant scenes found in any of the novels examined here. As a result, Slade ends up part Huey Long, part freak show attraction, and part carnival barker, an unrealistic but far more vibrant character than even *Cinnamon Seed*'s salesman-turned-statesman. On one point in particular, however, the novels coincide: for as does Brand before him, Slade both embodies and inspires the rising rabble, illustrates again what Basso considered the New South's lamentable but inevitable ascendancy over the Old.

What little we learn of Slade's political career deviates only slightly from Long's own. Introducing him to us at the beginning of the novel,

13. George Streator, review of *Sun in Capricorn*, by Hamilton Basso, *Commonweal*, 2 October 1942, 570; Rubin, 224; Joseph R. Millichap, *Hamilton Basso*, Twayne's United States Authors, vol. 331 (Boston: Twayne, 1979), 84; Lake, 187.

Hazzard dismisses Slade's first elected office as something as undistinguished as clerk of court. Long's first position was certainly more significant, but the railroad commissioner had run on the firmly entrenched Democratic ticket and had won only by way of a runoff—and, even then, by only a few hundred votes (*HL* 125)—whereas Slade had run on no ticket at all and had won by an overwhelming margin. Basso thus rewrites the record to give Slade as formidable, defiantly independent a political debut as possible. Long himself, at the time, would unquestionably have lost to him. By the time of his second run for governor in 1928, however, Long had made more of a name for himself. Keeping his clone as imposing as possible thus required less revision of the record. For instance, the fact that Slade, predicted to place last among three candidates, not only placed first but did so with such a plurality that the runner-up refused a runoff, is as true of Long as it is of Slade. Once in office, moreover, Slade never failed to entertain. So persistent a presence does he become that he soon seems what Hazzard calls "the central planet in our modest solar system," and Louisiana begins telling time by him, as it were. Slade's more infamous escapades—staging a national corn pone and pot liquor cook-off, receiving the Spanish ambassador dressed only in shorts and a T-shirt, ordering the legislature to pass bills without reading them—were far more memorable than the dates on which they occurred. Hazzard thus places his move to the country during Slade's third year as governor, by which point he "had brought the state under his own personal control by various means, legal and illegal."[14] Similarly, Hazzard remembers the morning he tried to resign from his uncle's law practice as that of the day Slade declared he would win a U.S. Senate seat and thenceforth run Louisiana from Washington. Occasional modifications notwithstanding, Slade's political career may as well be Long's own.

Just as he had populated *Cinnamon Seed* with Long's opponents, Basso surrounds Slade with thinly veiled versions of Long's closest associates. In one scene in particular we meet Abe Shoeman, a local merchant-turned-Slade-henchman, and Faber Meyerhold, a former barber now Slade's treasurer. The characters are based, respectively, on Abraham Shushan, a New Orleans merchant and Long insider (*HL* 421),

14. Hamilton Basso, *Sun in Capricorn* (New York: Scribner's, 1942), 40.

and Seymour Weiss, the one-time manager of the Roosevelt Hotel barber shop who later became Long's treasurer (*HL* 375). After singling out such characters, one reviewer wrote that, when we encounter them, "we feel pleasantly or unpleasantly at home, depending on our own memories of those days."[15] The reviewer fails to equate Hazzard's uncle Thomas with any such figure, but he in many ways resembles one of Long's most persistent enemies, Mayor Lee E. Thomas of Shreveport. Just as, in *Cinnamon Seed*, Basso turned Sanders into Janders, Wilson into Tillson, Kingfish into King-Frog, he seems to have turned a last name into a first in *Sun in Capricorn*. Slade's charges against Hazzard's uncle sound much like Long's against Shreveport's mayor. Just as Slade derides Uncle Thomas as "*a thieving bandit who's never done an honest day's work in his life*" (169), an "*aristocratic antique who sits on velvet and partakes of the fatted calf*" (171), Long charged Mayor Thomas with having "lived off the public during his entire adult life" (*HL* 220–21), often portraying him as a "perennial officeholder of the old [aristo-cratic] regime," a "pie eater and trough feeder . . . who has been suck-ing the pap for thirty-five years" (*HL* 269). In the case of one speech in particular, the issue is not similarity but equality. In the political rally that closes the novel, Slade regales his listeners as follows:

> "I know you good people didn't come here tonight to hear any funny stories. . . . But I heard a tale yesterday that I'd like to pass on. It'll help you folks understand what kind of candidate they've picked to run against your Leader. It seems that my honorable op-ponent, whose name you all know, made a bet with a Chinaman and a Fiji Islander as to which one could stand to stay locked up the longest with a pole cat."
>
> Laughter. He held up his hand for silence.
>
> "The Chinaman went in the room with the animal and stayed ten minutes. Then he had to come out. He couldn't stand it any longer.
>
> "Then the Fiji Islander went in and stayed fifteen minutes with the pole cat. He came out a very sick man.
>
> "Then my honorable opponent's time came. He went in and stayed five minutes—then the pole cat ran out." (252–53)

The anecdote is not only attributable to Long—Basso seems to have paraphrased it directly from *Every Man a King*[16]—but, Williams tells us, is one that Long once directed at Mayor Thomas at just such a rally (*HL* 269). Yet Basso does not stop there. Because *Sun in Capricorn* appeared after September 8, 1935, Slade can meet his end just as Long met his. Enraged by Slade's attack against his father, Hazzard's cousin Quentin takes up a revolver and, at a pivotal moment during the central rally, assassinates Slade in mid sentence. Just as Carl Austin Weiss had fallen, Quentin then falls the bullet-ridden victim of an overzealous bodyguard. When Basso moves from generalities to specifics, he approaches still closer the *roman à clef:* almost as much as it depends upon Basso himself, the novel depends upon details from the biographies of Abraham Shushan, Seymour Weiss, Lee E. Thomas, Carl Austin Weiss, and, of course, Huey Pierce Long.

In many cases, moreover, the most tyrannical of Slade's political pronouncements are but rough translations of Long's. Early on we learn that when he announced his candidacy for the U.S. Senate, Slade had proclaimed, "This is my state. . . . It belongs to Gilgo Slade. Without me running things it would fall to pieces" (42). Slade is also convinced that the people are of the same opinion. Just as Long once boasted, "[The people] like what I'm giving them and what they're getting" (*HL* 762), Slade proclaims, "The people know . . . there's nobody to take the place of Gilgo Slade. That's why I'm going to be their Senator and their Governor at the same time" (42–43). Slade is still more brash in private: in a speech that borrows almost directly from both Long and Brand, he rails, "When I say hop, those fellows [in the state legislature] hop. I can make 'em or I can break 'em and they know it. *I'm* the state legislature" (74). According to Hazzard—who, in saying so, sounds much like Basso in "Huey Long and His Background"—his chief sin is an almost Snopesian rapacity. What upsets him about Slade is his desire to own the world—an inevitably dangerous proposition because, however he accomplishes it, "people and the things they stand for have to be destroyed" (220). Because of what he represents, and despite both his appearance and public persona, Slade does not, when

16. See Huey P. Long, *Every Man a King* (1933; reprint, Chicago: Quadrangle, 1964), 100.

Hazzard observes him at the rally, "look comical. . . . Nothing about him was comical. It came to me," Hazzard concludes—in a comment that might well have come from *It Can't Happen Here*—"that too many people had thought he was comical for too long" (252).

Slade's talents as a master manipulator and first-rate rabble-rouser are what most belie this comical persona. As do both Windrip and Brand, he speaks to the masses as one of their own. More deviously than either, though, he reduces all sociopolitical conflicts to simplistic skirmishes between haves and have-nots. He begins a radio address as follows:

> My name is Gilgo. . . . I don't want any of you good people to call me Governor Slade or the Right Honorable Gilgo Slade or even plain Slade. I want you to call me Gilgo. It's a corn-pone name for a corn-pone man. Gilgo. That's my name. Lemme spell it out. G I L G O. . . . That's the way you spell it. That's the name of the man who is going to cast out the forces of corruption and greed. It is said in the Bible that there came a humble man to the temple and that the forces of wickedness fled before him. Remember that, you good people, always remember your Bible. And don't forget the name. It's Gilgo Slade you're listening to, that's who it is, Gilgo Slade. G I L G O. (46–47)

His final speech not only continues to pander to the angrily dispossessed and barely Bible-educated but becomes the first in the Long novels to employ one of Long's most effective stump tactics. As Williams explains, Long would first ask his listeners how many of them were wearing silk socks. When not a single hand shot up, he would dramatically pause, then ask them how many were wearing cotton socks. In response to the huge show of hands that inevitably followed, he would pull up a pants leg to reveal not the silk socks he alleged his opponents wore but the cotton socks his listeners had just admitted to wearing. Then, after seeing the same show of hands upon asking how many of them had holes in those socks, he would take off a shoe to reveal a big toe protruding from a huge, ragged hole. The crowd, of course, would burst into uproarious laughter and applause (*HL* 418). Similarly, Slade asks how many of his listeners own three suits of clothes. When none respond, he tells them that he had expected as much. When he asks how many own only the clothes on their backs, hands shoot up everywhere, and the candidate, leaning forward conspiratorially, jokes, "And you're mighty thankful to have one suit, ain't you, brothers!" (255). Unassuming laughter interrupts him, but only until he blasts into his main point:

> Greed! That's why you good people—my people—have only one suit of clothes. It's because of *greed*—the lustful and sinful greed of the privileged and powerful who sit on plush and partake of the fatted calf. How long, good people, how long? Do you remember what it says in the Bible? It says in the Bible that those who partake of the fatted calf shall bring whores and seducers into the temple. Do you remember? It says in the Bible that they shall befoul the temple and betray the people. It says in the Bible that a humble man shall come out of the multitude and do the bidding of the multitude. And who among you has come out of the multitude? Who have you called upon to do your bidding? Who else but Gilgo! It's GILGO you have called upon! GILGO SLADE! (255–56)

In that he portrays himself as one of the multitude, speaks their language, and backs up his only argument with cribbed paraphrases of the only book they know, Gilgo Slade is even more representative of the southern demagogue than his predecessor Harry Brand.

Just as he provides Slade Long's speeches, Basso also provides him Long's supporters. They, too, as Lewis described Windrip's followers, are the "[m]ost facile material for any rabble-rouser." We never see them categorized as schematically as in *It Can't Happen Here,* but Basso does introduce us to a few individual followers. He points out two "country" boys (247), a pair of overall-clad "countrymen" (252), and a woman in a faded calico dress at the rally, but the member of the masses on whom he most focuses is a man known only as Dent, whom Hazzard meets in Slade's hotel suite. One conversation is all it takes for both Hazzard and the reader to understand how leaders like Slade so easily arouse such a servile following. As Dent tells Hazzard, "You have to be a little fellow to appreciate Gilgo. . . . You have to be one of the little fellows like me. It's people like me he's looking out for." Dent goes on to tell him that he would have lost his home if it were not for Slade and his programs. "What I think is this," he concludes: "And I'm not the only one who thinks it either—believe you me I'm not. There are thousands of people who think the same way I do; hundreds of thousands. I think Gilgo Slade is the greatest man since Jesus Christ" (72–73). Despite the fact that one observer says he hardly looks like he can afford the sum, Dent spends a hundred dollars on one-dollar Gilgo Slade campaign ties. The day he met Slade, he confides to Hazzard, was the greatest he had lived. The day of Slade's assassination, it would follow, must have been the worst. For on the day after Slade's funeral, Hazzard reads of an unidentified suicide found face-down in a park pond. Attached to his coat is a note that reads, in part, "He was my Leader and I swore a Sacred Oath to follow him and I will follow him to the grave, keeping my Sacred Oath" (265). Nearby, police find eighty-nine Slade campaign ties in a ragged brown paper package. Slade's following, then—which Basso characterized in his letter to Cowley as "the worshipful dispossessed lower-middle class mass"—is but a multitude of Dents, so-called little people who follow him not only because they see him as one of their own but because, in no matter how small a way, they believe he has done something for their sake, not his.

Slade's politics and following might place him firmly alongside all other characters based on Long, but his physical appearance puts at least some degree of distance between them. He looks like Brand on the surface, but in *Sun in Capricorn* Basso takes his despot's characteristics to a particularly southern extreme. On first appearance, he looks much like Long. His hair is a ruddy brown, and his face, particularly his nose, would be easy fodder for satirists. On the afternoon Hazzard finds himself in his hotel suite, moreover, Slade appears, fresh from the shower, wearing a bright green robe and green bedroom slippers. Hazzard tells us that Slade enters with Long's "aggressive, almost brutal energy" (79) and that it quickly electrifies the room. What makes Slade unique, and at least temporarily places Basso in the company of such southern gothicists as Flannery O'Connor, is what Hazzard notices next. When one of Slade's slippers falls off, Hazzard is shocked to see that his left foot has only three toes. As a young man, Slade had slipped while chopping wood and had lopped off the other two— which a cat had spirited away and quickly eaten. The story proves difficult for Hazzard to forget, and when Basso reminds us of it later, he heavy-handedly draws for us the connection that more skillful artists like O'Connor would never need to. A still-queasy Hazzard confesses that he cannot stop thinking that "the misshapenness of his imagination, the will to destruction behind it, was but a reflection of the misshapenness of his foot" (104). Slade may look as much like Huey Long as Brand and many of his successors, but he is the only such character whose psychology is manifested physically. More than any of his fictional counterparts, he looks, and literally is, as unbalanced as he thinks.

What sets Slade still farther apart—and, indeed, what most makes the novel worth reading—is a pair of scenes in which he assumes center stage in a metaphorically political freak show. In Millichap's opinion, these scenes are nothing less than tours de force, the first even reminiscent of the party F. Scott Fitzgerald describes in the third chapter of *The Great Gatsby*.[17] It comes when Hazzard happens into Slade's hotel suite, a cluster of rooms characterized by even more commotion than that Lewis depicts in Windrip's suite. The meandering visitor cannot help but immediately notice a woman who must weigh four hundred pounds, "a perambulating mountain of fat dressed in hoop-skirts and a satire of pantalettes, wearing a pleated crinoline bonnet that framed a barely congealed jell of flesh held in a vague impress of the human face." Soon thereafter, as a girl with bright red hair leads several of the assembled in Slade's campaign song, "a bandy-legged dwarf with a great bulge of forehead" enters to join the festivities (68). The scene simply overwhelms Hazzard: he can never quite get a fix on it, and it remains for him more like a carnival sideshow than anything he would expect to find in a hotel suite. Yet he still has sights to see, for he soon spies a bodybuilder once billed as Strongo the Superman. After hearing one partygoer toast his fellow "fallen angels"—"I give you, gentlemen, the seven original sins" (76)—Hazzard overhears Slade dictating the text of a new handbill. It is to read, "'*Come One, Come All. See The Fat Lady And The Dwarf. See The Fire-Eating Cannibal From The Heart Of Africa. Hear Gilgo Slade's Champion Hill-Billy Band*'" (84). What he has witnessed, he realizes, are preparations for

17. Millichap, 87.

the debut of Gilgo's Old-Time Carnival Show, the vulgar bait Slade uses to draw the masses to his campaign stops. When Hazzard stumbles across one such show, a huge crowd has gathered, and after the fire-eater finishes the opening act, Slade himself takes center stage. He begins by introducing Madam Old-Time Politics, the four-hundred-pound woman Hazzard had seen in the hotel suite. Within moments, the woman's "offspring" appears: she screams, and the dwarf, this time clad in top hat and a ragged dress suit, runs out from under her skirts and jumps up onto a table to bow to the crowd. Slade introduces him as the son of Madam Old-Time Politics, his "worthy and venerable opponent, Thomas Hogswill Plushbottom" (258). Slade thus takes a more creative, even more entertaining route to claim of Uncle Thomas what Long often claimed of opponents like him: that, no matter how much they might seem improvements on their predecessors, they amounted to little more, in the end, than what Long too derided as "Old-Time Politics" (*HL* 70). Although engaged in much the same sort of character assassination that future Long figures would embody, Slade, in dramatizing them from the center of what once was called a freak show, also becomes the most garish of them all—a dubious achievement but, considering the competition, an achievement nonetheless. We know little more about his personality than we did upon his entrance, but what Slade so clearly lacks in depth is at least partially restored to him in volume and color.

Though much more showman than salesman, Slade, like Brand before him, also brings about a symbolic end to the South's old order. Constructed, like *Cinnamon Seed*, on distinctions between Old South and New, *Sun in Capricorn* presents as its most prominent embodiment of the former the unnamed family of Uncle Thomas, or more accurately, his wife's family, the Hazzards. Just after introducing himself as narrator, Hazzard explains that his family had lived in his home parish for several generations. As one of his maternal aunts is fond of pointing out, Hazzards "have *always* been in Montrose parish"—as if, Hazzard jokes, they had welcomed the Native Americans to the area and taught them how to hunt and fish. Hazzard himself is said to resemble his great-grandfather Edward, "the founder" (3)—of the local academy, not the country, Hazzard clarifies, although some among them seem to consider it the same thing. Hazzard seems to share John

Pine's attitude toward what Basso in *The View from Pompey's Head* (1954) would dub Shintoism, the almost Oriental, yet also characteristically southern predilection for ancestor worship. The representative of the younger generation who most embodies this attitude is Hazzard's cousin Quentin. As an engraving of Robert E. Lee and Traveller hangs on his father's office wall, a miniature of Stonewall Jackson sits atop Quentin's desk. To Hazzard—as, perhaps, it would also be to Dekker—this is "silly," just further proof of his cousin's "anachronistic turn of mind" (45). As it is to the Blackheaths, the past to Quentin's family is often more present than the present itself.

Just how anachronistic Quentin's mind-set truly is becomes most apparent during a conversation with Hazzard after Quentin discovers that his cousin Augusta has been dating Fritz Cowan, the scion of a locally ignominious family who is soon to become one of Slade's chief henchmen. After Quentin argues that Hazzard should forbid Augusta's dating Cowan, Hazzard plays Dekker to Quentin's Olivia, charging that "The time has come when you can stop trying to live up to your first name. A man named Coolidge is President, not Walter Scott." Quentin counters that the passage of time neither implies the decay of values nor makes it acceptable "for an alley-cat like Cowan to start prowling on decent people's front porches. . . . All I know," he argues, "is that I think people ought to have a code." Hazzard, with seemingly strained patience, responds,

> "So do I. Only—"
> "Only you think this isn't 1860."
> "I know it isn't."
> "And you think it's better the way it is now."
> "Better or worse, it just is."
> "But you think it's better."
> "It just is."
> "I'm not so sure it's better," he said. "I think the way it was might have been a better way. A man had his code and he looked after his name and he knew where he stood. I would have liked that. It would have suited me better than what we have now." (16–17)

Quentin casts Cowan in the same terms as Hazzard casts Slade, the same as those in which Basso casts Brand in *Cinnamon Seed* and casts

Long in his essays. The fact that he embodies something worse than what was is lamentable, but the prospects of a triumph over what he represents—whether by way of a clenched fist or some force more permanently formidable—are not promising enough to even initiate. Carl Weiss, after all, died in the attempt, and, according to most authorities on the era, succeeded only in ushering in a regime still more corrupt than Long's. For better or for worse, Hazzard repeats, the South is not what it was—and accepting and adjusting to that fact is both more realistic and more potentially productive than attempting to resurrect what, like Dixie itself, has been dead for years.

Though Basso appraises Slade's rise to power from a variety of damaging perspectives, all point to the victory of New South, Snopesian rapacity over such Old South honor as that to which Quentin clings. Slade is characterized from the outset as the antithesis of the Hazzards. In Uncle Thomas's words, he is a "peckerwood"—which Hazzard defines for all non-southern readers as "a man from the backcountry." They are called "hill-billys and red-necks" as well (9–10), he explains. To Quentin, of course, Slade is much the same, a "peckerwood," a "red-neck" (17). One of Uncle Thomas's friends, after learning of Slade's gubernatorial victory, echoes Basso's "Huey Long and His Background": "We'll have to fumigate the governor's mansion when we get back in. . . . There'll be roaches all over the place. . . . The walls will be stained with tobacco juice. They'll keep pigs in the dining room. That fellow will turn the mansion into a peckerwood's shack" (33–34). As Slade's opponent in the senatorial campaign, Uncle Thomas ends up defending a cause he had rarely had to defend before, having left much of that to his wife and son. To Hazzard, who sees the effort as futile, Uncle Thomas thus becomes a man being tossed in a raging hurricane, a man "caught in a flood, striving mightily, trying to save grandma's rosewood piano" (105). This somewhat curious symbol, as Hazzard explains later, is comparable, in a sense, to the Confederate statue in the Montrose town square. Extended to its utmost, it represents the rapidly vanishing old order, and in trying to protect it, Uncle Thomas is not only privileging the past over the present but engaging in what Basso considered an absolutely futile attempt.

Later in the novel, Hazzard extends these comparisons to connect the novel's title, its epigraph—"Capricorn is said to be the sign of ambition. It looks like the horns of a goat"—and the ruined plantation houses he and Erin pass as they flee New Orleans for Baton Rouge. Erin, he explains, is taken with one old place in particular. She sees in it, he imagines, a candlelit ball in progress, complete with string accompaniment. Hazzard immediately smashes these idealistic evasions by explaining that goats had probably taken over the old place. He knows they inhabit one in particular, for he had seen them befouling the ballroom that had since become their home. As if it were not already clear enough, Hazzard further explicates the novel's network of symbols. After commenting that his uncle "doesn't quite understand about grandma's rosewood piano or the goats in the ball-room," he tells Erin, "It's easy to understand. . . . There were not enough people invited to the ball. It was too exclusive. Too many of them had to stand out in the rain and look through the windows. That's why they're resentful. That's why they get a certain pleasure in watching a goat like Gilgo foul up the ball-room. That's why they want to junk grandma's rosewood piano" (170). In his 1939 *New Republic* essay "Huey's Louisiana Heritage," Basso describes Long as "a direct result of the Civil War," the "authentic voice of the lower and middle middle-class freed by the War from the economic and social repressions of the plantation caste system."[18] Slade, then, is still more the fictional counterpart of Basso's Long, for he too, as Hazzard explains him, is at the forefront of a historical movement by which the southern lower classes, dispossessed for generations, finally begin to demand attention. As Hazzard ventures after the speech above, "This fellow means something; he's no accident" (170). Instead, like Long himself, he is the result of generations of Dents—"those who were not invited to the ball"—waiting too long for, then finally demanding, admission.

Their invitation, however, never formally arrives. For when Quentin assassinates Slade for slandering his father—acting, as Hazzard sees it, and as many see Weiss acting, "in the unfortunate belief he was avenging the family honor" (264)—the New South ascendancy, along with Capricorn itself, at least figuratively begins to set. Yet even in doing so, Slade takes with him the novel's foremost representatives of the Old South mind-set: Quentin himself, gunned down within sec-

18. Basso, "Huey's Louisiana Heritage," *New Republic*, 30 August 1939, 99.

onds of Slade, and his mother Caroline, weakened first by the revelation of her nephew's all-too-public involvement with Erin, then left comatose after the murder of her son. Just as Brand brings on the death of the Blackheath patriarch Langley, hastens the degeneration of the Blackheath law firm and Carter Blackheath himself, and then threatens the destruction of the Blackheath estate, Slade, some seven years later, brings on the demise of those who, in *Sun in Capricorn*, most embody what Basso once referred to as Louisiana "tradition" and "ceremony." To Basso, then, though Brand may be more salesman than statesman, Slade more ringmaster than true reformer, both, above all else, hasten the demise of the South's old order. The Huey Long character in both novels is of the lower classes—he is "trash" in Cinnamon Seed, a "peckerwood" and a "red-neck" in *Sun in Capricorn*—and not only raises but leads the rabble, people more attracted to egg-laying contests, fat ladies, fire-eaters, and dwarves than to political issues per se. If we reduce them to their simplest terms, just as Lewis's Windrip becomes an American Hitler, Brand and Slade are exactly what Long was to Basso: a man who, after a decades-long tradition of refined gentlemen statesmen, spat tobacco juice on the walls of the governor's mansion, relied on his talents as a salesman and showman more than the skills of a statesman, and was, in short, a redneck in what had been a patrician's position—or as *Sun in Capricorn* puts it, a goat in what had been a grand ballroom. To paraphrase Hazzard, the modern South, thanks at least in part to men like Long, simply is what it is— not what it was or, worse, what its still-thriving population of evasive idealists have envisioned or attempted to resurrect.

In the end, what most distinguishes Basso's contributions to the fictionalization of Huey Long is not the trenchancy of his social commentary—more than a few have said what he did on the subject—but the rare vitality that emerges from the immediacy of his perspective. Both Dos Passos and Warren, as we shall see, would witness the Kingfish in action, but each did so only once, and neither walked away inspired or outraged enough to write novels that focus so predominately on the sociohistorical particulars of what he saw. Most of the works examined here rise and fall with what their authors achieve by way of transcending, instead of delineating, these particulars. One of the central commentaries on the subject, Rubin's "All the King's Meanings," in fact elevates *All the King's Men* so far above its predecessors because, as Rubin saw it, Warren is the only author who efficiently enough uses historical subject matter as a particular means to a universal end. *Cinnamon Seed* and *Sun in Capricorn*, it must be said, almost entirely fail to achieve this transcendence and more often comment on the historical moment than ask it to embody anything timeless. That being said, though, they also offer us an incorporation of both historical detail and the subjective impressions of being present, for instance, as Long held court in his hotel suite, that no other novel can rival. The objective may be available in any good biography, but the subjective is more difficult to find. Indeed, in a 1969 letter to Walker Percy, Shelby Foote pronounced T. Harry Williams's just-published *Huey Long*, now the best-respected of the more than half-dozen Long biographies, a "disappointment," for though the facts are "all there"—it is "[b]ig and fat and full of stuff," he conceded—there is "absolutely no feeling of [the] Thirties, and strangely none of Long himself."[19] One can hardly make the same criticism of *Cinnamon Seed* and *Sun in Capricorn*, for when Basso describes Brand disrupting the Senate or shows Slade stalking around his hotel suite in a brightly colored bathrobe and slippers, we get the feeling that this is what it must have been like, what Long himself must have been like, for Basso had been there to see him in action time and time again. These novels, *Sun in Capricorn* in particular, may therefore be of more interest to the historian than the literary critic—and even though they only rarely, if ever, transcend the particulars of the scenes they describe, there is much to be said for the fact that Basso was the one writer who was most often *there* to see the events upon which those scenes are based unfold, and for the now unrecoverable impressions of them, and of Huey Long himself, he brought to each novel as a result.

19. Jay Tolson, ed., *The Correspondence of Shelby Foote and Walker Percy* (New York: Norton, 1997), 138.

3 Manipulator of "Ruined Words": John Dos Passos's Chuck Crawford

IN "POST-WAR WRITERS AND PRE-WAR READERS," HIS CON-
tribution to the June 10, 1940, *New Republic*, Archibald MacLeish—
Librarian of Congress since the previous June—took up what to him
were two primary facts. The first concerned the attitude of young
Americans toward events in Europe and Asia that, before the end of
the following year, would precipitate America's entry into World War
II. The nation's youth, he found, were disturbingly skeptical of "all slogans, all tags—even all words," particularly those that constitute statements of "principle," of "conviction," and "of moral purpose." This,
MacLeish wrote, was a "sobering" discovery, for "[i]f all words are suspect, all judgments phony, all convictions of better and worse fake,
then there is nothing real and permanent for which men are willing to
fight." The second fact was that much of the responsibility for this attitude lay with "the best and most sensitive and most persuasive" writers
of the World War I generation, Ernest Hemingway and John Dos
Passos among the Americans singled out. What they had written,
MacLeish argued, were not just indictments of war itself but books
"filled with passionate contempt for the statements of conviction, of
purpose and of belief on which the war of 1914–1918 was fought." One
result of reading novels like *A Farewell to Arms* and *Three Soldiers*,
MacLeish contended, was the conclusion on the part of young
America that "not only the war and the war issues but *all* issues, all
moral issues, were false—were fraudulent—were intended to deceive."
Such works might express the "honest words of honest men . . . writers
of great skill, integrity and devotion," but as MacLeish saw it, those
same words had since borne "bitter and dangerous fruit."[1]

1. Scott Donaldson, *Archibald MacLeish: An American Life* (Boston: Houghton
Mifflin, 1992), 300, 334; Archibald MacLeish, "Post-War Writers and Pre-War Readers," *New Republic*, 10 June 1940, 789–90.

Edmund Wilson, among others, was quick to disagree, and in the next issue of the *New Republic* pronounced MacLeish's contentions both "absurd" and "extraordinarily confused." Objections of the sort notwithstanding, however, MacLeish does have something of a point. He may fall short of substantiating his claims about the effect of such statements on young Americans, but anyone reading the authors he cites can easily apprehend his more general line of reasoning. Even the most casual reader can recall Hemingway's Frederic Henry and his disgust for the words "sacred, glorious, and sacrifice," "honor, courage, [and] hallow," and for the phrase "in vain." That same reader, perhaps, can almost as easily recall how John Andrews in *Three Soldiers* similarly targets particularly American words and slogans, dismissing such World War I rallying cries as "Make the World Safe for Democracy" as the empty rhetoric of "bought propagandists." For Dos Passos, moreover, satirizing statements like these would become the stuff of an entire career. Even in a novel as late and relatively apolitical as *Chosen Country*, for instance, he introduces us to a character who finds "the footing of . . . old slogans" like "Liberty, Justice, Civilization, [and] Democracy melt[ing] into a slush of platitude under your feet," for those who most frequently uttered them "confidently mouthed the words but at the same time . . . let the substance dribble down their chins." What MacLeish seems to have missed, though, is Dos Passos's intent in making such statements. Far from condemning the "substance" behind them or, much less, attempting to undermine the values of young America—indeed, as Wilson wrote, "moral principles play a more serious part in [Dos Passos's] work than in that of almost any other important American novelist"—the satirist and reformer in Dos Passos was trying to recover their original meaning in the hope of doing the same for the "substance" behind them. His attempt, in short, was to restore, not destroy. As he argued in a relatively late essay, the "most valuable" role writers play comes in their looking beneath the superficialities of "the opinions, the orthodoxies, the heresies, the gossip and the journalistic trivialities of the day" to find and express not further worn-out "phrases" but "really and truly . . . liberty, fraternity, and humanity."[2]

2. Edmund Wilson, "Archibald MacLeish and the Word," *New Republic*, 1 July 1940, 30; Ernest Hemingway, *A Farewell to Arms* (1929; reprint, New York: Scribner, 1957),

There had been a time, Dos Passos believed, when such words meant more, when Saussure's signifier and signified had not been so deceptively split by two hundred years of political phrasemaking. There had been a time when phrases like those Jimmy Herf confusedly mumbles at a pivotal moment in *Manhattan Transfer*—"Pursuit of happiness, unalienable pursuit . . . right to life liberty and . . ."—were revered, had not yet become catchphrases bordering on cliché but remained single-minded declarations of faith. Both the phrases and much of the thinking behind them were still fresh, and those who uttered them in office did so with what Dos Passos found an integrity rarely glimpsed since, an honest attempt to elucidate meaning for the listener's benefit rather than obfuscate it for the speaker's. Dos Passos realized that, even by the early decades of the twentieth century, the words of Jefferson and Madison, of Patrick Henry and Thomas Paine had grown "old and dusty and hung with the faded bunting of a thousand political orations." At their core, however, they still were "sound." Yet the problem remained: not only did twentieth-century phrasemakers use them as ostensibly patriotic window dressing for their often underhanded intentions, but their listeners "failed to notice that the words don't apply any more to the facts they are supposed to describe." The War to End All Wars didn't, after all—nor did it make the world safe for democracy. Elaborating elsewhere, Dos Passos wrote, "Slogans and phrases that yesterday pointed steadily toward the lodestar of good today spin waveringly around the compass and tomorrow may have taken on meanings opposite from the meaning they started with." His history of the United States, accordingly, not only tells the old tale that begins in Jamestown, Virginia, but tells the more recent one of how the "old American speech of the haters of oppression," as he describes it in *The Big Money*, increasingly itself becomes a tool of oppression.[3]

184–85; John Dos Passos, *Three Soldiers* (1921; reprint, New York: Modern Library, 1932), 221; John Dos Passos, *Chosen Country* (Boston: Houghton Mifflin, 1951), 466; John Dos Passos, "The Workman and His Tools," in *Occasions and Protests* (Chicago: Henry Regnery, 1964), 13.

3. John Dos Passos, *Manhattan Transfer* (1925; reprint, Boston: Houghton Mifflin, 1953), 365; Dos Passos, "Workman and His Tools," 13; John Dos Passos, "A Question of Elbow Room," in *Occasions and Protests* (Chicago: Henry Regnery, 1964), 59; Floyd Watkins, *The Flesh and the Word: Eliot, Hemingway, Faulkner* (Nashville: Vanderbilt Univer-

Likewise, the thrust of his career is in large part a campaign against those who corrupt the original meanings of once-genuine words, phrases, and slogans. His hope, to return to the language of *Chosen Country*, was to remind us of their true "substance" and in so doing to rouse readers into demanding that those who employ them in elected office make that "substance" as authentic as originally intended.

Dos Passos first woke to widespread perversions of such language as a volunteer driver for the Norton-Harjes ambulance service during World War I. Hardly a partisan back home, upon shipping overseas he quickly came to see the war not as politicians and propagandists portrayed it, as a valiant attempt to halt German aggression, but as a bloodily Pyrrhic attempt to promote American capitalism—"the great God of our times," as he once satirized it. Almost as trying as the reality of the war itself was the disparity he found between signifiers back home and their ostensible signifieds on the fields of France. "The joy of being on the front," he wrote just after arriving there, "is that one is away from the hubbub of tongues, from the miasma of lies that is suffocating the world like . . . waves of poison gas." We find him particularly incensed by the official use of religious, patriotic, and more generally humanitarian terms to justify the carnage he was shipped over to clean up. A diary entry dated July 1917 reads, "How damned ridiculous it all is! . . . All the cant and hypocrisy . . . all the vestiges of old truths now putrid and false infect the air, choke you worse than German gas—The ministers from their damn smug pulpits, the business men—the heroics about war—my country right or wrong—oh infinities of them!" America, he concluded, was foundering unaware in an "orgy of patriotic bunk," in "lies & hypocritical patriotic gibber." This "gibber" served its purpose, however, as illustrated in the case of the enthusiastic but naïve American soldier Dos Passos watched arrive with the fervent belief that "he would be engaged in constantly snatching half-raped Belgian women from the bloody claws of Huns; that all the Germans spent their time in atrocities and that the American soldiery . . . actually would step in every few minutes and cry, 'Shoot not

sity Press, 1971), 5; John Dos Passos, "The Changing Shape of Institutions," in *Occasions and Protests* (Chicago: Henry Regnery, 1964), 201–2; John Dos Passos, *The Big Money* (1936; reprint, New York: Modern Library, 1937), 463.

this old grey head' etc." For this and a million other cases of brain-washing, Dos Passos made plans, in a 1918 letter detailing his postwar writing projects, to "make their ears tingle . . . by God, if I die in the attempt. I'll dust their coats with a clanking of printing presses." He would show them, he vowed, that "things are not what they seem."[4]

Making good on these threats of course won his fictional protests a larger audience than his letters and diary would ever find. Published in 1920, *One Man's Initiation: 1917* is an autobiographical novel that tells of six unsettling months in the life of an American ambulance driver stationed at the French front. If Martin Howe seems at first more naïve than Dos Passos did in the same situation—he merely nods in embarrassed acquiescence when a more experienced soldier de-nounces the "ocean of lies" necessary to foment and maintain the war effort—he soon finds himself seeking refuge from just such "stupidity" and government-engendered "cant." Six months later, Howe has de-veloped the insight to think beyond what his superiors tell him and his peers all too willingly accept, and what at first had inspired only half-hearted assent becomes the subject of his own increasingly vocal pro-tests. "I shall never forget the flags," he begins his most self-assured speech, "the menacing, exultant flags along all the streets before we went to war, the gradual unbaring of teeth, gradual lulling to sleep of people's humanity and sense by the phrases, the phrases. . . . People seem to so love to be fooled. Intellect used to mean freedom, a light struggling against darkness. Now the darkness is using the light for its own purposes. . . . We are slaves of bought intellect, willing slaves." On the final pages of *One Man's Initiation,* one of America's most cherished symbols is thus exposed beside all "the phrases, the phrases" as mere camouflage for that same "ocean of lies."[5]

Dos Passos tells a similar story in *Three Soldiers,* which followed a year later. John Andrews begins military life much as had Dos Passos himself, horrified by the anti-German hatred whipped up by Allied

---

4. John Dos Passos, *The Fourteenth Chronicle: Letters and Diaries of John Dos Passos,* ed. Townsend Ludington (Boston: Gambit, 1973), 152, 90, 93, 219, 239; John Dos Passos, *John Dos Passos' Correspondence with Arthur K. McComb, or, "Learn to Sing the Carma-gnole,"* ed. Melvin Landsberg (Niwot: University Press of Colorado, 1991), 64, 57.

5. John Dos Passos, *One Man's Initiation: 1917* (1920; reprint, Ithaca: Cornell Univer-sity Press, 1969), 60, 81, 159.

propaganda. He ships over and, for the length of his stay at the front, remains a man apart. Others in his unit can find comfort in YMCA platitudes about their involvement in "a great Christian undertaking," can find justification in the phrase "*Make the world safe for Democracy*," but Andrews cannot. Instead, he finds such platitudes "shams" and desires above all not to strafe Germans in the name of "brave little Belgium" or lockstep his way into Army hierarchy but to make others aware of "the falseness of the gospels under the cover of which greed and fear filled with more and yet more pain" the everyday lives of those torn by war.[6] His enterprise ultimately fails—he deserts and begins to spread his message but is soon captured and imprisoned—but he does save himself from the mindless conformity of his fellows, that unthinking acceptance of authority and its "shams" that Dos Passos would continue to excoriate in his fiction.

What remains the most oft-quoted example of this protest came five novels and fifteen years later in the final volume of the *U.S.A.* trilogy, *The Big Money*. Professional and political phrasemakers in *Manhattan Transfer*, *The 42nd Parallel*, and *Nineteen Nineteen* are far from immune to this kind of criticism—in the latter, for instance, Dos Passos characterizes Woodrow Wilson as a speaker for whom the phrase "*New Freedom*" actually means "*Conscription*," "*Democracy*" means "*Win the War*," and "*Reform*" means "*Safeguard the Morgan Loans*"—but none receive the kind of scathing treatment he unleashes upon the officials at the heart of *U.S.A.*'s final Camera Eyes. Camera Eye 49 compares the Plymouth, Massachusetts, of America's founding to the Plymouth, Massachusetts, of the novel's 1927 setting. The former is where "the immigrants landed the roundheads the sackers of castles the kingkillers haters of oppression," the latter where Bartolomeo Vanzetti, "another immigrant . . . hater of oppression," had lived and worked before his arrest alongside Nicola Sacco. As he watches a train depart the local station, the Camera Eye's unnamed narrator glances up at the passengers on board and dejectedly apostrophizes:

> how can I make them feel how our fathers our uncles haters of oppression came to this coast   how say   Don't let them scare you   how make them feel who are your oppressors America

6. Dos Passos, *Three Soldiers*, 166, 174, 215.

rebuild the ruined words worn slimy in the mouths of lawyers districtattorneys collegepresidents judges   without the old words the immigrants haters of oppression brought to Plymouth how can you know who are your betrayers America

    or that this fishpeddler you have in Charlestown Jail is one of your founders Massachusetts?

Camera Eye 50, set immediately after the immigrants' executions, continues this argument: "America our nation has been beaten by strangers who have turned our language inside out who have taken the clean words our fathers spoke and made them slimy and foul."[7] Dos Passos's point is clear: the values upon which America was founded—freedom from oppression in particular—had been so perverted by the elected officials since entrusted to safeguard them that the effects had been felt on even the linguistic level. If a nation of immigrant haters of oppression can openly and with impunity oppress fellow immigrant haters of oppression, what, if anything, does the word "oppression"—or, by extension, its specifically American converse, "life, liberty, and the pursuit of happiness"—actually mean? Over the course of three hundred years, the "old words," the "clean words our fathers spoke" have been "turned . . . inside out," made "slimy and foul," have become the words of oppressors, rendering them essentially meaningless, "ruined." "[B]etrayers" thus seem saviors, for they use the same words, and both use them in the service, ostensibly, of the American people. The jury who convicted Sacco and Vanzetti and the advisory committee who later upheld the conviction are thus not only dishonest trustees of the public faith but traitors both to those they represent and to American English itself—which must now be "rebuil[t]." Only then, Dos Passos implies, will we be able to tell who our oppressors are; only then will we be able to express solidarity with the oppressed without sounding like oppressors ourselves.

A biography entitled "Kingfish the First" originally was to have followed Camera Eye 50 and concluded *The Big Money*. According to

7. John Dos Passos, *Nineteen Nineteen* (1932; reprint, New York: Modern Library, 1937), 105; Dos Passos, *Big Money*, 435–37, 462.

Donald Pizer, whose *Dos Passos's U.S.A.* presents the most detailed study to date of the trilogy's notes and manuscripts, *The Big Money* began as a list of fictional characters—some new, some retained from *The 42nd Parallel* and *Nineteen Nineteen*—and a list of historical figures to serve as thematic counterpoint. After generating these lists, Dos Passos compiled tables of contents, elements of which juggled back and forth as his conception of the novel changed. "Kingfish the First" appears in the first three tables, disappears from the fourth, and reappears in the fifth and sixth, but is replaced in the seventh and all subsequent tables, as well as in the published version of the novel, by "Power Superpower," his biography of Samuel Insull. We can perhaps hypothesize that Dos Passos dropped the Long biography because its subject matter, which truly begins to build to its 1935 climax only after 1928, would have clashed with the novel's pre-Depression setting. We can also hypothesize that Dos Passos abandoned the piece before so much as even drafting it. In his notes for *The Big Money,* now housed at the University of Virginia, references to Long occasionally appear in the margins and on the inside cover of one notebook, but there is no draft proper of the intended biography. All that remains—if anything else ever existed—is a single sheet of typing paper, its bottom quarter torn off, with a dozen or so lines of handwritten notes for what Dos Passos, contrary to what his tables of contents imply, seems to have at least considered calling "The Free State of Winn." That, at any rate, is the first line on the page, and the next few lines that follow, after references to "Callie" and "Old Man Long," refer to Winn's geography— "backwoods and pinescrub hills"—and to its infamous political reputation—"antisecession," "populist," "socialist." The notes then jump to Long himself. "Huey's circulars" refers to his primary means of early self-promotion, "Railroad Board" to his first elected position, and "1929—when . . . legis [*sic*] started going against him" to his impeachment.[8] This, though, is probably all of "Kingfish the First" that ever made it to paper. Whatever Dos Passos would have written about Long in the roughly half a decade before his assassination is at best, therefore, a matter of conjecture.

8. Donald Pizer, *Dos Passos' U.S.A.: A Critical Study* (Charlottesville: University Press of Virginia, 1988), 86–87, 102–9; John Dos Passos Papers (#5950), Albert and Shirley Small Special Collections Library, University of Virginia Library.

Inherent anachronisms notwithstanding, the material could easily have continued Dos Passos's fervent debunking of "ruined words." Share Our Wealth and its attendant propaganda, its claims of saving America from the grip of the Great Depression, after all, were quite likely to Long just "bullshit" to "get attention." The Huey Long of Dos Passos's nonfiction, moreover, understood all too well the way language works: in "The Use of the Past," Dos Passos perpetuates the myth of Long's cleverly speculating that fascism, if and when it arrives in America, will do so as "antifascism," an ideology identical in all but name. In the same essay, Dos Passos goes on to argue that the "history of the political notions" of many if not most twentieth-century Americans "is largely the record of how far the fervor of their hopes of a better world could blind them to the realities under their noses."[9] So it was, apparently, with the nearly eight million registered members of the Share Our Wealth Society. So strong were their hopes, so persuasive Long's claims to be working in their interests, that what doubts they had about his record ultimately did not matter. The possibilities of a novel about such a gifted manipulator of empty signifiers were apparently too promising to pass up, for even if Dos Passos dropped "Kingfish the First" from *The Big Money*, he returned to the material some six years later in the second volume of his second trilogy. More than a mere continuation, however, *District of Columbia* is an intensification of his protests against public officials who destroy once-revered words. His central characters, no longer the relative outsiders we find in Martin Howe, John Andrews, and the nameless narrator of Camera Eyes 49 and 50, are now insiders, often devoted followers of those they only later realize are such shameless betrayers of the public trust. The result of their awakening to their mentors' deceptions is not just the indignation of Howe, Andrews, and the nameless narrator, but abject disillusionment only further magnified by the immediacy of their associations with the officials in question. And though they realize it only after the fact, their involvement—their collusion, in effect—makes them unknowing conspirators, complicit participants despite themselves in the very betrayals that ultimately so disgust them. "King-

9. John Dos Passos, "The Use of the Past," in *Occasions and Protests* (Chicago: Henry Regnery, 1964), 36–38.

fish the First" would no doubt have been critical enough of Long, but as Dos Passos's incriminations of politicians who so unconscionably ruin words are only redoubled in *District of Columbia*, Long's appearance in this second trilogy probably casts him as a more perfidious figure than he would have been if written into the first, as originally planned.

Adventures of a Young Man, the first volume of *District of Columbia*, is the story of Glenn Spotswood, a Washington, D.C., native who early on renounces his middle-class capitalist upbringing to aid in the plight of the common laborer. After years of unfulfilling, often failed attempts to improve life among the working class, Glenn finds himself embroiled in a standoff between labor and management in the coal mining center of an unnamed Appalachian state. As a lower-level organizer in the communist-affiliated American Miners Union, he puts much of his hope in Irving Silverstone, a party litigator ostensibly dispatched to help the miners resolve the conflict. Glenn's placing faith in either the party or Silverstone—who, speaking to jailed miners, assures them that "what we want to do is get you boys out of jail as soon as we can"—quickly proves ill-advised, for those who control the party are there only to organize the miners, not actually to free them. As Elmer Weeks, Glenn's superior, explains, their primary purpose is "to educate the American workingclass in revolutionary Marxism." They are not interested, he reminds him—despite Silverstone's impassioned promise—"in the fates of individuals." Dos Passos puts what seems his perspective on the proceedings in the mouth of Harve Farrell, the novel's most outspoken critic of the American Communist Party. Farrell accuses party representatives of making the trip to Appalachia only "to raise a big political stink and git yourselves a new crop of martyrs to raise money . . . for your own mealtickets." What Silverstone and his comrades care most about, Farrell argues, is "words": "that's what you'll get," he tells his fellow miners, "a big talkfest," and "the boys'll stay in jail."[10] In the end, as one familiar with Dos Passos's experiences in Harlan County, Kentucky, might imagine, this is exactly what happens. Disillusioned and finally disheartened by his complicity in what

---

10. John Dos Passos, *Adventures of a Young Man* (New York: Harcourt, Brace and Co., 1939), 182, 201, 187, 206.

Farrell correctly condemns as a communist betrayal of the party's constituency, Glenn disavows party politics altogether and crosses the Atlantic to assist the Spanish Loyalists, hoping that with them he can at last contribute to an authentic fight against fascism. The true fight, he discovers, is not to be found in America. Between the early 1920s and late 1930s, Dos Passos may have changed his target from World War I military propaganda to that of the American Communist Party, but his message remains much the same: all too often those sworn to support their constituents only turn them into martyrs for their leaders' meal tickets.

One of Dos Passos's most succinct expressions of this evolving argument—he had progressed, after all, from youthful antiwar protest to more sophisticated dissections of the politician-constituent contract—comes in "To a Liberal in Office," an open letter he published two years after *Adventures of a Young Man* in a 1941 issue of *The Nation*. "No matter how good the intentions of a man in public service are when he starts out," he began, "I think you'll agree that it's exceedingly difficult for him to avoid leading a double life. While with one side of his mind he's trying to fulfil [*sic*] his duty to his fellow-citizens, with the other he's busy with his career and with the demands of the organized group he belongs to. Only too often the members of the aggregations of men that make up a government lose all contact with the public needs they were got together to serve." Just as his charges apply to the unnamed, perhaps generic liberal of the title—as well as, by extension, virtually every politician and propagandist from *One Man's Initiation* to *Adventures of a Young Man*—they also apply to Senator Homer "Chuck" Crawford, the title character of Number One, the second volume in *District of Columbia*. Crawford is a politician who, with the help of his wife Sue Ann and his confidential secretary Tyler Spotswood—Glenn's alcoholic older brother and the self-proclaimed black sheep of the family—rises to the rank of United States senator.[11] Along the way, he makes the standard demagogic promises, portrays himself as a politician who, unlike his opponents, is "workin' in [the] interests"

---

11. John Dos Passos, "To a Liberal in Office," in *John Dos Passos: The Major Nonfictional Prose*, ed. Donald Pizer (Detroit: Wayne State University Press, 1988), 198; John Dos Passos, *Number One* (Boston: Houghton Mifflin, 1943), 258.

of the "plain folks" because he is "one of 'em" himself (36). Yet, just as much as there is "ole Chuck . . . doin' chores for the American people" (15), there is also Number One, doin' numbers on the American people. The public claim permits—for it almost completely disguises—the private crimes, ruining the relevant, once-revered words in the process. Much like Dos Passos's Liberal in Office, Crawford works to deliver on his promises with, at most, only half of his mind. For in the process of living the other half of what Dos Passos referred to as the politician's double life, Crawford, tempted by the excesses increasingly within his reach, soon begins sacrificing those he most owes his success. The first to go is his wife Sue Ann, overlooked amidst ever more frequent after-hours activities with call girls and lounge singers. Next to be betrayed are his constituents, the "plain folks" for whom he so hypocritically professes to be working. In order to remedy a desperate lack of cash, Crawford devises a plan by which he can profit by leasing oil rights to the state's public parks. When, toward the end of the novel, a grand jury threatens to expose the scheme, Crawford also turns his back on Tyler. As one of those taking the fall for Crawford's corruption, he becomes, in the senator's public pronouncements, one of the deceivers instead of the deceived. His younger brother Glenn admonishes him in a letter written just before his death on the war-torn fields of Spain not to let his boss "*sell out too much of the for the people and by the people part of the oldtime United States way*" (282), but the message arrives too late to prevent his undoing, and Tyler ends up yet another martyr to the self-serving double-talk of a politician whose private actions increasingly contradict his public pronouncements.

This pattern finds further expression in *The Grand Design*, the third volume in *District of Columbia*, a novel that begins with an epigraph from Mother Goose: "A man of words and not of deeds / Is like a garden full of weeds." The novel proper begins as Millard Carroll and Paul Graves leave lucrative jobs in the private sector and, at the behest of their newly elected president, move to Washington, D.C., to try to rebuild Depression-wracked America from within the Department of Agriculture. On the subject of this new, more altruistic approach to government service, Dos Passos's unnamed representation of President Franklin Delano Roosevelt comments, "*In the building of [public] service there are coming to us men and women with ability and courage from every part of the Union. The days of the seeking of mere party advantage through the misuse of public power are coming to a close.*" This is far from what Carroll and Graves find at their new posts, however. During the decade they occupy them, they repeatedly find their superiors forgetting their purported beneficiary—"the poor devil in the field being moved around by forces too big for him to understand"—only to return to the same old party politics the president had forsworn upon inauguration. Every four years, he shoves all other efforts aside to ensure his reelection; almost as often, his secretary of agriculture shrugs off his own slate of commitments to lobby for the best position in the oft-reconfigured administration; worse still, the administration as a whole almost entirely forgets that "poor devil in the field" as the nation begins preparing for World War II. Carroll and Graves approach the contracts the impending conflict will necessitate as their best chances to impose New Deal standards of labor on suppliers and manufacturers worldwide, but the president appoints a known profiteer as coordinator of his War Procurement Board. Initially outraged over the nomination, even the secretary of agriculture, who had once affirmed that "Government must look out for the little people," quickly buckles under the president's wishes, and as he quickly resumes life as an "Administration zombie," business returns to normal. Their determination to raise the global standard of living now all but unattainable as they find themselves among the few even interested in the attempt, Carroll and Graves both resign. The sacrifice of the "poor devil in the field" for the rich man in the big office proves too much for either to stomach. Even as late as the mid-1940s, as Dos Passos puts it in his final prose poem, Americans had yet to learn *"how to put power over the lives of men into the hands of one man / and to make him use it wisely."*[12]

Long before *The Grand Design* winds down to these, among its final passages, Dos Passos begins the novel—as he would also begin subsequent editions of *Number One* and the omnibus edition of *District of Columbia*—with a disclaimer. "Although the frame of this story is the history of our time," it reads, "the characters are inventions through and through and any resemblance to real people alive or dead is acci-

---

12. John Dos Passos, *The Grand Design* (Boston: Houghton Mifflin, 1949), 1, 14, 162, 206, 370, 418.

dental." To accept this statement blindly is to apply Dos Passos's arguments throughout not to what actually was, but only to what he imagined could have been, to read the trilogy not as the work of a self-styled "second-class historian" but as that of a novelist of pure imagination. To do so, more specifically, is also to rebut dozens of critics and scholars who find in *Number One*'s Chuck Crawford not an "invention through and through," as the disclaimer puts it, but a thinly veiled fictional portrait of Huey Pierce Long. Still more concretely, it is to contradict Dos Passos's own admission, hedging though it may be, that "[t]he nearest I ever came to a character completely from life was Huey Long in 'Number One.'"[13] It is also, finally, to withhold from Dos Passos much of the credit he deserves for his efforts as a "second-class historian." For in casting Huey Long in the role of Chuck Crawford—the single politician in *District of Columbia* who most unconscionably sacrifices the masses for his meal ticket, most egregiously ruins once-meaningful words and phrases—he offers us not such sensationalistic, at times overdrawn incarnations of Long as Berzelius Windrip and Gilgo Slade, but a more realistic version of the man historians tell us Long was, an incarnation that on occasion approaches, at times even threatens to surpass the realistic incarnation Hamilton Basso gives us in Harry Brand. The threat he embodies, in other words, is real, more factual, in the end, than fictional.

In *Number One*, the most oft-manipulated phrases are "of the people" and "for the people"—as in the Gettysburg Address's "of the people, by the people, for the people." Lincoln's words are invoked on three separate occasions, Lincoln himself on one. Emphasizing, especially, the first syllable of the word "populist," Dos Passos keeps "the people" continually before our eyes, particularly in the italicized prose poems that introduce each chapter and conclude the novel. Each begins with the phrase "*When you try to find the people*" and then introduces us to individual segments of "*the people*." In the first chapter, we meet a

13. Dos Passos, *Grand Design*, n.p.; John Dos Passos, "Statement of Belief," in *John Dos Passos: The Major Nonfictional Prose*, ed. Donald Pizer (Detroit: Wayne State University Press, 1988), 115; John K. Hutchens, "On the Books," *New York Herald Tribune Weekly Book Review*, 30 January 1949, 10.

farmer plowing a field behind a team of mules; in the second, an auto mechanic wearing a union badge; in subsequent chapters, a seventeen-year-old clerking in a chain store, a coal miner slowly starving while holding out hope for something better, and a businessman beginning another day at the office. The sixth and final prose poem even approaches the texture of a Walt Whitman catalogue:

> *When you try to find the people,*
> *always in the end it comes down to*
> *the old man with chalk in his knuckles selling pencils on a windy*
> *streetcorner, the sweaty small boy with grime behind his ears who runs*
> *lugging the heavy pack of evening papers, the girl in a scurry to get*
> *home after ten hours in a department store raising her patent leather*
> *handbag to signal the streetcar, the foxyfaced young man with a lunch-*
> *box under his arm hurrying to his job on the night shift, the ruddy man*
> *who's just been commissioned a major sitting bolt upright in the back of*
> *the taxi looking joyfully forward to the cocktail lounge where at five-*
> *fifteen he's going to meet the girl he's going to marry before Christmas,*
> *the stoopshouldered convict on parole dragging his feet with his eyes on*
> *the curb, the stout mother of many children who's waiting for the bus;*
> *she's been shopping; her legs are heavy; one heel's run down; her arms*
> *are full of bundles; she has two smeary brats in tow:*
> *when you try to find the people, myriadfigured pyramid precariously*
> *balanced on every one*
> *alone:*
> *lathe operator, welder, bench hand, mechanic, filing clerk, brake-*
> *man, lawyer, cook, girl in a beauty parlor, doctor, barber, radio repair-*
> *man, truckdriver, rigger, watchmaker, seaman, babbiter, farm hand,*
> *tester, surveyor . . .* (301–2)

Dos Passos not only gives faces—or at least ages, genders, and occupations—to the populist's abstraction of "the people" but rouses our support and even sympathy for them; for in the process of the novel—if not American politics as usual—each is potentially the victim of a politician employing "the people" as a catchphrase only to earn their trust, which, all too often, he will eventually betray. Indeed, many subjects of the early prose poems are in the presence of a radio, soon to be Crawford's chief means of public promotion. The farmer, for instance, hears a local program each time his mules pull him past his open door. Among the scraps of what he catches is a political address with "*the voice direct from me to you of a candidate who wants to be nominated*" (3). From the radio in the mechanic's garage come

> *voices that lull, insinuate, incite the mind*
> *to grow new tendrils of appetite, sow sets of words like seeds at random in the ears of a man alone with his hands grimed with carbon and grease* . . . (47)

Dos Passos thus connects flesh-and-blood Americans in need with "the people," the dangerously abstract phrase that so consistently and conspicuously appears in Crawford's public pronouncements. "The people" to whom Long addressed his own claims, of course, were in no less need, an inevitably dangerous situation for both constituencies.

In the opening chapters of Crawford's life, Dos Passos keeps as close to the Horatio Alger as to the Huey Long tradition. Born five years after Long in the fictional town of Texarcola—whose name implies more about its location than Dos Passos ever divulges—Crawford was raised the son of a small-town lawyer and dabbler in local politics. Because of a particularly well-read mother, Crawford, like Long, grew up in an unusually well-educated family for their time and place. Yet Crawford's family was in no way as well-off financially as Long's: in Crawford's words, "My folks never had a piece of change in the house from one week's end to the other. If I wanted any money, I jess had to go out an' make it" (21). So, beginning at age ten, make it he did, selling everything from newspapers to ice cream. What eventually proved his forte was not sales, however, but management—politics, in a sense. As Crawford explains to Ed James, the local reporter assigned the research and writing of his campaign biography, what would become a career in politics essentially began with a local church's efforts to buy stained-glass windows for its sanctuary. Against his better judgment, Crawford's boss let him talk him into donating the ice cream for the benefit. So successful did Crawford's plan prove that it not only financed the new windows but eventually turned a local ice cream stand into a statewide operation. More significantly for him, Crawford learned what may have been his most valuable lesson in the process: that "people's minds are full of mean lil barbwire fences"—fences like those his boss had built up against the idea of giving ice cream away free—and that "[t]he thing to do when you are tryin' to talk folks into somethin' is to kinder fool around till you find a gate or a break in one of them fences" (25–26)—a gate or a break like that Crawford confesses to subsequently forging by quoting scripture on the stump as often as possible. Later, of course, he would add "of the people" and "for the people" to his public repertoire. The most valuable part of what he learned is that "once you've gotten through them fences, it's like breakin' a colt, you kin ride him easy" (26). The stained-glass window benefit thus gives rise to what will become Crawford's political philosophy: first find, then appeal to, then exploit the desires of the people.

The novel's record of Crawford's young adulthood reads like selections from Long's biography. Crawford's years at an unnamed state university were punctuated, as were Long's, by serious financial difficulties. In the midst of a dire financial bind, Crawford had won one hundred dollars at the kind of debate Long himself often won, addressing an issue like those Long addressed, the federal ownership of railroads. Consequent stints on the debate team and as a cheerleader did little to alleviate his perennial cash flow problems, so Crawford, after a disastrous attempt at staging his own raffle, left both the college and the town. Soon thereafter, again like Long, he found employment as a salesman traveling for a hardware store and, later, for a manufacturer of kitchen appliances. That was when he "started to canvass the voters," Crawford jokes. "[I]t was the customers in those days," he says, "but it's the same thing." Both his manner of speaking and his method of canvassing voters resemble Long's in his early days:

> I used to be on the road day an' night. Instead o' stoppin' in hotels I stopped in farmhouses so's to git to know the folks, see how they lived, see what they needed. I was always ready to chop a little wood for 'em or help the misses light the stove or clean the lamps or take the swill out to the pigs . . . Wasn't a damn thing I wouldn't do . . . I got up contests at county fairs an' all that crap. Took 'em out of themselves a little . . . It's easy to git on the right side of plain people. (32)

If he sounds condescending, possibly even contemptuous, he did not at the time offend Sue Ann Jones, an attractive young woman who entered a waffle-making contest contrived to promote his company's waffle iron. More impressed with the promoter than the product, she soon became Mrs. Homer T. Crawford. This episode, as it so clearly parallels the meeting, courtship, and marriage of Huey and Rose Long, proves Dos Passos as conversant as Basso not only with the broad outline of Long's early adulthood, but with the more private, relatively obscure facts of his life. As his notes for *The Big Money* demonstrate, Dos Passos had done his research on Long, and even though "Kingfish the First" never materialized, Dos Passos made extensive use in *Number One* of the information he had earlier uncovered.

Dos Passos also shadows the record when sketching in Crawford's years as a young lawyer and politician. Not falling for the myth that so many others did, Dos Passos says nothing of Crawford's completing a law program in any span of time whatever. Instead, he has Crawford avoid advanced schooling altogether and simply read law, alongside his wife, under the tutelage of her father's attorney. Once the Crawfords are admitted to the bar, their first case, much like some of Long's own, accused a utility company of unfairly suspending the service of an underprivileged customer. Next, upon the death of the local county road commissioner, Crawford nominated himself for the office, bought a car, and "drove around . . . an' said Howdy to folks I used to be friendly with when I was on the road" (35). He won easily, and in the process brought in voters who for decades had avoided the polls. Much the same can be said of Long's entrance into state politics. A post on the State Utilities Commission came next, one that brought with it a battle against Crawford's own version of the Old Regulars, an unnamed machine Tyler refers to as "one of the most entrenched political gangs in the country." Crawford emerged unscathed, however, for he could always count on the support of the people: "the plain folks knowed I was workin' in their interests," he explains; "why shouldn't I, when I was one of 'em?" (36). Dos Passos also sticks to the record as the novel assumes the immediate present—when Crawford, upon the death of a sitting U.S. senator, begins running for the right to assume his vacant seat.

Crawford's résumé, appearance, and personality all resemble Long's. The Chuck Crawford campaigning for the U.S. Senate both looks and acts like the Huey Long who won election to the same body.

His face is "rosy" and "boyish," and he often has "an impudent kind of grin on his full lips" (126). He has "dark" hair that has "a mussed steamy look" (14) and "big bright popeyes that seemed to be looking in all directions at once." His cheeks are "full of color," his jaw is "heavy," and his neck is "thick" (39). He walks with Long's characteristically "easy short fast steps" (126). Dos Passos, it should be noted, had seen Long in action—more or less—on Capitol Hill in early 1934. Having spied the senator napping through an ongoing session, Dos Passos described him in a *New Republic* article as "an overgrown small boy with very bad habits indeed."[14] Even more reminiscent of the Kingfish is Crawford's taste in clothes. At various points in the novel we find him wearing purple-trimmed white silk pajamas and red morocco slippers; a double-breasted blue suit with a pink shirt and a blue bow tie; and a double-breasted brown suit with a pale blue shirt and breast-pocketful of blue-bordered silk handkerchief. Still more characteristic of Long— again proving Dos Passos familiar with the minutiae of his material— are Crawford's eating habits. Though displayed in only one scene, they convey the overt gluttony and blind indifference to others with which Long himself apparently gorged (*HL* 319–20). As Dos Passos describes him at one point, Crawford with one hand crams part of a triple-decker sandwich into his mouth and with the other catches and crams back into it the pieces of meat that had fallen out. Moments later, upon catching sight of Tyler and Ed James, he signals to them with both hands and mouth full of food and attempts to grunt through it for more. Mrs. Roosevelt's question upon encountering Huey Long at her dining room table—"Who is that AWFUL man?"—apparently would apply just as well to Chuck Crawford.

Yet just such boorishness is part of Crawford's appeal. Like Windrip, Brand, and Slade before him, no matter what position he might aspire to or attain, Crawford strives to appear in public what Lewis dubbed the Professional Common Man. Dos Passos makes this point early on when, in response to Ed James's claim that a railroad boardinghouse is an inappropriate birthplace for a national leader, Tyler disagrees, countering that Crawford had been born exactly where he should have been, "right out in the middle of the American people" (5).

<hr>

14. John Dos Passos, "Washington: The Big Tent," *New Republic*, 14 March 1934, 120.

And Crawford fights to remain—or, more accurately, to be perceived as—the product of just that kind of environment. Before the end of his first scene in the novel, he has claimed to be either of, or working for, the American people some half-dozen times. We soon realize, however, that he does so only in public and, even then, only in the presence of potential supporters. He tries to substantiate his claims in more than just words, as well. When Crawford, just after stuffing himself full of sandwiches, notices the arrival of newspaper photographers, he arranges for one a scene in which he dramatizes, beside a stiffly posed waiter, his complaint that the stylish hotel in which he finds himself does not serve hog jowls and turnip greens. Crawford defends these acts, much as Long defended the corn pone–pot liquor debate, by arguing that, though some might find them "all horsin' an' demagogue foolery," they serve an altruistic purpose. "Down where we come from," he tells Ed James, "there's a lot of pore people don't eat the proper food." But they "listen to what I say because they know I'm their friend," Crawford explains, so he promotes such dishes in what he claims is the hope that "they'll start to git the proper vitamins an' all that" (19–20). His pose on the bandstand is no less calculated or contrived. As he explains to one crowd,

> I ain't askin' you to elect me to the U-nited States Senate. I ain't got the high toned eddication for the job to tell the truth. You all know me I'm jess a small town salesman with a smatterin' of law. All I know's how to keep my hands outa the other feller's pockets . . . To tell the truth I ain't really well enough off to keep up appearances like I'd oughto in a capital city like Washington D.C. A position like that's likely as not to be the ruination of our kinds of folks . . . All I'm askin' you-all to do is to think of your own interests. (68)

One can see the same strategy at work when, at another rally, Crawford shouts, "[I]n the face of God and man . . . I can't stand these store clothes . . . these lies." He then tears off his coat and tie and, in plain white shirt and suspenders, launches into a speech about saving "the home an' the little white church where we gather together on the Lord's day to worship the Lord of all harvests an' blessin's" (84)—although he is not, the novel implies, a religious man. U.S. senator though he may be, Crawford never wants his constituents to see him as anything other than that product of the railroad boardinghouse, that hog jowl– and turnip greens–eating "small town salesman with a smatterin' of law." His intent, of course, is for them to trust him as one of their own, to take as gospel truth the patent lie that he is one of them and working for them. "This is the time," he tells the crowd assembled at one speech, "to elect plain folks, who will stand up for the rights of plain folks an' who will see that government of the people, for the people an' by the people, shall not perish from the earth" (121), invoking Lincoln's words—another once-esteemed phrase ruined by a duplicitous politician—for the second time in the novel.

Having broken through their "mean lil barbwire fences" by convincing his constituents that he is every bit as common as they, Crawford saddles them up and gets ready to ride. One of the easiest ways to do so, he explains, is to appeal to their love of spectacle. As he tells Ed James in an early conversation, "Down home I step out an' lead the band. Give the folks a time for their money, that's what I say" (34). What he really does, of course, is distract them from the fact that all his style only masks a complete lack of substance. And he does so as often as possible. The number and variety of stops on just one day's timetable recall the frenzied rush of Long's own campaigns, the schedule for the day Dos Passos most fully details calling for some half-dozen speeches, a barbecue, a baseball game, an auction, and a torchlight parade. The larger events draw tens of thousands of spectators, for what Crawford offers is little less than Gilgo's Old-Time Carnival Show itself. The barbeque, for example, treats them to a backwoods spectacular. It begins as Tyler, fearing that a less-than-engaging opening speaker will lose the crowd, brightens upon the arrival of a vehicle like one Long himself invented (*HL* 466), a sound truck that drives up blaring the sounds of Klaxons and a so-called hillbilly band playing "O Susanna." The band breaks into "Every Man a Millionaire" (Crawford's version of "Every Man a King") as the truck pulls to a stop, and the candidate, flanked by his wife and three young sons, all waving tiny American flags, appears alongside it in an open convertible. Crawford jumps out onto the back of the truck, shouts, "All right, boys . . . Let 'em have it" (104), picks up an ocarina, and leads the band in his campaign song as the people join in, clapping and stomping. That night, a torchlight parade offers still more spectacle. Beginning with snare drums and the sound truck, Klaxons and car horns, it features a procession of bunting-draped cars, legions of marchers, and enough torches to brighten the bottoms of the lowest-hanging clouds. As the parade comes to a stop in front of the designated hotel, spotlights explode upon the featured attraction himself, standing high above the crowd on a hotel balcony. The sound truck blasts into "Every Man a Millionaire," and a massive roar fills the streets. As Tyler puts it, and as Long might well have, "We're great believers . . . in getting some oldtime showmanship back into politics" (120).

Crawford's words and beliefs—not just the dialect in which he expresses them—also sound something like Long's. True to his stand in his first big court case, he remains—at least on the bandstand—an enemy of corporate interests and a friend of the common man. One of the most oft-sounded notes in his public repertoire is that "it's the plain people that produce all the riches there is," and that what he most wants is to help them "jess git together an' freeze out of our government the bankers an' usurers an' predatory interests that never did a lick of real work in their lives" (53). His professed aim is to help "establish the victory of the common man, the reconquest of his government an' of his whole civilization by the plain or'nary citizen" (121). His explanation of how he will bring this about sounds much like Share Our Wealth. He argues that "every man who's put in a lifetime of hard work ought to have something to show for it" (61), for "if every man who sows in a field or store or a business got the full value of his production back we could all have a standard of livin' like a millionaire's today. That means livin' better than Solomon lived in all his glory" (62). The speech showcased as Crawford's first is still more specific, as well as more akin to Long's favorite stand on the stump: "Why should one million people in this country have all the good things of the world while the other hundred an' nineteen million go naked an' hongry an' destitute? It's against common sense an' it's against revealed religion. Don't the Bible lay upon us the injunction . . . to spread the good things of the land equally among the people of the land?" (13). Though Crawford rarely expands upon these ideas, Long, we must remember, was reluctant to do so himself. Not until his second year as a U.S. senator did he begin to refine the ideas that, for the previous several years, he had pitched almost as broadly. Chuck Crawford, significantly, never does.

Just as Crawford often espouses Long's general ideas, he sounds even more like the Kingfish and makes still further use of his tactics as he campaigns for the Senate. He spends less time addressing issues than baiting his opponent, portraying him not just as an enemy of the common man, but a comical one at that. Using caricature, even slander to distract his listeners from the gaping holes in what, like Long's, is only the sketchiest of platforms, Crawford argues that "the first step in loosenin' the stranglehold these interests has got on the produce of this country is to drive their willin' tools an' henchmen out of office. The first one we're a-goin' to drive out of the public trough," he tells a group of farmers, "is Mr. Fatty Galbraith":

> One of the dumbest an' bluntest tools that ever touched his hat to a banker, who's had the gall to present himself, in spite of what every man woman an' child in the country knows about his record, to the voters of this state for the Democratic nomination for United States Senator. Here he's been eatin' an' fattenin' off the green things of this land worse than the crickets . . . an' now he's askin' us to send him up to Washington to go sell out what's left to the big Eastern interests. Well what we're a-goin' to say to him is "No Mr. Fatty Galbraith it ain't good for your health to run for no nomination in this hot weather. Ain't good for your shortness of breath. You go back to your nice cool office an' go on representin' your wealthy clients in the courts an' not in the U-nited States Sen-ate." (53–54)

Expecting Galbraith to retaliate by alleging that he has African American blood, Crawford draws up a phony physician's affidavit certifying that three members of Galbraith's family are patients in a state insane asylum. The campaign may be fictional, but many such details come from Long's own battles. Just as Long, as we have seen, ridiculed Joseph E. Ransdell because of his particular physical characteristics, he parried another foe by threatening to expose the fact that his brother was a patient at a state mental institution (*HL* 351). Again, Dos Passos proves himself conversant with both the broad outlines and more obscure details of Long's biography.

As Crawford's tactics are, in many ways, the same as Long's, those who respond to them are much like Long's followers. In Crawford's words, his message is not for millionaires but commoners, "the real people whose work an' brains on farms, in factories, in millions of small businesses throughout the land, have made this country what it is" (89). Among his constituents we therefore find a wilted man in a sweat-stained straw hat and a simple blue work shirt and an ancient farmer in overalls who, at one of Crawford's speeches, listens with a work-contorted hand cupped behind one ear. En masse, Crawford's constituency is not diverse, lacking even the idealists Buzz Windrip attracts. At one point, Dos Passos characterizes Crawford's followers by their modes of transportation. There is occasionally a stray motorcycle among them, but far more prevalent are dilapidated cars, farm trucks, and wagons hitched to mules. In many ways, what his followers see in the man on the platform is but an angrier, more ambitious, smoother-talking version of themselves: someone with beginnings much like their own who has dedicated his life, as they see it, to improving the lot of all like them. What they do not understand, though, is that this is but the public persona of a professional confidence man, a face he has to work to compose before turning it toward his audience, and that the words he speaks are also just part of the act. For in private this politician is someone quite different, not so much "ole Chuck," the friend of the common man, as Number One, the backstage manipulator given to comment that his followers—whom he refers to in at least one instance as "crackers" (78)—will "go to the polls an' vote when I tell 'em to an' . . . stay away when I tell 'em to. An' if I tell 'em to give their chillen castoroil, they'll give 'em castoroil. If I told 'em to go jump in the crick I bet a whole lot of 'em would jump in the crick" (248). As was Long himself, and as are Windrip, Slade, and Dos Passos's Liberal in Office, Crawford is yet another politician split between public and private personae, and the largest part of *Number One* concerns his struggle to keep his private crimes from tarnishing and ultimately destroying his public image. For when his career begins to unravel, what Crawford most risks, in the end, is exposure: revelation of the fact that he is neither of nor for the people but just another politician who claims to be both so he can maintain his ill-gotten meal ticket.

As readers, we see much of what Crawford's constituents see, for Dos Passos shows us much of what Crawford shows them, yet we also see what they do not see, what they cannot see, for Dos Passos also shows us what Crawford does not show them, the dissembling politician behind the common man persona. One of the most subtle ways he does so is by providing us glimpses of the machinations involved in securing what Crawford's followers see as the fervent support of more established politicians. At the beginning of the novel, when Crawford's constituents see a newspaper photo of him alongside the widely respected and rarely photographed Senator Johns, they do not know that the venerable old statesman had started for the door upon seeing the photographer arrive, and that the senator, "with the face of a child who's been tricked into swallowing castor oil" (18), almost had to be forced into the frame. Nor do they see the scheme involved in getting Governor Steve Baskette onto the balcony beside Crawford at the end of the torchlight parade. Tyler has to ask a mutual friend to convince the governor even to travel to the same town; then, once Baskette is at the hotel, Crawford has to lure him outside by sparking his interest in the balcony's view of the crowd below. When the spotlights flood the two figures on the balcony, the governor is as shocked as if someone had pointed a gun at him, and when Crawford throws his arm around him in a gesture of what the crowd mistakes as solidarity, Baskette's lips form a terse, black line. The governor waves stolidly to the masses with barely suppressed chagrin, then moves as quickly as he can out of the crowd's line of sight. As often proves the case in politics, what Crawford's followers see is only the end of a long, carefully orchestrated, at times even underhanded series of events. Rather than an up-and-coming politician with the support of his seniors, Crawford is only a wilier conniver than those already in power, just a master manipulator of what only seem authentic signifiers.

Another early veil to drop for insiders and readers is the one concealing Crawford the deceitful husband. Behind the man who in public so often claims to support home and church is the man who in private spends far more time with other women than with his wife. Most if not all of his affections in the novel are directed toward other women. To Crawford, Sue Ann is not so much a wife as a prop, a comforting symbol to others of a warm and stable home and family life. On the campaign trail, he demands that she and their sons sit next to him on the platform, asking Tyler at one point, "What do you think we brought 'em for?" (70). Just hours after spieling on about his indebtedness to her at the beginning of the novel, Crawford takes Tyler and Ed James to a Washington, D.C., brothel and shortly thereafter begins a relationship with a lounge singer. When reminded of Sue Ann in the midst of such affairs, Crawford is prone to comment, "Jeez, I'd almost forgotten I was a family man" (218). In a scene that illustrates many of the reasons Sue Ann eventually abandons him, much like Rose Long abandoned her husband, Dos Passos translates into fiction the Sands Point incident—as well as, perhaps, some of Long's brother Earl's infamous carryings-on with New Orleans stripper Blaze Starr. Egotistically believing that all are amused as he is by his relationship with the lounge singer, Crawford jumps up on stage during her act one night and, after attacking a group of hecklers with his ocarina, ends up with a black eye and a bloody lip. Coupled with his ever-increasing status as a public figure, the incident leads to rumors of a foiled assassination attempt and an immediate increase in the presence of his bodyguard. Not only is the ostensible family man an adulterer, but the ostensible man of the people is a man increasingly afraid of the masses. Dos Passos thus employs three of Long's more infamous escapades both to further define Crawford's character and further delineate the split between his public and private personae.

What nearly proves his public unmasking—and what does prove his ultimate, but much more private betrayal of his constituents—is Crawford's involvement in what Dos Passos calls the Struck Oil Corporation. Long dubbed the factual version of this enterprise the Win or Lose Oil Corporation, but the names themselves are the biggest difference between them. Their proceedings are so similar that an individual analysis of each is unnecessary. In the novel, when a dire need of cash necessitates a frenzied search for funds, Crawford strong-arms his State Utilities Commission into selling the subsoil rights to specified sections of state park lands to Struck Oil, a dummy corporation whose paperwork bears the name Tyler Spotswood, not Chuck Crawford, just as Win or Lose's bore the name Earle Christenberry, not Huey Long. Struck Oil immediately sells those rights, and Crawford's financial problems just as immediately disappear. The implications of the deal are identical to those of various Win or Lose transactions. As Williams explains, the corporation succeeded because those who managed it were high-ranking Louisiana officials with inside information about state oil deposits and all the power necessary to demand leases to them. Their actions may not have been beyond the law—the company acquired the properties on opprobriously favorable terms, but did not do so illegally, exactly—but they were not entirely ethical, either (*HL* 825–27). Dos Passos opens up the morality of Struck Oil to even further question, for the sale allows Crawford to buy a radio station, WEMM—named for his "Every Man a Millionaire" program—to spread his message to a still larger audience. Crawford thus uses his elected position not only to cheat his supposedly beloved "plain people" behind their backs but to steal from a two-party electorate to further disseminate his decidedly one-party platform. His knowledge of his treachery, despite his refusal to admit wrongdoing, is clear. In response to Tyler's protesting, "Chuck, we can't do it like that," Crawford replies coolly: "Ain't no harm in a profit. We sell out to the best businessman . . . The people gits the wells developed . . . the royalties lower their taxes. Ain't nobody going to squawk. It's clean as a hound's tooth" (136). Although he tries to rationalize his wrongdoing, the fact that he worries more about the legality than the morality of the deal reveals that Crawford clearly knows, and is trying to cover up, his real crime: selling out "the people," the very constituency he so often promises his efforts.

Then, just as profits from Win or Lose encouraged the Internal Revenue Service to initiate a case against the Long administration (*HL* 826), the IRS, largely as a result of what an unnamed state newspaper calls a bitter and final break with the White House, begins an investigation of Crawford administration records, the most suspicious of which concern Struck Oil. After the investigation, like that of Long, leads to the indictment of assorted administration cronies, the same newspaper reports that Crawford himself, unsurprisingly, had been found innocent of all charges. And Crawford clearly would prefer that public perception remain that way. Coaching Tyler before his appearance in front of a federal grand jury, Crawford's soullessness, the unblinking ease with which he so callously asks a colleague, proponent, and old friend to take the fall for him, is flagrant even for him:

"Toby," he said quietly. "You've always been a drinkin' man, we mustn't suppress that . . . It's too bad . . . but it's true. . . . It's notorious that any soak's memory's weak . . . I used to be a drinkin' man myself, so I ought to know . . . I shouldn't wonder if you couldn't remember a goddam thing. . . . Now Norm Stauch . . . He's a gambler an' a brothel keeper an' a lowlife, you know that. What he did was to throw a lot of wild parties an' had you signin' documents you wasn't fit to read . . . You don't remember a goddam thing. You signed 'em by the yard. Tell 'em to ask Stauch why he tried to debauch my private secretary . . . Wouldn't be surprised if the interests put him up to it." (244–45)

Just before Tyler enters the courtroom, Crawford's defection becomes complete. Tyler learns that the resignation Crawford had earlier forced him to sign—standard operating procedure for Long as well—had been dated and accepted during a recent secret meeting. And after the trial, Crawford goes still farther. In a radio address that night, one that Tyler overhears much as the prose poems' farmer and mechanic over-hear similar orations, he characterizes himself as "one of the few who reachin' high office does not forget the people from which he came" and depicts Tyler as one of those he trusted "as Caesar did Brutus," who delivered "the unkindest cut of all, the stab in the back from a friend" (294). When we leave him, Tyler has thus become yet another martyr to a politician's meal ticket—and not just as an onlooker, but a supporter, ultimately even an unknowing conspirator—Chuck Craw-ford himself but another politician who ruins once-revered words and phrases to serve his own selfish interests.

Dos Passos's Crawford is thus easily a more realistic version of Long than either Lewis's Windrip or Basso's Slade. Though born in a differ-ent state than Long, he is born into a family of similar socioeconomic status and is therefore forced early on to go on the road to earn a living. Both Crawford and Long also turn early business lessons to their full political potential and later claim among early constituents customers from their days as traveling salesmen. As young lawyers, both earn rep-utations for defending the poor against predatory interests and later make the most of their renown by beginning political careers with seats on relatively minor commissions. They go on to hold different positions as state politicians, yet their careers are similar in that each spends much of his time fighting an entrenched political machine and protecting the common man from corporate interests. In their campaigns for U.S. senator, both propose wealth redistribution schemes while slandering their opponents more than actually addressing issues. Each fights to maintain his image as one of the people, excites a largely poor rural populace with campaign stops more akin to carnivals than rational examinations of political realities, and easily wins election to the U.S. Senate. Both also are split between public and private personae, show weaknesses for adultery, tendencies toward paranoia, and the ability to shamelessly manipulate whomever they need whenever they want, often by way of what Dos Passos called "ruined words."

If this sketch seems the biography of many an American populist, Dos Passos incorporates into *Number One* details that remind the informed reader of no politician but Huey Pierce Long. First, there is the hint inherent in his politician's name: on *Amos 'n' Andy*, the Kingfish's partner in crime is named Crawford. The way Crawford met his wife alludes to one particular historical fact, Long's meeting his own wife-to-be when she entered a bake-off staged to promote Cottolene. Upon her introduction, Sue Ann also wears a crown-shaped brooch, a resonant symbol replicated in the insignia of the crowned machine gun that tops chapter titles in the novel's first edition. Crawford's slogan may be "Every Man a Millionaire," but allusions to "Every Man a King" abound. Other such facts also refer to Long alone. In 1932, Crawford finds one of his most arduous challenges seating his delegation at the Democratic National Convention (*HL* 571–81); toward the end of the novel, an increasingly bodyguard-surrounded Crawford finds in a preacher-turned-radical one of his most staunch supporters (*HL* 699–700); and the event that most clearly signals his break with the federal administration is an infamous one-man filibuster (*HL* 811–12). What proves more significant, though, is Crawford's version of the Win or Lose Oil Corporation. As Dos Passos admitted, again—despite the fact that his subsequent disclaimer holds that his characters "are inventions through and through"—"The nearest I ever came to a character completely from life was Huey Long in 'Number One.'" The fact that he speaks of Long himself as a character, never so much as mentioning the name "Crawford," only makes the argument all the more unassailable. Dos Passos may not use this material to create quite as consistently close a copy of Long as Basso does in Harry Brand, but the relative obscurity of much of the historical material he incorporates proves him a more ambitious researcher than any other author examined here. Hamilton Basso may have been there, but Dos Passos seems to have read more about it.

Previous authors, as we have seen, translated similar material into fiction, yet Crawford is hardly the dictatorial tyrant of *It Can't Happen Here*, the redneck buffoon of *Cinnamon Seed*, or the rabid grotesque of *Sun in Capricorn*. Instead of a man merely power-mad, he is closer to what the real Huey Long seems to have been—a brilliantly gifted but increasingly wrongheaded politician who may have started out working for the people but ended up taking advantage of them. One of the most striking facts about *Number One* is the presence throughout of the judgment many during Long's life uttered about him: that he was unquestionably a masterful politician, but at the same time had in him a bit too much of the snake oil—or perhaps Wine of Cardui—salesman. Dos Passos allows Crawford only one speech to reveal his hidden potential, but it takes him no more than a few hundred words to prove that, even if not exactly erudite, he is far from the "small town salesman with a smatterin' of law" he makes sure his followers see on the stump. At the same time, the speech also proves just how much his public persona is a carefully crafted farce designed to get him cozy with the contingent he will soon betray. "[O]ne reason why reformers in politics lose out," he tells a small gathering of insiders, is that

> It's easy enough for 'em to tear things down; Henry George criticised the moneymad society of his day beautifully . . . Marx's strictures on the industrial system of England were profoundly just . . . Men with brains an' plenty of spare time kin always show us what's wrong with the system, but where they always fail is on the constructive side . . . I've laid awake nights thinkin' about this thing time an' again an' I've come to the conclusion that one reason they turn out such small potaters an' few in a hill is that they bend their erudite gaze on society from the outside . . . they are never on the inside where the plain or'nary run of the mill citizen is strugglin'

with the day to day business of livin', doin' his fall plowin' or sellin' some product from door to door, payin' his family's doctor's bill, gettin' his children schoolin' or maybe just scrapin' up a lil fatback an' hominy grits to keep his belly from hurtin' so bad . . . Well, by the time they've thought up all their high intellectual theories about society . . . society's a plant like a cornstalk or an oak tree. It grows an' bears fruit an' flower . . . it's changin' all the time . . . by the time they've got their theories ready out of a lot of fivedollar words all tacked together, the plant's grown into something quite different. Society's got to be reformed by practical politicians who keep track of it from day to day. If you want to raise a crop of corn you go out an' hire you a good tenant farmer, you don't engage a cryptogamic biologist. (197–98)

This is one of the few times Crawford speaks without being deceitful, slanderous, or self-serving, one of the few times he demonstrates any real thought for anything other than furthering his own interests. The venerable Senator Johns, who addresses the subject twice, perhaps best gauges Crawford's ultimate potential. On the first occasion, the old man argues that Crawford could have "one of the greatest careers this country ever offered a man of genius" if only he would "grow up and come out of the foothills." Instead of "trying to ram all this nonsense about Every Man a Millionaire down our throats," he asserts, "he ought to settle down to study and think" (202). In the end, it seems, both Long and Crawford were gifted with perhaps unprecedented potential that neither, sadly, realized in full. As Basso wrote in his 1935 *New Republic* essay "The Kingfish: In Memoriam," the "great tragedy" of Long's life "is that he could have been, as has already been said, the foremost American democrat. Much was lost when he chose to go in the opposite direction."[15]

Aside from what such parallels reveal of Dos Passos's judgment of Crawford—and, by association, Long himself—discrepancies between them are also illuminating. Most glaring is the fact that, though Crawford is far from the political or, much less, social threat Lewis and

15. Hamilton Basso, "The Kingfish: In Memoriam," *New Republic*, 18 December 1935, 177.

Basso make of Windrip, Brand, and Slade, he is also a politician with no political accomplishments whatsoever. He has none of Long's achievements to his credit. Even Buzz Windrip has a successful road construction program—not so Chuck Crawford. He paves no roads, constructs no new capitol, establishes no adult literacy programs. This is in keeping, of course, with the judgment Dos Passos pronounces upon Crawford: that, more than anything else, he is a confidence man of the worst kind, a shyster who sows promises only to reap votes, not actually to serve the people. Coupled with the fact that, of all the many politicians in Dos Passos's corpus, Crawford commits one of the most egregious betrayals of any single constituency, he becomes the one character most guilty of selling out the little man to maintain his status as a big man, of—as Dos Passos puts it in *Adventures of a Young Man,* again—making martyrs of the masses to ensure his own meal ticket. Yet the fact that *Number One* is the only such novel written after September 8, 1935, that does not include an assassination scene illustrates the most significant omission. Apparently Dos Passos wanted us to realize that threats such as those Crawford embodies in no way died with Long and that politicians, propagandists, and phrasemakers, if not kept in constant check, will continue to cloak their dissembling in the storied words of their more earnest predecessors. In that Dos Passos ends the novel proper with Tyler's agonized realization that "We can't sell out on the people" (297) and then concludes the final prose poem with the lines "*weak as the weakest, strong as the strongest, / the people are the republic, the people are you*" (304), he draws us into the novel beside his central character, warning us that we too—for we also are the people—might not realize Tyler's fate. To keep politicians like Crawford from "*sell[ing] out too much of the for the people and by the people part of the oldtime United States way*" (282), we all must begin—as Tyler finally realizes—with the acknowledgment that number one is not an elected official, not a "big wind" like Crawford (297), but the people themselves—or as Dos Passos implies in the novel's last line, the people *our*selves.

In the end, the Huey Long material in *Number One* may lack the power "Kingfish the First" might have had had it concluded *The Big Money,* as originally planned, but Dos Passos's message is much the same in both novels. His critique in *Number One* is not nearly as indignant as that to which he subjects politicians and propagandists in his previous works—Woodrow Wilson and other World War I–era leaders in particular—nor, of course, does he so boldly name names. As a result, we can see that his vehemence, the passion that had once ignited such scalding passages as those in Camera Eyes 49 and 50, had waned to a significant degree. *Number One*, it must be said, ultimately lacks the force, the outraged and righteous protest of *Three Soldiers, The 42nd Parallel, Nineteen Nineteen,* and *The Big Money,* yet just as the author calling for correctives is rarely as impassioned as one proposing outright revolt, neither is a series of oil transactions the potential betrayal of public trust that Dos Passos considered World War I. Dos Passos's purpose in addressing each in fiction, though, remains much the same. As Tyler's brother Glenn puts it, *"it's what you do that counts, not what you say"* (282)—and what Dos Passos tells the American electorate it must do, above all else, is prevent its leaders from *"sell[ing] out too much of the for the people and by the people part of the oldtime United States way."* Such had always been the case, as Dos Passos saw it, but the politician-constituent contract was far flimsier in the mid-twentieth century than it had been when Abraham Lincoln first uttered the storied phrase about "government of the people, by the people, for the people." The young rebel is almost always more romantic than the aging patriot, but Dos Passos issued the same challenge both early and late, consistently proclaiming perhaps the signal requirement of American constitutional democracy: that the people make sure they see their leaders' signifiers signified.

4 Neither Family Man nor Man of the People: Adria Locke Langley's Hank Martin

IN MID-1995, AS THE CRITICAL REPUTATIONS OF LEWIS, Basso, and Dos Passos continued the decline they had suffered for decades, an article in the June 26 *New Yorker* proved that of Adria Locke Langley as stable as it had been for the previous forty years. Lewis, with 1920s modernists continuing their depredations of what once might have been his readership, made fewer and shorter appearances in literary anthologies. Basso, just four decades after the estimable success of *The View from Pompey's Head,* was all but out of print. Dos Passos, even as *U.S.A.* held tight to its status as one of the landmark—though now increasingly unread—works of twentieth-century fiction, found himself relegated to progressively smaller niches in the canon. Adria Locke Langley, however, was still to most readers what she had been for decades: as most had never heard of her, they could hardly ignore her more. Indeed, only twelve years after her death, that 1995 *New Yorker* article, the first in years to so much as mention her name, could not do so without simultaneously implying her obscurity, could not refer to her as any more conspicuous a quantity than "someone named Adria Locke Langley." Today, even such quizzically oblique consideration would be a windfall for the Langley camp—if in fact one still exists. What remains in print of her now, even biographically speaking, is little more than the occasional, far-flung sketch:

> Born c. 1899 in Iowa; died August 14, 1983, in Los Angeles, Calif. Educator and author. Langley was best known as the author of the 1945 best-seller *A Lion Is in the Streets.* Based on the life of the flamboyant former governor of Louisiana Huey Long, the book was translated into fifteen languages and was adapted as a motion picture starring James Cagney. Langley, who also gained fame for

her support of the repeal of prohibition, helped found the Women's Organization for National Prohibition Reform. In [her later] years the author supported herself by teaching writing.[1]

Biographers and journalists add only so much to such sketches, sparse though their details may be. An earlier, only slightly more enlightening look at her life reveals that Langley's interest in American politics dates as far back as 1929, nearly two decades before she would publish *A Lion Is in the Streets*. A divorced traveling saleswoman with an infant daughter at her side, she spent what rare moments she could steal from her New York-to-Texas sales route at town meetings throughout the South. Later, more settled and already something of an anti-Prohibition agitator, she enlisted some 200,000 recruits for the Women's Organization for National Prohibition Reform, weathering an arrest and even dodging a bullet along the way. Next came fieldwork for a consortium of anti-Prohibition congressmen, a stint as publicity director for the New York State Democratic Committee, and a leading role in the 1934 battle New York dairymen waged to secure a minimum price for their products. So outraged was she over the state's offhand treatment of its farmers that, when the case went to trial, she testified, just days out of the hospital, from a wheelchair. The seasoned reformer then turned novice writer, publicizing the cause of impoverished urban New Yorkers in a series of articles for the *New York Post*. *A Lion Is in the Streets*—written over a period of years, mostly between midnight and 5 a.m., while Langley lived her days as everything from a psychology teacher to a wartime munitions riveter—followed shortly thereafter. It was an almost immediate best-seller—initially the most popular of all the Long novels, *All the King's Men* included—and the film rights alone netted her $250,000, a record sum for the time. Further sketches tell us that after this she taught writing in California, but they add little to what we know about her life thereafter. Profiles published at the height of the novel's popularity tell us that its author "is forceful and direct; she has a warm personality; and she usually gets what she

1. Anthony Lane, "Warring Fictions," *New Yorker*, 26 June 1995, 72; *Contemporary Authors*, vol. 110, s.v. "Langley, Adria (Locke)."

goes after,"[2] as one can perhaps glean from what biographical detail survives, but in the end, they tell us little more. In one of these articles, Langley comments that the two "great sores" afflicting 1930s and 1940s America were poverty and demagoguery,[3] and if her articles for the *New York Post* take up the poor more than the exploited, *A Lion Is in the Streets* more than makes up for her earlier focus on the former. Yet poverty and demagoguery are only two of the novel's concerns. Though primarily the story of a demagogue's rise to power on the backs of his poor constituents, in that its central character is not the demagogue himself but his wife, the novel cannot help but address her role (which is disappointingly more passive than Langley's, however) in the largely male world of 1940s politics. On the novel's dust jacket Langley comments, "I can never say enough for the fighting spirit of women. They will risk today's bread and a boycott if it will do anything for the next generation." Though speaking, it seems, of her colleagues at the Women's Organization for National Prohibition Reform, she may as well have been describing her own central character, known first as Verity Wade. The proverbial Yankee schoolmarm moved South to teach in a rural schoolhouse, Verity adopts a new surname within weeks of meeting a backwoods peddler named Hank Martin. Initially inspired by his devotion to friends and local customers, which, early on, manifests itself in a battle for fairer crop-weighing practices and a one-man campaign to bring electricity to the rural multitudes, she later grows disillusioned as her new husband increasingly casts aside his peddler's pack for the professional politician's bag of tricks. Hank's political success soon becomes perhaps the most accurate measure of his marital and familial failure. The closer he gets to the governor's mansion, the farther he strays from his wife and their daughter. More faithful in the end to her first name than her last, Verity soon condemns Hank as a man more politician

2. *Current Biography: Who's News and Why*, 1945 ed., s.v. "Langley, Adria Locke"; Louis D. Rubin, Jr., "All the King's Meanings," in *The Curious Death of the Novel: Essays in American Literature* (Baton Rouge: Louisiana State University Press, 1967), 225; Alice Payne Hackett, "New Novelists of 1945," *Saturday Review of Literature*, 16 February 1946, 8; Clip Boutell, "A Literary Lion Cleans Up," *New York Post Magazine*, 29 June 1945, 25.

3. *Current Biography: Who's News and Why*, 1945 ed., s.v. "Langley, Adria Locke."

than husband or father, more demagogue than authentic champion of the poor, and she ultimately even condones his assassination by affirming a witness's comment that the anonymous gunman had acted in the spirit of "all the men of the Boston Tea Party . . . the men at Valley Forge . . . all the liberty-loving men who live by Patrick Henry's words."[4] *Sic semper tyrannis,* she essentially affirms, even if the tyrant happens to be her own husband. True to her fiercely moralistic perspective, Verity risks more than just "today's bread and a boycott" to do something "for the next generation," going so far as sanctioning her husband's sacrifice to a certain belief in the abstract cause of justice. In *A Lion Is in the Streets,* the "fighting spirit of women" thus proves a weapon against more than just poverty and demagoguery.

As inspiring as this "fighting spirit" may be at times, whether embodied in the book or its author's life story, it is ultimately not enough, unfortunately, to redeem the novel itself. One reason Langley is not better known today is perhaps the fact that, as Louis D. Rubin has charged, *A Lion Is in the Streets*—her only novel and most conspicuous achievement—is simply a "badly written" book. It follows as if by explicit design the formula for historical romances once derisively outlined as follows: "Take one part of warm-blooded heroine and one part of devil-may-care hero, add a generous portion of violence and drop after drop of tantalizing sex, and you may concoct a synthetic marvel that will be distributed by the Literary Guild and immortalized in Technicolor Vistavision." Though originally applied to a different novel, the description fits on all counts. The heroine is Langley's heroine, the hero her hero, and *A Lion Is in the Streets* indeed became both a Literary Guild edition and a popular film. And to call its plot formulaic is still to say nothing of its florid prose, its hackneyed attempt at southern dialect, its lapses in accuracy about the southern landscape in general. One review, fittingly entitled "Whey Down South," describes the novel as such "a splash of drunken color" that, when one puts it down, "one marvels that his hands do not ooze gold and purple and crimson and jade." Few reviewers overlooked Langley's attempt at rendering regional dialect, the kindest referring to it as "flowery" and "ex-

4. Adria Locke Langley, *A Lion Is in the Streets* (New York: Whittlesey House, 1945), 479.

aggerated," Rubin writing that it "approaches the burlesque," Basso, characteristically direct, calling it simply "baffling." Nearly six decades later, the novel's dialogue would border on the riotous if not so degrading, particularly to its African American characters, those "minstrel cartoons" one reviewer found "vastly depressing." Roark Bradford, writing in the *New York Times Book Review* upon the novel's appearance, had still more to say on the subject. As a sort of addendum to his review, he detailed a number of "trivial slip-ups" Langley makes in trying to detail her southern setting:

> Among these little blunders which needlessly detract from one's interest in the story are: Snuff, as used in the South, does not make one sneeze. Pot-licker is not stewed, it is the liquid that gathers in the bottom of the pot when vegetables are stewed with side-meat.
>
> Also: In the sharecropper system, the seed for planting cotton is [usually] supplied by the landlord, and is one of the least expensive items encountered in making a crop; the "bucketful of seed" so generously given the Ribidoux family by her hero would hardly have been enough to plant a medium-sized victory garden. And the speech of illiterates in the South is something more than mere bad grammar, and all illiterates do not speak exactly alike. Unhampered by syntax, they frequently turn a phrase that is musical, poetic and at times more forceful than the same thought expressed in a formally correct manner.

Bradford concluded with a wish that Langley's otherwise "talented and industrious pen" would take leave of the South—through which she may have traveled, but not to much profit beyond sales, it would seem—to take up material a bit closer to home. Another reviewer, citing the novel's general effusiveness, advised her to put down that same pen and pick up a paintbrush.[5]

5. Rubin, 226; Nelson Manfred Blake, "How to Learn History from Sinclair Lewis and Other Uncommon Sources," in *American Character and Culture in a Changing World: Some Twentieth-Century Perspectives,* ed. John A. Hague, Contributions in American Studies, vol. 42 (Westport: Greenwood Press, 1979), 111; Hackett, 8; J. Saunders Redding, "Whey Down South," review of *A Lion Is in the Streets,* by Adria Locke Langley, *New Republic,* 18 June 1945, 852; review of *A Lion Is in the Streets,* by Adria Locke Langley, *Booklist,* 15 May 1945, 269; Hamilton Basso, "The Huey Long Legend," *Life,* 9 De-

Not all of the novel, though, conflicts so clearly with reality. Ironically, some of what Langley would most wish unfamiliar is what readers have found most familiar. As we saw earlier, she begins with a disclaimer: "This novel is fiction and intended as such. It does not refer to real characters or to actual events. Any likeness to characters either living or dead is purely coincidental." As is often the case in such works, however, many allegedly fictional elements bear likenesses beyond the coincidental to both real characters and actual events. Indeed, so many reviewers challenged Langley's assertion (Bradford, for instance, argued that she "unquestionably . . . employed as a springboard the more blatant and well-known episodes" from "the spectacular rise and fall of Huey P. Long") that, eventually forced to defend herself, Langley reiterated in an interview that *A Lion Is in the Streets* was not meant to be "a fictionalized account of the career of Long," nor was Hank Martin meant to represent anyone beyond "the universal demagogue." She had once dodged a bullet; now, it seems, she was trying to dodge a libel suit. Warner Brothers Studios had good reason to rewrite and delay for nearly a decade the film version of *A Lion Is in the Streets.* Though they bought the screen rights almost upon the novel's publication, threats that Long's survivors might sue—his son Russell, more than likely, leading the charge—kept the film unreleased until 1953. *A Lion Is in the Streets* may not be a strict *roman à clef,* as more than one critic has asserted, and Langley may have made what one critic calls "conspicuous departures from the actual Huey Long story" at several points during the novel, but Hank Martin's story is more than that of "the universal demagogue." Basso, one of the few to investigate the novel's integration of fact and fiction more fully, writes that *A Lion Is in the Streets* is not a work of invention so much as one of "transmutation." Langley's method, he finds, "while not altogether lacking in the imaginative process, consists of little more than sugarcoating the facts." She "begins with fact," he writes, but "ends with candy."[6] *A Lion Is in the Streets,* therefore, is not nearly as fictional as

cember 1946, 112; Lane, 72; Roark Bradford, "Life and Death of a Demagogue," review of *A Lion Is in the Streets,* by Adria Locke Langley, *New York Times Book Review,* 13 May 1945, 20.

6. Bradford, 3; *Current Biography: Who's News and Why,* 1945 ed., s.v. "Langley, Adria Locke"; Hackett, 8; "Prohibition Foe, Writer Adria Langley Dies at 84," *Los Angeles Times,* 17 August 1983, national edition; A. Fred Sochatoff, "Some Treatments of the

its author would have us believe. For while Langley may change names and disguise locales, may substitute metaphorical equals or rough parallels for major events, the fact remains that, although they sometimes end up saccharine-sweet, the actual events beneath the candy coating often bear unmistakable likenesses to those in the personal and professional life of one particular, rather than just the so-called universal, demagogue, Huey P. Long of Louisiana. Langley tells a tale told often, and, even if she does so from a feminine, if not broadly feminist, perspective—devoting as much attention to home as to statehouse—she makes few significant changes to the tale her more numerous male counterparts had told and would tell.

Some of the earliest candy she confects concerns her demagogue's upbringing. Born in the northern pine hills of what she calls the Magnolia State—which has far more in common with the Pelican State than with Mississippi—Hank was one of seven children fathered by a poor farmer upon a woman who often worked harder in the fields than her husband. Poverty and despair were what most characterized the Martin household. Hank recalls his mother often looking out their ramshackle front door and quoting her mother's favorite psalm, "How shall we sing the Lord's song in a strange land?" only to be echoed by her mother herself, who would join her to stare out over the barren fields and intone, "We want t' go back to Zion, Lord" (42). Hank blames most of their problems on his feckless father, a man who, when Hank was only twelve years old, bound him out to another local farmer for the sum of one dollar per month. He worked sunrise to sunset, day in and day out, and at night slept on a rough pallet in a bare outbuilding. When his father suddenly appeared to claim his son's wages some fourteen months later, Hank learned his first lesson in the employment of power. Strengthened by his time in the fields, he knocked the old man unconscious and reclaimed his fourteen dollars. He later recalls the moment clearly, for that was the one time, he says, when he saw his mother stand proudly. She told him to forget the family, to leave home and make something of himself, concluding, "I'm a-thinkin' I birthed one as c'n mebbe git back t' Zion" (47). Thus the fitness of

Huey Long Theme," in *All the King's Men: A Symposium* (Pittsburgh: Carnegie Institute of Technology, 1957), 6; Basso, "Legend," 110, 112.

Basso's comments on the novel, both its "baffling" dialect and its sugar-coated sentimentality. Since Long's upbringing did not require of him such outraged and righteous rebellion, Langley places Hank in circumstances Long would find alien, circumstances straitened just enough to inspire youthful heroism. Barely a teenager, Hank had won praise and recompense from his first exercise of power, inevitably casting himself in the role he would play until assassinated decades later: that of a newly empowered David against a formerly more powerful Goliath.

With fourteen dollars in his pocket and his mother's exhortation in his ears, Hank left the farm for a career in traveling sales. Like Long, Brand, and Crawford before him, he finds himself better fit for peddling than for farming. For the next several years, he treks from northern pine hill to southern bayou selling general merchandise including Sizzle, the fictional twin of Long's Cottolene. Yet peddling was not only the way he earned his daily bread: for as Martin, just as Crawford, Brand, and Long himself well knew, it was also a way to befriend the local poor and broaden what would one day be his constituency. "I'm their friend," he tells Verity at one point; "Hell, I'm a event in their lives" (19). We see that he speaks the truth when he rides into apparently uninhabited country one day, blows on a tin whistle, and waits. A woman and her eight children—all of whose names and ages Hank readily recalls, for he also has Long's fabled memory—soon surround Hank and Verity and excitedly see them back to the sharecropper's shack they call home. The next morning, when the man of the house tells Hank he has no seed to plant his crop, Hank supplies it, free of charge. For reasons like this, "[m]en greeted him with love as a kinsman who always brought laughter and pleasure," and "women greeted him with a love sweetened with an anxious yearning to serve him" (95–96). We soon realize, though, that Hank's motives are not entirely altruistic, that he is not nearly the man of the people he may seem. As he explains to Verity, "[I]t's gonna mean everythin' t' me, this here peddlin'. I know near 'bout every damn swamp angel in this here state. 'N someday . . . I'll run this state! 'N d'you know why? 'Cause I'll know what folks think. I'll know what they feel. I'll know what they want." Williams would write much the same of Long's approach to his own years on the road, as would Basso of Brand's, Dos Passos of Crawford's. Martin's final comment is still more revealing: "[W]hat's more," he concludes, "I'll be a-knowin' just how much they gotta have give to 'em afore they'll be a-givin' their vote t' me" (7). Martin, therefore, is already the cynical pragmatist that Long seems to have become only gradually.

What his constituents "gotta have give to 'em" is a long, complicated list of items, for Martin's Magnolia State looks much like Long's Louisiana. Though Langley refuses to refer to it as anything else, Hank's Magnolia State is clearly Huey's Pelican State. Divided into parishes instead of counties, it is home to northern farms that give way to southern swampland, and its cultural center, a vibrant mix of French, Spanish, African, and American influences, is named Crescent City. And conditions in the Magnolia State are as deplorable as they also were in Louisiana at the time. The poverty of the people seems "like a fever" (97) to Verity, and Saber Milady, a northerner imported to serve as Hank's press agent—and whose name seems a play on that of Long supporter Swords Lee—finds his first visit to the backcountry nothing less than bewildering. Verity's school houses no textbooks; local children are no more literate than their parents; roads are unpaved and vary from "six inches a' dust" to "twelve a' mud" (94). Yet there is but one central reason for the people's copious needs: the aristocracy's control of state and local legislation. The upper classes suppress the lower by refusing support to state schools—which keeps the local populace, one generation after the next, both illiterate and tied to their lives as sharecroppers—then by defeating all attempts to improve state roads—which keeps them dependent on only the closest cotton gins, the property, of course, of the local aristocracy. In the absence of a state bureau of weights and measures, moreover, these gins favor the upper-class buyer more than the lower-class seller. What his constituents need, in short, is a complete overhaul of a long-standing social structure much like that Long himself fought to dismantle. The time was right, then, for Martin to engage Goliaths far greater than just his father.

As he begins this fight, Martin both looks and dresses like Huey Long. Langley spends less time describing the man than his clothes, but both are evocative of our one particular, now-familiar demagogue. Early on we are told that Martin is a "dark bulky" man with "thick, dark, wavy" hair, a "ruddy outdoor" face, and "beaming" eyes (6). Soon thereafter, we find him in an ill-fitting suit with a tacky purple stripe, a loud purple tie, and still louder yellow shoes. Upon his first trip to a local estate, Hank wears a similar outfit, a striped purple suit and a pink shirt that are a "rude insult" to the stateliness around him (50). One guest looks at him—as Mrs. Roosevelt looked upon Long—"as he might look at a freak" (59). Much later, we find him in a bright blue suit, a lavender shirt, a tie of assorted purples, blues, and yellows, and later still we find him wearing a green-striped gray suit with a shirt "of too bright a blue for good taste in men's wear" (411). Langley, unlike her fellow novelists, at least attempts to justify this wardrobe: "Hank had an eye for color," Verity rationalizes. He has "remarkably good taste in everything except his own clothes," she thinks, but then realizes that men's clothes were "awfully patterned," and that "Hank's love of color couldn't be satisfied within the boundaries set for gentlemen" (106). This attempt at understanding, though, is almost all of what differentiates these descriptions from those in *Sun in Capricorn, Number One,* and any number of Long biographies. Physically speaking, Hank Martin is as much Chuck Crawford, Harry Brand, and Huey Long as any one of the four is any other.

After long hours contemplating his state's socioeconomic disparities, Hank declares one evening that, though he may not run for office for several years, he will start campaigning the following day. As usual, he does what he says. The next morning, in the blacksmith's shop at the village crossroads—Longfellow's idyllic "The Village Blacksmith" seems to have made a strong impression on Langley—he makes his first speech. Already renowned as "the most describin' talker in the state" (33), he does not disappoint. He tells the hopeful locals that his aim is to be their governor. "I wanta see folks like to you 'n me get a chancet in this world!" he tells them. "I wanta see the young'uns get free schoolbooks. I wanta see folks able t' read so's they can understand good enough t' fight for what they should oughta have!" (79). Several similar assertions later, he promises to "take on m'self the burden a' freein' the likes a' you! . . . the burden a' seein' yore young-'uns gets a chancet at some a' the good things a' this here world," and closes with a question: "Now, friends, I'm a-askin' you, straight 'n simple—you for me or agin me?" (80). Their answer, of course, is that they are for him—for as one follower puts it, "He c'n kindle a dream in men, he can" (114). Enthusiasm of the sort soon inspires him to found the Hank Martin Organization, an almost identical twin to Long's Share Our Wealth Society. Its dues a scant dollar per year, its membership within a quick year is nearly 4,000. As one member offers, "A mite a' hope's plumb worth a dollar a year" (84). The Great Emancipator of the Magnolia State's poor whites—Martin too is fond of alluding to Lincoln—thus corrals his followers and, as Crawford would have put it, saddles up and gets ready to ride them into office.

Martin then hoodwinks them with a wealth redistribution scheme almost identical to Long's. Not content to demonize the aristocracy for their control of the legislature alone, he soon begins attacking them for the size of their wallets as well. The idea comes to him at a local plantation, Cypress Bend. Led into the library, Hank sees the thousands of books housed there as wall after wall of shelved insult. "God'l-mighty," he erupts, "what the hell right you got to all these here books whilst kids can't get ary one to git a edgucation. No money in this state for books!" he rages—and, of course, much to Verity's embarrassment—"Roarin' thunderbolts! Why the hell didn't they take some a' these!" (51). The outburst leads his more refined host, Jules Bolduc, to tell him of Claude Henri de Rouvroy, Comte de Saint-Simon, the eighteenth-century Frenchman who, as Bolduc explains, proposed that "riches should be better divided through the reorganization of society, taking labor for the basis of the new hierarchy" (57). As it coddles the lower classes while spurning the upper, the idea inspires Hank to read an essay Jules had written on the subject. More satire than apology—the aristocratic Bolduc accuses Saint-Simonians of nothing more noble than covetousness—the piece so angers Hank that, kicking the kitchen table hard enough to awaken his sleeping wife, he calls Jules a "sneerin' sonuvabitch" (67). Upon further reflection, though, he realizes that the same material, stated somewhat differently, just might serve his larger purposes. The next morning, back at the crossroads blacksmith's, he therefore announces his Divide the Earth's Riches plan. "I'm gonna take on m'self the burden a' findin' a way t' divide the riches a' this earth" (80), he crows. "Why, I betcha iffen the rich a' this here state hadda spew into one pot all the money they got, 'n it was divided even 'mongst everybody, you folks'd get enough t' be a-ownin' yore own land." When one listener exclaims, "Wouldn't that be a wonderful thing!" (82–83), we are perhaps reminded that in 1934 and 1935 almost eight million Americans reacted the same way to Long's propositions—and perhaps foresee that, just as Share Our Wealth did little for them but incite false hope, Divide the Earth's Riches will probably do little more for their fictional counterparts.

The character who initially plays villain to Martin's hero is Robert J. Castleberry IV. An embodiment of 1920s and 1930s Louisiana aristocrats, Castleberry owns everything from cotton gins to banks and indirectly controls much state and local legislation. To Hank, Castleberry and his cronies are human incarnations of the black skimmer, an indigenous bird that flies so fast that, even upon dipping its beak into the water below to scoop up smaller, slower creatures on the surface, it hardly slows its pace. All within earshot affirm the fitness of the metaphor and respond to it precisely as one would expect. "You know, don'cha, that year by year the Black Skimmer is a-forcin' you down his gullet for to feed and fatten hisself on?" Martin asks them. "You know, don'cha, that he's a-doin' it withouten never havin' t' slack his speed? . . . Well, I say birds like to him should oughta be squeezed till he spews back some a' his takin's" (78). Hank's specific charge is that Castleberry and the other Black Skimmers are "short-weightin'" (129)—that they have rigged their scales to weigh light so they have to pay less per actual pound of cotton. He soon learns that five years earlier, when the governor had tried to create a bureau of weights and measures, the Black Skimmers had been the lobby that had prevented him. As the Hank Martin Organization's "first step t'ward gettin' the little fellers their rightful share—t'ward keepin' the little fellers outen [the Black Skimmers'] gullets a piece longer" (133), Hank organizes followers in five parishes to forge their own weights, pre-weigh their cotton, and, with rifles at the ready, watch closely as the Black Skimmers weigh it. The result is exactly what Hank had predicted: the big man had indeed been cheating the little, and for years, if not decades. Though the conflict concerns cotton rather than oil, Martin's championship of the little man because of it closely parallels Long's crusade against interests like Standard and other large conglomerates. The names may differ, but the players are almost identical.

Just as Long engaged early opponents across courtrooms instead of cotton gins, Martin soon does the same. Before Martin can prove his charges, Castleberry attempts to silence him by trying to have him arrested. In the ensuing skirmish, one of Hank's men, Harry Disbro, shoots one of the deputies Castleberry had recruited for protection while he delivered the arrest warrant. Hank now has reason to force Bolduc to make good on his promise to tutor him in law. What follows is Langley's version of Long's legendary run at the Louisiana bar, as well as a candy-coated profusion of scenes featuring the burgeoning rustic scholar at the books. To Verity's question, "Doesn't it take four years to become a lawyer?" Hank scoffs, "I aim t' cut that in half" (161). To do so, he not only studies while driving his sales route but, back at home, clears a space in his barn and, for months on end, reads, recites, and often addresses invisible juries there. Two years later, he passes the bar exam with the highest score recorded in years. When the time comes to apply his new expertise during Disbro's trial, though, he tricks Bolduc into taking the case himself. Hank may have needed help with his studies, but he needs none with public relations. He realizes that, since his constituency is limited to the lower classes, he needs influence among the middle and upper if he is to ever run for state office. Bolduc and Martin—their names now linked in the minds of voters, no matter their socioeconomic standing—soon win the case, both exposing the Black Skimmers and the short-weighing scandal and generating statewide publicity for the Hank Martin Organization. Though once a politician who at least seemed to fight for the little man, Hank quickly comes to see the little man's misfortune as an opportunity to profit far more than assist. Chuck Crawford, in other words, has little to nothing on him.

Years earlier, just after the Martins had moved into their first home, Hank had offered to his new bride a glimpse of this same side of himself, which would remain hidden from all others until the Disbro trial. That day, while the newlyweds had watched their new neighbors paint their house—Hank had offered them a cast-off carpet if they would paint the decrepit building and clean up the yard—Hank had asked Verity to take note of what was happening. "Lookit them a-hustlin' here all in a herd," he had said. "Ain't airy a one got the gumption of nutted cockerel, but in herds they fancy theirselves t' be gamecocks. . . . I see plain ain't a one a' 'em worth a dang. Not a dang.

But in herds they got a use to a man like me. I been a-thinkin' on it for years. . . . [A]in't a one worth a dang, still 'n all, I'm right partial to the dumb sonsabitches. B'God, sometimes I think I'm full 'n runnin' over withen love for 'em" (31–32). In private, the ostensible champion of the poor has never been anything but his own champion—and, years later, after Harry Disbro's trial, he proves it to more than just Verity. Earlier, while he had been reading law, Hank had also been studying utilities regulations. Poring over the franchise records of the local electricity provider, he had uncovered a forgotten clause that promised service to any community producing a petition signed by 10 percent of its residents. As soon as the trial ended, he took to the road once more, this time traveling the countryside in search of signatures. Several months, six parishes, and one lawsuit later, however, he returns to reveal that, after meeting with executives from Southern Light and Power, he had dropped the lawsuit and accepted a $50,000 contribution to the Hank Martin Organization. He had had them where he had at least said he wanted them, where, clearly, the people themselves truly did want them, but he accepts what amounts to a bribe. All answers to Verity's questions ("Had he really been bought? Had he really roused his people to love and dreams only to use them? To sell them out when it met his needs? When it profited him?" [257]) undoubtedly in the affirmative, Hank implicitly reveals how, "in herds," as he had put it earlier, the "dumb sonsabitches" can be useful to him. He had stopped, the day of the painting party, before explaining why he sometimes feels "full 'n runnin' over withen love for 'em," but we quickly realize that it is not because of what he can accomplish for them but because of what he can attain by them.

In the aftermath of the Disbro trial, Martin's name becomes known statewide and soon appears on election ballots after he begins campaigning for an office like Long's first. On any number of stumps, in any number of rural parishes, his promises are what they had been at the crossroads blacksmith's and are framed in the same language—Long's promises, framed in Langley's attempt at Long's language:

> I'm aimin' to run for Commissioner of Public Works 'n Highways. Every one a' you has got to go t' the nearest pollin' place 'n help me with yore vote. 'Cause in me is yore salvation. In me is

yore young'uns' salvation. 'Cause as God is a-listenin', I'll get yore children the schools they should oughta have. 'N they'll have every schoolbook free—free! No longer will a young'un not be able to go to school 'cause you can't buy his books. That buyin' a' schoolbooks is a disgrace as will be a thing a' the past when Hank Martin is runnin' this here state.

I'm a-promisin' you roads. Thousands a' miles a' fine, reliable roads. Roads, b' God'lmighty, that'll make it possible for you to laugh at rain 'n blackjack mud! Roads that'll let you take yore cotton 'n cane 'n beans 'n strawberries out to the best market when they should be took. Roads that'll free you from the likes a' men liken to Robert Castleberry, him I call a Black Skimmer, him as was a-thievin' you outen life 'n bread for yoreselves 'n yore young'uns.

'N that ain't all I'm a-promisin'. Lissen close, my friends, for I'm a-tellin' you 'bout a gift I'm gonna make to every man as can acquire a home he holds title to. Are y' liss'nin'? Well, I'm gonna pass a law someday that'll make them big bastards as own the corporations pay the taxes in this here state 'n every man jack a' you shall have his own home tax free!—'N that's a promise from Hank Martin to you. 'N I don't never make a promise I don't keep. Now you make me a promise—will you promise to vote for me so's I can do all this for you? Will you? Will you? (284–85)

In the country, because of steps he takes to circumvent state voting regulations, Hank counts on as positive a response at the polls as to these questions. For if he does not actually teach his followers how to read—votes come much cheaper than that, he soon discovers—he does teach them how to recognize his name on a ballot. As identifying the letters H-A-N-K M-A-R-T-I-N does not exactly constitute literacy, though, Hank, unlike Long, proves himself no more a friend of the rural illiterate than do the state's aristocrats, who, even if they try to disguise their underhandedness, at least make no secret of their unconcern. His worries about voters in the city, however, remain as persistent as ever. Complicating the fact that he had never appealed as much to urban as to rural folk is the fact that the mayor of Crescent City, hardly a Martin partisan, completely controls the urban vote. Thus Hank's deal with Guy Polli, a Crescent City bootlegger: in exchange

for a significant percentage of city votes statewide, Hank promises
Polli a portion of the proceeds from his sale of oyster shells (acquired
the same way Long and Crawford acquired oil leases) to a pending
coastline reclamation project. On election day, both the country and
the city vote come in, shocking even the most knowledgeable observers, and Hank Martin, much as had Huey Long before him, proceeds
to a post on the Public Works and Highways Commission.

Compared to the scenes in which Martin campaigns for this position, the scenes in which Langley shows him acting in it are relatively
few. The state functionary, obviously, is not as romantic—or, to paraphrase Basso, as candy-coatable—as the country stumper. All scenes
of the sort, though, show an official who, like Long during his second
term as public service commissioner, spends less time fulfilling campaign promises than working to amass personal power. As offhandedly
as Langley dispenses with Long's popular and productive first term,
Hank dispenses with his inner circle of neighborhood friends and
would-be advisors, replacing them with career politicians who teach
him how to maximize power and profit, even if at the people's expense.
Just as Governor Long required state employees to "contribute" part of
each paycheck to what he called the "de-duct box" (*HL* 821–22), Commissioner Martin begins speaking of kickbacks—"I can allus force the
feller as owes his state job t' me t' pay into a sorta welfare vacation
fund" (391)—and devoting more energy to divvying up patronage than
actually improving the state. The most likely candidates for government projects, he stipulates, will be those who most influence the vote.
"There was nothing like putting people on the pay roll . . . to make
them and all onlookers jump on the band wagon and vote right from
then on" (390), Langley explains. Even the one official act we see
Commissioner Martin carry out amounts to little more than a power-
grab. While campaigning for the position, he had uncovered a long-
overlooked ordinance that, in defining as highways all inland waterways and the first fifteen miles of gulf, subjected them to the regulation
of his Public Works and Highways Commission. Once in office, he
fights first to reclaim this lost control, then to extend the commission's
reach still farther, declaring that, since waterways are once again highways, and since highways are state property, all seafood harvested

within fifteen miles of shore is state property and therefore taxable as such. Instead of working, as he claimed—and as first-term Commissioner Long actually did work—for the poor and the powerless, Commissioner Martin—as did second-term Commissioner Long—works mainly to strengthen his political machine. His cry on election day thus proves true for several months thereafter: "The big lion—that's me, 'cause I'm sure as hell king a' this jungle! . . . 'N, by God'lmighty, this here whole state'll know it come nightfall. Hank Martin, the Big Lion, starts ruling this here jungle right now!" (370–71).

If the comment sounds like the one Basso heard on a similar night in Long's life, the rest of *A Lion Is in the Streets* reads much like what Basso and the rest of the world witnessed from that point on. After two years as commissioner, Martin begins his long-promised campaign for governor, much of which he conducts via radio. Langley's disclaimers to the contrary, the one speech she quotes from this campaign follows the same outline as Long's basic script. After introducing himself as the commissioner of Public Works and Highways and a candidate for the office of governor, Martin, as did Long (*HL* 629), asks listeners to tell their friends and neighbors to tune in, then pauses to wait for them to do so. After a few minutes pass, he launches an appeal and an argument that also might as well be Long's:

> [M]ebbe you, like me, didn't have enough t' eat when you was a young'un. Mebbe you, like me, look around y', 'n are a-seein' of great riches. 'N mebbe you, like me, are a-thinkin' them riches should oughta be divided so yore young'uns'll have the chancet you didn't never have—well, I'm yore friend! I'm the feller as comes a' the plain people. I can see that not merely has the pore a' the hills 'n the swamps never had the right chancet—but you fellers in the towns 'n the cities ain't had it neither! Should you oughta be workin' for some rich 'n mighty feller a-lettin' him take a profit off a' the salt a' yore tears! (401)

Soon after this speech, Hank wins the governorship much as Long did—with some of the urban vote and most of the rural vote—and on the day of his inauguration inspires a scene reminiscent of Long's. As Langley describes it, it looks like the one Forrest Davis witnessed, with legions of followers arriving by wagon, mule cart, even pirogue. Basso's claim that in *A Lion Is in the Streets,* the reader "runs into incidents based upon Long's life on almost every page"[7] is only a slight exaggeration. When the commissioner of Public Works and Highways begins running for governor, much of what follows can hardly be called fiction.

Martin's postinaugural record looks even less like work of the imagination. Hank might spend six instead of four years in the governor's mansion, might even win election to a second term, but virtually all other details are mere transcriptions of Long's own record. Martin's primary accomplishments are the least fictional of all. As a new capitol building climbs to its full height, new roads stretch out across the previously unpaved state. Since Langley's focus, however, is not Hank's accomplishments as much as his increasingly heavy-handed use of power, we learn more about how the Big Lion rules this jungle than what he accomplishes for it. Like Long, he fills his state legislature with bought sycophants and spends more time eliminating than trying to cooperate with his adversaries. "I don't aim t' give the opposition time t' grow nobody of a size t' even compete with Hank Martin" (427), he says. When he encounters an opponent of almost any size, he invites him to the capitol, installs him on a committee, and then, by placing a pro-Martin man on either side of him, effectively silences both his voice and his vote. Within a term or two, he reasons, whatever opposition remains will have no one to run against him. But these tactics ultimately backfire, as they lead to the desertion of Hank's earliest supporters. Charging that his economic policies are bankrupting the commonwealth, Bolduc is the first to break. After Martin threatens to run Saber Milady out of the state if he publishes Bolduc's charges, Saber also departs the Martin camp. Lieutenant Governor Varick Kirkendall attempts to resign, but when Hank threatens to expose evidence that will send his son to prison if he does not help him win reelection, Kirkendall changes his mind. Hank amasses unprecedented power and wins a second term as governor, but whereas Chuck Crawford actively abandons his earliest supporters, willfully leaving them behind, Martin inadvertently drives his away by offending their sense of justice to such a degree that they all but flee his corrosive presence.

7. Basso, "Legend," 116.

In response to Hank's assertion that he had "plumb carried the people a' this state on my back from the backwoods t' modern glories," Bolduc had once added, "and 'they who ride lions can never dismount'" (436). The proverb becomes the slogan of Hank's remaining opposition, who soon see it proven false. The day after his reelection, as he begins dreaming of leaving the Magnolia State for Capitol Hill, Hank is assassinated. The details, again—though Langley, of course, would deny it—are much like those of Long's assassination. Her *Los Angeles Times* obituary even claims that she wrote the scene in 1933, supposedly predicting Carl Austin Weiss's gunshot some two years before he fired it.[8] As Hank gets out of his car and begins making his way toward the capitol, an unknown assailant fires one shot and disappears inside, dodging bullets with every step. The fatal bullet strikes the same spot as Weiss's and, as did Weiss's, fails to immediately dispatch its victim. In his last moments, Hank is concerned more for his machine than his family or constituents: just as Long on his deathbed worried about the whereabouts of the de-duct box (*HL* 876), Martin worries about the disposition of various secret documents. Two days later, with his body lying in state in the rotunda of the new capitol, a five-hour-long line of "hillbillies" and "swamplanders" files by to lay on his casket a virtual garden of cheap but dearly bought flowers (2). Off to one side, Saber Milady broadcasts to a national audience his version of the life of the late governor, the most important words of which come upon the discovery of Hank's assassin. Just as Weiss was rumored early on to have drawn a short straw (*HL* 872), the nameless assailant, Saber discovers, had drawn a slip of paper marked with a crude drawing of stick figures climbing off the back of a dead lion. To a small assemblage of friends, Saber remarks of the assassin, "There are thousands and thousands like him—men who do not hold with killing. But when a ruler . . . has spread an organization like a choking octopus—when the courts are corrupted and there is no justice, when he has blackmailed and bribed the judges—when his organization is so great and corrupt that a people cannot get rid of him at the polls—how else do a people dismount such a lion?" (479–80). Even in the opinion of those initially his closest and most loyal friends, in the case of a

8. "Prohibition Foe, Writer Adria Langley Dies."

tyrant like Hank Martin, assassination is not only acceptable but imperative.

His creator's comments to the contrary, Hank Martin is but an initially romanticized, increasingly realistic incarnation of Huey Long. Both begin life on the farm, and both leave it early on to earn a living on the road. As traveling salesmen, both befriend the poor, who later become their primary constituents, in the process familiarizing themselves with the concerns that later constitute their political platforms—free schoolbooks, better roads, and greater equity for the poor chief among them. Both take unconventional paths to the state bar, inspire a mostly lower-class following by waging war against the aristocracy and corporate interests, and expand their constituent base with a scheme calling for a more equitable distribution of wealth. Both begin their political careers on a public services commission and then proceed to the governorship, from which—though they do bring the populace certain benefits—they spend most of their time building the most firmly entrenched political machine they can manage. And though Martin wins reelection while Long won the U.S. Senate seat to which Martin only aspires, the capitol buildings whose construction they had supervised, soon thereafter the destination of hordes of the rural poor paying tribute to their fallen leaders, is later the scene of their assassinations. Perhaps the best that can be said of either is that he had an almost unprecedented potential for leadership—but that, in each case, an increasingly perverted lust for power spoiled it. In *A Lion Is in the Streets*, some of the final words on Martin the politician are left to Jules Bolduc. Early in Martin's career he had told him that, "truly, I have never met any man with a larger degree of potentiality for greatness. You can be a great man. A great leader, Hank" (225). In the end, Bolduc ignores that forfeited future to focus on the past: addressing a politician who, he asserts, has "grow[n] drunk on power," he laments, "You had the gift, Hank. . . . this is the generation in which much could have been done" (439). So Basso said of Long, so Senator Johns said of Crawford, so Burden would soon say of Stark.

More than just the story of Hank Martin the traveling salesman, public works commissioner, and two-term governor, *A Lion Is in the Streets* is the story of Hank Martin the suitor, husband, and father. Initially, he excels in private life as easily as he does in public life. He may begin as a poor, ill-clad traveling salesman, but Verity sees him as "a magnet with a warm radiance," nothing less than a "glowing god" (6). A resident of the South for but two months, she had found little to her liking before Hank's appearance. Three weeks later, with Hank "the very sun of her world," she feels a "pulsing excitement" she previously thought beyond her experience (9). In the early sections of the novel, following the formula of the pulp romance, Langley devotes a great deal of space to this "excitement." As the newlywed Mrs. Martin first approaches Cypress Bend, just looking into her husband's eyes is enough to start a "fever . . . burn[ing] in her middle, shooting a paralyzing weakness down her legs and a delirium of desire up to her brain," a fever that "should not be in a body . . . clothed in chaste white" (17). Martin similarly brings new life to their first home. His methods in organizing the painting party that revitalizes it, though, cause Verity, still very much against her will, to entertain her first doubts about him. She knows she should, but she does not yet object to his treatment of the people he refers to as "dumb" but "use[ful]" "sonsabitches." In retrospect, this is one of the few times Verity will silence herself on the subject; when Hank leaves Cypress Bend in his attempt to transform not just a house but a statehouse, she increasingly disagrees with the husband who will soon be governor.

Many of her early complaints against Hank the family man come during his last years as a traveling salesman, his first as a state politician. Excited though she may be to move into a new home, she quickly becomes lonely after Hank begins leaving her there during his frequent and increasingly extended travels. Before one trip she even begs, "[P]lease take me with you. My life has been very lonely. Lonely and empty. Only living when you are home. Living a few days and just waiting emptily months and months on end" (287). Her loneliness only grows greater when Hank's responsibilities at home expand alongside his responsibilities in the state. When Verity discovers she is pregnant with their first child, she does not even tell Hank, for she knows his every thought is trained on the short-weighing scandal. When their daughter is born, he is not at his wife's side but away supervising the Hank Martin Organization. "Womans bust derese'ves birthin' babies," their maid Selah complains, "an de mens . . . runs away ter mak deres-

e'ves full uv big impo'tance. . . . Ain' no man good 'nuf fo' no woman"
(192). And Hank's responsibilities as a political leader only pull him
farther away from his family, no matter how large it threatens to grow.
Two years later, when Verity nearly dies during the stillbirth of a second child, Hank is absent yet again, this time engineering the Southern Light and Power sellout, thus simultaneously proving himself a
traitor to both party and family. (Dante, therefore, would have been
doubly justified in sentencing him to the ninth circle of Hell.) A few
days later, while Verity struggles to accept her baby's death, Hank's
defense of his actions does little to pacify her growing disillusionment:
"I had a thing t' do," he explains. "I just couldn't deefen myself to the
callin' 'n the drivin' inside a' me" (254). Though that "drivin'" may be,
early on, one of the characteristics that most attracts Verity to Hank,
as his political career increasingly monopolizes his time—time that
could have been their time together—it becomes one of the characteristics that most drives her from him.

A weakness for other women is another shortcoming for which
Verity condemns Hank. Wary from the day of the painting party, when
she notices how neighborhood women color upon Hank's approach,
she grows increasingly jealous as Hank's political career puts him in
more frequent contact with his constituents, roughly half of whom are
female. As Selah puts it, when Hank appears, "womens jes' plumb git
dat lolly-gag look" (123). Verity begins to see her worst suspicions realized when, a few years later, she arrives unannounced at a Martin campaign stop and hears of Hank in the company of Sylvia Hylen, the
stylish kinswoman of one of the Black Skimmers. Verity later hears her
claim that Hank had dismissed her, but a scene she soon interrupts
implies much the opposite. Spying on Hank at another stop farther
down the road, she is shocked to find him in the company of Sunny
Lou McMenimee, a startlingly beautiful young woman who has never
recovered from her childhood infatuation with the traveling salesman
who did business with her father. Upon seeing her, Hank forgets his
work and, poring over every inch of her, begins quoting verses from
the Song of Solomon—which Sylvia Hylen, also hidden, angrily takes
up before stomping out. Verity thus realizes what she had long suspected, that she is hardly the only woman to hear Hank speak those
words. Much later, she detects between Hank and Sunny Lou "the

mystic looks which pass only between a mated man and woman, a sort of communion of possessiveness, when in spite of all other urgencies they hunger each for the other"—and "envy came desolately in Verity's breast" (422). Their affair eventually even takes on a quasi-official nature: just as Long named Alice Lee Grosjean his secretary of state, Hank names Sunny Lou his commissioner of the Department of Cosmetic Sanitation, a post he creates especially for her. But Hank has not yet pushed Verity to her limit. For to Verity, as we shall see, there are far worse crimes than abandonment and adultery.

Chief among those crimes is dishonesty, an offense than encompasses Hank's shortcomings in both personal and professional arenas. As Verity at one point explains to him, her primary desire is that he be "the finest, most honest man in the world" (216), for "[l]earning that one's husband is dishonest" is "a blow no woman should have to sustain" (225). Even before Hank begins his first campaign, though, Verity begins bracing for that very blow. When their new neighbors begin to contribute their scarce dollar bills to the Hank Martin Organization, Verity cries out, "[T]his is homage. . . . This is homage!" (84). Later, she even wonders if Divide the Earth's Riches, the most trod-upon plank in Hank's platform, is anything more than an empty attention-getter, anything more than the very "bullshit" a Long insider pronounced Share Our Wealth. Their first significant disagreement over these matters comes after the Southern Light and Power sellout. What most upsets her is the shameless delight Hank takes in his dishonesty. He sees himself as a champion of the people, she as an abject fraud. When he argues that, because she is his wife, she should never express opinions of the sort, Verity firmly, quietly responds, illustrating again the "fighting spirit of women":

> "Yes, I am your wife. And I love you more than anything else in all this world. I—I love you too much, I sometimes think." She hesitated, then went on, flailing herself to make the words come. "But you just remember this—I will say to you whatever I think I must say. And I say you sold out your people because the fifty thousand was a quicker start. Because it felt good in your own pocket. Oh, Hank, please don't be mad at me. . . . Hank, Hank, darling!" she pleaded desperately, "I couldn't stand it if this is the straw that shows which way the wind is blowing." (271–72)

Though the Southern Light and Power sellout is precisely that, Verity manages to maintain the status quo a little longer. She tells herself that, if she cannot either change Hank or abandon him altogether, she must learn to accept him. This line of thinking, however, will last her no more than a few days.

Verity soon reaches a crossroads at which she can no longer accept Hank's politics, and after trying but failing to change them, she decides to leave him. She is appalled at his machinations in buying the commissionership from Polli—"Great God!" she exclaims, "so this is how it is done!" (305)—and soon thereafter his every act begins to "threaten . . . her very soul's fiber" (312), so much so that she begins to question exactly how much she supports him. She still shares his ostensible beliefs, still naïvely supports his campaign for the poor, but she begins wondering if Hank's ends justify his means. Soon she decides they do not. Hank pushes her too far when he tries to force her to accept what he calls nictitating—in his words, the act by which certain high-flying birds draw a "kinda third eyelid" across their eyes "[s]o's they can rest them sharp eyes whilst still a-goin'—so's they can shut out what ain't worth the seein'" (320). In practice, nictitating lets Hank focus only on ends, even when the means include murder. Verity's discovery of Hank's involvement in a double homicide devastates her, and his attempt at justification does little to pacify her horror. "I want lotsa things," he explains to her. "I aim to fly high. 'N iffen a couple off-color gents is killt in the process. . . . Then I'm nictitatin'. 'N that's how it's gotta be, Verity" (321). This argument soon leads to an inner battle between Verity's allegiance to Hank and her allegiance to her own integrity, a war punctuated by frequent disagreements, occasional abandonments, and, upon yet another threat of bloodshed, her anguished realization that she would "rather see him killed than killing" (361). At the end of the novel, as she tearlessly takes her last look at his coffin, she hesitates only a second. "She loved him," Langley writes, "she loved him; but justice was justice. She breathed deep and walked on" (481).

Much more than Windrip, Brand, Slade, and Crawford, Martin finds himself wholeheartedly condemned for both personal and professional failings. Langley thus makes use of material her fellow Long novelists mostly leave fallow, material that dramatizes in a different, more intimate arena betrayals that metaphorically represent the more frequently dramatized breaches of faith their politicians' constituents so often suffer. In the end, though, it is difficult to determine which side of Hank's character Langley treats most critically, whether she considers his crimes against the people or his crimes against his wife and daughter the most unforgivable. For if Martin the politician is a man who makes empty promises to the people, Martin the husband is a man who disregards his vows to his wife, Martin the father a man who ignores his responsibilities toward his daughter. Initially, he is guilty only of neglect, of putting career before family as he builds a broader client and constituent base, but Verity soon finds him guilty of abandonment and adultery, and on more than a few occasions. As both a man of the people and a family man, then, she finds him degenerating: he may begin with laudable aspirations, but as his quest in their name increasingly brings him political and sexual reward beyond what she will countenance, as he begins to concentrate only on ends, letting means be what they may, she consciously sacrifices family for justice. The most prominent female perspective in the novels examined here thus reinforces the judgments of most of her male counterparts, who analyze their Long characters according to mostly professional criteria. Adria Locke Langley, by way of Verity Martin, might subject her Long figure to both personal and professional scrutiny, but she comes to much the same conclusion as those who subject him primarily to the latter: she is unique in that she addresses the family man as much as, if not more than, the so-called man of the people, unique in that she does so from the woman's perspective she so trumpeted outside the text—and more loudly there than in that text, unfortunately—but, from both perspectives, she pronounces a condemnation we have heard before. It may derive from a different source—a different voice, even— but the message itself is essentially the same.

5 Philosopher King(fish): Robert Penn Warren's Willie Stark

HIS CURRICULUM VITAE WAS HARDLY THE PROBLEM. BE-fore he had turned even thirty, Robert Penn Warren could boast of degrees earned at Vanderbilt, California-Berkeley, and—as a Rhodes scholar, no less—Oxford; the publication of a biography, a novella, several essays, and an array of poems; and a teaching career that already included three years of service to his undergraduate alma mater. Even so, Warren still found himself jobless at the end of spring semester 1934. As one given the date might expect, the national economy, not his professional record, was the problem. A victim of the Depression, Vanderbilt had had to downsize, and the twenty-nine-year-old acting assistant professor had been one of many junior faculty who had been let go. Later that summer, though, Dean Charles W. Pipkin of Louisiana State University had come to Warren's rescue and had offered him a full-time assistant professorship in the LSU Department of English, which Warren thankfully accepted. It was "a much-needed job," he later wrote, one at a university that, as a result of increased attention from the state administration, was "definitely on the make—with a sensational football team and with money to spend even for assistant professors at a time when assistant professors were being fired, not hired." He was not without his reservations about teaching there, however, for even if the state's newest U.S. senator had previously been for him "only an occasional headline," Warren knew full well that his move from Nashville, Tennessee, to Baton Rouge, Louisiana, would also mean his entrance into what he termed "the orbit of Huey P. Long."[1]

1. Joseph Blotner, *Robert Penn Warren: A Biography* (New York: Random House, 1997), xi–xii; Albert J. Montesi, "Huey Long and *The Southern Review*," *Journal of Modern Literature* 3, no. 1 (1973): 67; Robert Penn Warren, "*All the King's Men*: The Matrix

As Warren was well aware, there was a reason LSU was known as "Huey's University." But at the same time, he "had been assured that Huey would not mess with my classroom" and that Long "wanted a 'good' university almost as much as he wanted a winning football team." And such, according to all accounts, was the case, even when the assistant professor clashed with one of the senator's prized football players. Warren writes that, after he kicked a "hulking brute of a young man" out of his class one day—a student who, as he soon found out from the startled classmates left behind, was an LSU Tigers standout—he heard nothing from either university or state administration. "A man as smart as Huey," Warren reasoned, "was well aware that the American Association of University Professors would like nothing better than to blacklist his university" and knew better, therefore, than "to mess with classrooms." Even when Long's daughter Rose enrolled in one of his courses, even when Warren, as one of the founding editors of the *Southern Review,* solicited an essay from Norman Thomas— thus funding with money Long appropriated the work of one of his most fierce ideological adversaries—Warren heard nothing, again, from either school or state official. Indeed, during the one year Warren spent in what he called Long's orbit, the senator remained to him more a public figure than a personal or even professional acquaintance. He saw Long only once: he writes that, at a banquet celebrating LSU's seventy-fifth anniversary, the Kingfish strolled in as unannounced as uninvited, picked his way through the crowd to the head table, insinuated himself among the disconcerted guests and dignitaries, and sat down "as calmly as though coming into his own kitchen late at night for a snack." Warren goes on to write that on another occasion he perhaps saw Long ride by in a car, but even though he spent his first year as an LSU professor in the city where Long spent much of the last year of his life, the two never met, neither as state employee and state official, professor and concerned father, nor editor and, in a sense, benefactor.[2]

---

of Experience," *Yale Review* 53 (1963): 161; Robert Penn Warren, "The World of Huey Long," *London Times,* 5 January 1974, Saturday Review section.

2. Warren, "Matrix of Experience," 161; Robert Penn Warren, "In the Time of *All the King's Men,*" *New York Times Book Review,* 31 May 1981, 9, 39; Montesi, 71.

Yet even if Long never made an appearance in either Warren's classrooms or his office at the *Southern Review,* he—or a figure that in many ways resembles him—made numerous incursions into the more private recesses of the young professor's mind. Warren writes that during the winter of 1937–38, some three years after his arrival at LSU, he found himself inspired to write a verse drama about "a Southern politician who achieved the power of a dictator, at least in his home state, and who was assassinated in the Capitol which had been the scene of his triumphs." He began writing the play the following summer, calling his politician Willie Talos—or, according to a recent scholarly account, Willie Strong—calling the play itself *Proud Flesh.* Two years later, though, during the summer of 1940, he set it aside to concentrate on what would become his second novel. He had no way of knowing it at the time, but *Proud Flesh* had reached its final form under that title. Even before he had finished that second novel, *At Heaven's Gate,* he had found himself rethinking the material behind the shelved play, and in a letter dated November 8, 1941, he for the first time mentions in print a second, similar-sounding work, an untitled novel to be "based on [the] Huey Long situation, but not an exposé—on theme of power versus values, means versus ends." Even while at work on *At Heaven's Gate,* he had come to see the subject of *Proud Flesh* as material fit more for a novel than a play. "I felt the play too constricted to provide the human context that made possible the rise of the man of power," he would later explain, for "the man of power must fill, in some deep and secret way, some blankness in each person of his world."[3] To broaden that "world," Warren substantially changed both the form and content of his story. Whereas the play focuses almost exclusively on a corrupt southern governor's dream of building a charity hospital, the novel expands perhaps tenfold, adding an entire assembly of characters whose blanknesses the central politician, soon to

3. Robert Penn Warren, introduction to *All the King's Men* (1946; reprint, New York: Modern Library, 1953), i–iii; James A. Grimshaw, Jr., and James A. Perkins, eds., *Robert Penn Warren's "All the King's Men": Three Stage Versions* (Athens: University of Georgia Press, 2000), xxiv; William Bedford Clark, ed., *Selected Letters of Robert Penn Warren,* vol. 2, *The "Southern Review" Years, 1935–1942* (Baton Rouge: Louisiana State University Press, 2001), 341; Warren, "Matrix of Experience," 166; Warren, "World of Huey Long," 5.

be named Willie Stark, was to fill.[4] The most significant such expansion is the role of Jack Burden, who leaves the periphery of *Proud Flesh*—he appears in only the last two scenes and utters no more than a dozen lines—for a role that, in *All the King's Men,* all but pushes the politician out of what had been his spotlight. Yet that politician also benefits from the revision, and greatly: more singular, far more fully realized, Willie Stark is less what Adria Locke Langley called the universal demagogue—for whom theatergoers may easily have mistaken his predecessor—but more, at the same time, what reviewers quickly called another fictionalized Long.

Unlike *Proud Flesh, All the King's Men* is the story of Jack Burden as much as of Willie Stark. A tough-talking but on occasion surprisingly thoughtful newspaper reporter, Burden first meets Stark while investigating a political skirmish in a small southern town. Stark, at the time a county treasurer, is not The Boss he would become but "Cousin Willie from the country," a man who looked as if "he never had been and

4. In the restored edition of *All the King's Men* (Harcourt, 2001), editor Noel Polk returns the text of the novel to that of the typescripts Harcourt's Lambert Davis and David Mitchell Clay read and edited from June 1943 until its publication in August 1946. Polk not only appends the novel's original opening and restores the thousands of variants between typescript and first edition but resurrects what Warren asserts was Willie's original surname, Talos. "Talos" was the name Warren preferred, Polk argues, as well as a name freighted with more literary allusiveness than "Stark." While the critical community at large has been receptive to most of these restorations, Polk has drawn little but criticism for his decision to return "Stark" to "Talos." His most vocal critic thus far has been Joyce Carol Oates, who, in the 28 March 2002 *New York Review of Books,* took him to task for preferring "a showy, pretentious, rather silly name in the 'Stephen Dedalus' tradition"—a name Warren himself agreed to abandon, she emphasizes—over a name she finds "effective without being an outright nudge in the ribs." "It's a measure of the enduring worth of *All the King's Men,*" she concludes, "that Willie Stark has entered our collective literary consciousness, in the company of Captain Ahab, Huck Finn, Jay Gatsby, Holden Caulfield, Rabbit Angstrom, and very few others. Set beside this . . . 'Willie Talos' hasn't a chance" (48). I agree, and have therefore elected to refer to Willie throughout as Stark, not Talos. I am not without my appreciation for the bulk of Polk's work, however: though all quotations from *All the King's Men* herein derive from its first edition, all significant variants found in Polk's restoration will be noted. (For Polk's response to Oates's review, as well as Oates's defense of her initial comments, see the Letters section of the 27 June 2002 *New York Review of Books.*)

never would be in politics."⁵ Time soon proves this early assessment incorrect, though, for as a result of his growing reputation for integrity in a state and county government collapsing under the weight of its own corruption, Stark gains local renown as a "spokesman for the tongue-tied population of honest men" (68).⁶ The next time the two meet, Stark is a candidate in the Democratic gubernatorial primary, Burden the reporter covering his campaign. As did Long, Stark fails in his first bid for the office but succeeds in his second, at which point he hires Burden—like Tyler Spotswood to Chuck Crawford—to serve as his confidential secretary. What Burden witnesses from that point on is much what Earle Christenberry, Long's own confidential secretary, witnessed upon his boss's ascension to the governor's chair: a social and political revolution that, like several examined here, comes only at the cost of an array of abuses punctuated by an underhandedly quashed impeachment attempt. At the end of the novel, as Burden's own, more private dilemmas threaten to draw the reader away from his boss's more public predicaments, Stark falls victim—as did Long, as does Slade—to a vengeful, gun-wielding young patrician, leaving Burden with questions assuaged only by writing Stark's story, becoming his boss's final judge, if not, in spite of himself, his boss's final apologist.

What Joseph Blotner has called "a part of modern literary folklore" began on August 18, 1946, the day before *All the King's Men* went on sale. Even more than they had done with its predecessors, reviewers emphasized similarities between its fictional politician and one factual politician in particular. The *Philadelphia Inquirer* began, "The shadow of the late and unlamented Huey Long has appeared, in recent years, in novels by John Dos Passos, Hamilton Basso, and Adria Langley Locke [*sic*], to name the more superior offerings, and now the examination is continued in this superlative performance by Robert Penn Warren." The *Chicago Sun Book Week* found Stark "a Huey Long–like governor," while the *New York Herald Tribune Weekly Book Review* found *All the King's Men* "in many respects" another fictionalization of "the Long story and legend." The most infamous notice came from the *New York Times Book Review*. Refusing to separate fact and fiction,

5. Robert Penn Warren, *All the King's Men* (Harcourt, Brace and Co., 1946), 21, 22.
6. Polk's restored edition reads, "tongue-tied and encephalitic population" (90).

even insisting on outright collusion between Warren and Long, Robert Gorham Davis begins,

In 1935, the year that Huey Long was shot and killed, Robert Penn Warren, a distinguished poet and associate [*sic*] professor at the University of Louisiana [*sic*], began editing the Southern Review with Cleanth Brooks. It was one of the best and purest literary quarterlies in the United States, and it was paid for by a brilliant and unscrupulous vulgarian who had imposed a naked dictatorship of fraud and force on the State of Louisiana, and who was now reaching out, through undercover alliances and Share-the-Wealth Clubs, for national power.

The Southern Review was completely free to print whatever its editors, men of integrity, thought best, and yet by that very fact, and by the presence of such men at the University of Louisiana, Long's ambitions were being served. He had poured millions of dollars into the university with a Fascist's love of buildings, particularly of stadiums. He had some of his happiest moments parading his heavily mechanized ROTC before visiting celebrities and personally conducting the huge bands and the elaborate cheering at football games. But his larger purpose was to win over the ambitious youth of the State and make them leaders in his national Share-the-Wealth program. Half the students at L.S.U. were getting money from State jobs, with all the corruption and intrigue inseparable from such an arrangement in Long's Louisiana.

Moreover, Huey Long interfered in university affairs in characteristic fashion. He forced the illegal award of a degree to a supporter in jail for obscene libel. He expelled honor students for criticizing his rule over student organizations. Such acts naturally aroused great protest. To forestall blacklisting by national educational organizations and to placate intellectuals, Long was shrewd enough to have able writers and teachers brought to the university and given freedom of expression and teaching as long as they let him have his way in politics.[7]

7. Joseph Blotner, *The Modern American Political Novel, 1900–1960* (Austin: University of Texas Press), 219; Frank Brookhauser, "Rise and Fall of a Southern Dictator in Tradition of Long," review of *All the King's Men*, by Robert Penn Warren, *Philadelphia Inquirer*, 18 August 1946, sec. SO, p. 17; Laban C. Smith, "A Wily Political Boss: From

This is a book review, remember, not an editorial. Nearly four hundred words into it, Davis has yet to mention either the name of the novel or even the fact that a novel was the inspiration for this diatribe. His main point, however, is clear: Huey Long had hired and granted freedom of speech to professors like Warren only to avoid educational blacklisting long enough to lure LSU students, already seduced by state paychecks, into his grasp. In addition to distracting critics from the corruption rampant beyond the classroom, Warren had also conspired with Long, Davis claims, by agreeing to be shushed politically so that he might say what he wanted in the classroom and on the pages of the *Southern Review.*

When Davis finally addresses the novel itself, he suggests far more than the correspondences between Stark and Long his fellow reviewers had mentioned:

> Robert Penn Warren is writing about the real Huey Long even more frankly than Adria Locke Langley was in her very successful "A Lion Is in the Streets." The details of the hero's education, mannerisms and features, of the impeachment proceedings and assassination, put this beyond question. The novel must be judged, then, in political as well as literary terms, for its total effect is to justify Long and the intellectuals who played ball with him; to romanticize him; to have a kind of love affair with him through the three women who adore him. . . .
>
> Robert Penn Warren is fascinated by the strong man of action, as many of our war novelists were fascinated by romanticized Nazis. And the question of "All the King's Men" is solely whether the man of ideas can work with the dictator in the interests of historic change; whether, in carrying out that change, the unscrupulous vulgarian is not really a better man than the selfish, dignified, discreet and also immoral politicians from whom he seized power. Warren

Lincolnesque to Huey Long–Like Role," review of *All the King's Men,* by Robert Penn Warren, *Chicago Sun Book Week,* 18 August 1946, 3; Fred Marsh, "Demagogue's Progress: A Novel of American Politics Following the Huey Long Story and Legend," review of *All the King's Men,* by Robert Penn Warren, *New York Herald Weekly Book Review,* 18 August 1946, 2; Robert Gorham Davis, "Dr. Adam Stanton's Dilemma," review of *All the King's Men,* by Robert Penn Warren, *New York Times Book Review,* 18 August 1946, 3.

does not ask—the question apparently has no imaginative appeal for him—whether American tradition does not demand that we fight men like Long with the utmost resolution and with all the democratic means at our disposal, in order to preserve in this country and in the world free, open, pluralistic societies in which ultimate control is invested below in the people and not above in Willie Stark.[8]

Davis does grudgingly admit that *All the King's Men* should be judged as a novel, but what rings clearer and ultimately more shrill is his patent insistence that, since Warren has written a book about "the real Huey Long," we should first approach it as we would a political tract. For Warren, he argues, is not only trying to "romanticize," not only trying to "have a love affair with," Long, but, more than anything else, is trying to "justify" Long's actions to readers—for Warren, according to Davis, is one of the bought intellectuals who toed Long's line in exchange for professional gain. Warren himself—not Adam Stanton, as the novel would have it—is the idealist who has sold out to the dictator in an attempt to influence history. And if Warren does not turn jingo in the name of "American tradition" and exhort his readers to overthrow leaders like Long, it is because he had been secretly fighting alongside him since signing on at LSU.

Though no other reviewer would insist on outright collusion between Long and Warren, many would continue to connect Long and Stark. A selection of the nearly sixty notices the novel drew upon publication reveals that, like those quoted above, reviewers generally found at the heart of *All the King's Men* the "Huey Long theme with slight variations" and a story "[b]ased on . . . the career of Huey Long," one in particular concluding that, though "Mr. Warren's Huey" is called Willie Stark, similarities between the two are "so obvious that you inevitably think of him as Huey." This resurgence of interest in Long and fiction—sparked the year before by the success of *A Lion Is in the Streets*—soon brought Hamilton Basso out of his relative silence on the subject. Four months after *All the King's Men* appeared, he published "The Huey Long Legend," the *Life* magazine article that would

8. R. G. Davis, 24.

so anger Russell Long. The first of several essays on the Kingfish's fictionalization, it cites *All the King's Men* as the most recent of the four
novels that, since 1942, had taken up "what has come to be called the
Huey Long story." Basso argues that "even though Mr. Warren has
gone to great pains to bury Long under several layers of disguise and
has draped yards of literary invention about him, he follows the basic
outline of Long's biography almost as faithfully as Mrs. Langley." By
the end of the decade, considerations of the novel began appearing in
scholarly journals and monographs, their conclusions rarely differing
with those of the reviews preceding them. One referred to Stark as
"Huey Long's surrogate," one as a character "obviously and closely
modeled on Huey Long," and another corroborated Sinclair Lewis's
praise on the novel's dust jacket, adding that "he ought to know, for
he wrote *It Can't Happen Here* with the same governor in mind."[9] According to reviewers, scholars, and even the author of the first Huey
Long novel, Long's life had unquestionably inspired yet another work
of fiction.

Seven years after the novel's appearance, in the summer 1953 number of the *Sewanee Review*, Warren further fueled debate with "A Note
to *All the King's Men*," an essay reprinted as the "Introduction" to the
Modern Library edition of the novel, published later that year. He begins the essay by discussing the story's genesis as *Proud Flesh* and its
subsequent translation into *All the King's Men*, but he soon responds
to Davis and all the others who, for the past seven years, had consid-

9. Saxe Commins, "Some Powerful Variations on a Huey Long Theme," review of
All the King's Men, by Robert Penn Warren, *Cleveland News*, 7 September 1946, Book
Review section, 3; Ethel Hathaway Dexter, "Robert Penn Warren's *All the King's Men*:
Southern Poet's Novel a Dramatic Story Based on the Real Life of a Famous Dema-
gog—Many Characters Add to Interest," review of *All the King's Men*, by Robert Penn
Warren, *Springfield (Mass.) Sunday Union and Republican*, 1 September 1946, 4d; Lewis
Gannett, "Books and Things," review of *All the King's Men*, by Robert Penn Warren,
New York Herald Tribune, 19 August 1946, 17; Hamilton Basso, "The Huey Long Leg-
end," *Life*, 9 December 1946, 106, 116; Parker Tyler, "Novel into Film: *All the King's
Men*," *Kenyon Review* 12, no. 2 (1950): 370; Orville Prescott, *In My Opinion: An Inquiry
into the Contemporary Novel* (Indianapolis: Bobbs Merrill, 1952), 25; Joseph E. Baker,
"Irony in *All the King's Men*," in *Robert Penn Warren's "All the King's Men": A Critical
Handbook*, ed. Maurice Beebe and Leslie A. Field (Belmont, Calif.: Wadsworth,
1966), 99.

ered the book more a biography or political tract than a work of fiction. "One of the unfortunate characteristics of our time," Warren writes,

is that the reception of a novel may depend on its journalistic relevance. It is a little graceless of me to call this characteristic unfortunate, and to quarrel with it, for certainly the journalistic relevance of *All the King's Men* had a good deal to do with what interest it evoked. My politician hero, whose name, in the end, was Willie Stark, was quickly equated with the late Senator Huey P. Long, whose fame, even outside of Louisiana, was yet green in pious tears, anathema, and speculation.

This equation led, in different quarters, to quite contradictory interpretations of the novel. On one hand, there were those who took the thing to be a not-so-covert biography of, and apologia for, Senator Long, and the author to be not less than a base minion of the great man. There is really nothing to reply to this kind of innocent boneheadedness or gospel-bit hysteria. As Louis Armstrong is reported to have said, there's some folks that if they don't know, you can't tell 'em.

But on the other hand, there were those who took the thing to be a rousing declaration of democratic principles and a tract for the assassination of dictators. This view, though somewhat more congenial to my personal political views, was almost as wide of the mark. For better or for worse, Willie Stark was not Huey Long. Willie was only himself, whatever that self turned out to be, a shadowy wraith or a blundering human being.

This disclaimer, whenever I was callow enough to make it, was almost invariably greeted by something like a sardonic smile or a conspiratorial wink, according to what the inimical smiler or the friendly winker took my motives to be—either I wanted to avoid being called a fascist or I wanted to avoid a lawsuit. Now in making the disclaimer again, I do not mean to imply that there was no connection between Governor Stark and Senator Long. Certainly, it was the career of Long and the atmosphere of Louisiana that suggested the play that was to become the novel. But suggestion does not mean identity, and even if I had wanted to make Stark a projection of Long, I should not have known how to go about it. For one reason, simply because I did not, and do not, know what Long was like, and what were the secret forces that drove him along his violent path to meet the bullet in the Capitol. And in any case, Long was but one of the figures that stood in the shadows of imagination behind Willie Stark. . . .

Though I did not profess to be privy to the secret of Long's soul, I did have some notions about the phenomenon of which Long was but one example, and I tried to put some of those notions into my book . . . [which] was never intended to be a book about politics. Politics merely provided the framework story in which the deeper concerns, whatever their final significance, might work themselves out.[10]

Several points here deserve reiteration. Willie Stark, Warren argues, is not Huey Long, but that does not mean that the two are antithetic. Long and Louisiana, he admits, "suggested" the play that became the novel. But, he stipulates, "suggestion does not mean identity," and even if he had been actively trying to turn *Proud Flesh*'s Talos into a fully realized fictional "projection" of Long, he says he would not have known how to do it. Long may be one of many figures who contributed to Stark's characterization, and Warren may have addressed in the novel some of the larger historical forces he found Long embodying— populism, certainly, even incipient American fascism, perhaps—but Willie Stark is not Huey Long, and *All the King's Men*, Warren stresses, is not a Huey Long biography.

Though it is all but impossible to causally link Warren's introduction and the arguments that soon issued from critics, those writing about *All the King's Men* during the next decade often implicitly accepted Warren's position, often rejecting the views of their predecessors, even upbraiding them on occasion for ever putting them on paper. One found the novel a fictional appraisal of native American populism, "far more," he contended, than "the narrow context of the life of Huey Long, as too many have mistakenly supposed." Cleanth Brooks, who had taught at LSU and edited the *Southern Review* alongside Warren, took such arguments farther. Scholars who had

10. Warren, introduction to *All the King's Men* (1953), v–vi.

mistaken Stark for Long "should have known better," he scolded, and had "disgraced themselves by their inability to make a distinction between the character of Willie Stark and that of the late senator from Louisiana." *All the King's Men*, he reminded them, "is a novel, not a biography." In other, less acquiescent quarters, though, Warren's essay inevitably inspired some of the same "sardonic smile[s]" and "conspiratorial wink[s]" it was intended to dispel. Seven years after the introduction's appearance, one scholar argued that, since so much of the novel is "derived from Long's career," Stark is undeniably "modeled on" the late senator. Three years after that, another critic argued that "[t]here is no doubt" that "Warren is writing with Huey Long in mind," for Stark's appearance and mannerisms, his educational and political careers—the impeachment proceedings in particular—"all point to the former Governor of Louisiana."[11] Though beginning to lean toward Warren's position on Stark-Long correspondences, the scholarly community as a whole had not been entirely convinced even a decade after "A Note to *All the King's Men*."

After writing the all but unseen introduction to an Italian translation of *All the King's Men: A Play* (1960)—in which Warren makes his most questionable statement on the subject: "my Willie Stark is no more like Huey Long than he is like Mussolini"—the 1963 *Time* Reading Program Special Edition of the novel allowed him to further clarify his position on the debate, then in its seventeenth year. He begins his "Introduction" by quoting the series editor, who had asked him to comment on "the 'Huey Long' side of the story" and "the thinking and feeling that led to the writing of the book." Initially, he had little new to say about the former. "I can be sure," Warren began, "that if I had never gone to live in Louisiana and if Huey Long had not existed, the novel would never have been written. But this is far from saying that my 'state' in *All the King's Men* is Louisiana, or that my Willie Stark is the late Senator. What Louisiana and Senator Long gave me was a line

11. Malcolm O. Sillars, "A Study in Populism," in Beebe and Field, 117; Cleanth Brooks, *The Hidden God: Studies in Hemingway, Faulkner, Yeats, Eliot, and Warren* (New Haven: Yale University Press, 1963), 105–6; Willard Thorp, *American Writing in the Twentieth Century* (Cambridge: Harvard University Press, 1960), 253, 335; Keith Beebe, "Biblical Motifs in *All the King's Men*," *Journal of Bible and Religion* 30 (1962): 130.

of 'thinking and feeling' that did eventuate in the novel." Long and Louisiana, then—if we conflate statements from Warren's first and second introductions to *All the King's Men*—may have "suggested" the novel, may have inspired in its author the "line of 'thinking and feeling'" that ultimately resulted in the novel, but, again, that does not mean that Willie Stark *is* Huey Long, or that *All the King's Men* is even set in Long's home state. Lest he be accused of repeating himself throughout the second introduction, Warren offered us at least some new insight into the way he approached the Long material:

> How directly did I try to transpose into fiction Huey P. Long and the tone of that world? The question answers itself in a single fact. The first version of my story was a verse drama. The actual writing began in 1938, in the shade of an olive tree by a wheat field near Perugia. If you are sitting under an olive tree in Umbria and are writing a verse drama, the chances are that you are concerned more with the myth than with the fact, more with the symbolic than with the actual. And so it was. It could not, after all, have been otherwise, for in the strict, literal sense, I had no idea what the then deceased Huey P. Long had been. What I knew was the 'Huey' of the myth, and that was what I had taken with me to Mussolini's Italy. . . .
>
> In 1942 I left Louisiana for good, and when in 1943 I began the version that is more realistic, discursive and documentary in spirit (though not in fact) than the play, I was doing so after I had definitely left Louisiana and the world in which the story had its roots. By now the literal, factual world was only a memory and therefore was ready to be absorbed freely into the act of imagination.[12]

According to its author, therefore, what we have in *All the King's Men* is not the Huey Long of record but "the 'Huey' of the myth" first "absorbed freely into," then transformed by, "the act of imagination"—a "Huey" twice removed, as Warren would have it, from the strictly historical Huey.

Unlike his first introduction, Warren's second elicited a direct re-

12. Grimshaw and Perkins, 9; Robert Penn Warren, introduction to *All the King's Men* (1946; reprint, New York: Time, 1963), xi, xvi–xvii.

sponse: critical commentary was divided and at times almost antagonistic. Among those who accepted its claims, one scholar wrote that
though "the real Huey Long has been often seen as the historical basis
for Willie Stark," those "who read the work carefully should be per-
suaded by it to accept the author's disclaimers of such an intention,
even as we recognize the biographical and political realities in the
'germ' of the novel." Another agreed: "Warren correctly believes," he
asserted, "that the fact that he stimulates his imagination with real
events, contemporary or historical, in no way effects [*sic*] their being
classed as imaginative creations." More adamant, however, were those
who rejected Warren's assertions, critics like Gordon Milne, who argued in *The American Political Novel* that though Warren "has always
denied making Stark a fictive disguise for Long . . . critics and readers
alike have gone on making the association, and I choose to join them."
Richard Gray put it still more emphatically: "What was true of Huey
Long is also true of Willie Stark, no matter how much Warren may
alter or condense specific details to make his point." Yet no one would
state his case more relentlessly than Ladell Payne, author of the most
thorough examination to date of correspondences between Stark and
Long, "Willie Stark and Huey Long: Atmosphere, Myth, or Suggestion?" The core of Payne's argument is as follows:

> While it is undoubtedly true that *All the King's Men* is not a
> literal biography of Huey Long, and equally true that much of the
> novel's literary value comes from the philosophical cogency of its
> subject matter . . . *All the King's Men* is much more directly based
> on the historical Huey Long than the words "suggested," "atmo-
> sphere," "line of thinking and feeling" and "world of myth" can pos-
> sibly imply. Whether or not Warren tried "to transpose into fiction
> Huey P. Long and the tone of that world," the fact remains that
> he succeeded in doing so. For in the novel's sequence of events,
> in the subordinate characters and in the characterization of Willie
> himself, so much is drawn directly from the publicly-known career,
> cohorts and character of Huey Pierce Long that Warren's state-
> ments, while not false, nonetheless have been misleading.

Striking intent from the debate altogether, Payne more forcefully reiterated Basso's argument that "once a writer begins to write about these

Hueys-who-aren't-Hueys, the real Huey jumps up and clings to his back like the old man of the sea."[13] Warren may not have intended it, Payne contended, but Willie Stark nonetheless became Huey Long.

Although it would continue for decades, Warren's half of the debate might as well have ended five years earlier, with his 1963 introduction to the *Time* edition. The next twenty years would bring three further introductions, as well as a handful of relevant but mostly unenlightening interviews (though Warren himself refers to Stark in one as "the Huey Long figure") but none significantly alter the author's stance. Secker and Warburg's mid-1970s reissue of *All the King's Men* elicited his third introduction, which first appeared in the January 5, 1974, *London Times* as "The World of Huey Long." More an attempt to introduce Long to the British reading public than further refute strict parallels between fact and fiction, it begins with something of a fatigued confession: "After all these years," Warren wrote, "I have little inclination to reopen old controversies about *All the King's Men*." What follows, consequently, is not new material as much as a further revision of earlier introductions. "Long and the world he dominated did provide the original stimulus" for the novel, Warren wrote, "and did suggest some of the issues that emerge there," but "[t]he definition of the nature of Huey Pierce Long is . . . far from the concern of my novel, and even today I have not the ghost of a notion of what he in truth was." Revisiting his second introduction, Warren wrote, "What caught my eye . . . and imagination" was not the actual Huey Long but "the myth that I saw growing before my eyes."[14] Except for the phrase "original stimulus," the third introduction's relevant detail may further

13. Murray Krieger, *The Classic Vision: The Retreat from Extremity in Modern Literature* (Baltimore: Johns Hopkins University Press, 1971), 296; L. Hugh Moore, Jr., *Robert Penn Warren and History: "The Big Myth We Live"* (The Hague: Mouton, 1970), 44; Gordon Milne, *The American Political Novel* (Norman: University of Oklahoma Press, 1966), 153; Richard Gray, "The American Novelist and American History: A Revaluation of *All the King's Men*," *Journal of American Studies* 6 (1972): 302; Ladell Payne, "Willie Stark and Huey Long: Atmosphere, Myth, or Suggestion?" *American Quarterly* 20 (1968): 582; Basso, "Legend," 117.

14. Marshall Walker, "Robert Penn Warren: An Interview," in *Talking with Robert Penn Warren*, ed. Floyd C. Watkins, John T. Hiers, and Mary Louise Weeks (Athens: University of Georgia Press, 1990), 152; Warren, "World of Huey Long," 5.

clarify but essentially only restates what Warren had offered us before: an admission of inspiration, a qualification via disclaimer, an emphasis on intent, and a profession of interest in myth rather than fact.

In his fourth introduction, the "special message to subscribers" appended to the 1977 Franklin Library edition of the novel, Warren describes *All the King's Men* as "an intersection of Louisiana, Huey P. Long, and me." In some of the most evocative prose ever to address the subject of Depression-era Louisiana, he then takes up his mid-1930s arrival at LSU and the thoroughly trampled ground of his position on parallels between Stark and Long. He offers us little new detail but nonetheless aids our overall insight: "I do not pretend to be privy to Long's soul," he reiterates, "and I never spent five minutes in anything that might possibly be called research. . . . I simply lived in the world in which his legend took shape. And certainly I had, and have, no desires to whitewash whatever may need whitewashing in Long's human frailty, arrogance, self-absorption, cowardice, vanity, and cynical use of his all too corruptible tools. . . . In *All the King's Men* what I was concerned with was, ultimately, the myth not the man, the melodrama of the modern state, society and not politics as such, and more generally, the question of human integrity and responsibility in the modern world." From this we learn that he absorbed more than investigated and concerned himself more with universals than particulars, but we hear relatively little that we have not heard before. Much the same is true of his fifth and final introduction, that to the Book-of-the-Month Club's thirty-fifth anniversary edition of the novel. Adapted and published in the May 31, 1981, *New York Times Book Review* as "In the Time of *All the King's Men*," the essay at least begins more promisingly: "Thirty-five years ago, 'All the King's Men' was published. With any event in your life, you know more after 35 years than after one. . . . [I]n the course of time, strange odds and ends—or even fundamental facts not recognized in the noonday sun—may, out of blank idleness of a later mind, rise up, trailing God knows what. . . . What rises so gratuitously out of the deep of time may be a set of relationships and connections of which you had been unaware when things were fresh." Despite this playful—if not slightly tormenting—hinting at long-awaited revelation, what follows is mostly a still further reworking of previous introductions. If Warren had realized anything about *All the King's Men* in the four years since his last introduction, it was not any "set of relationships and connections" he had not previously noticed or admitted. Instead, what Warren ultimately offers us is yet another focus on myth rather than fact ("In one sense I wasn't really much interested in [Huey Long] as a man" but "as a focus of myth") and another rephrasing of what he was doing under that olive tree in Umbria ("trying to organize the speculations provoked by Huey").[15] Thus concluded the authorial half of the debate, often rephrased since 1953 but essentially unchanged since 1963.

Despite two further considerations of Long's connections to fictional offspring—Robert E. Snyder's "The Concept of Demagoguery: Huey Long and His Literary Critics" (1976) and Luther Stearns Mansfield's "History and the Historical Process in *All the King's Men*" (1978)—critical debate has similarly stabilized since Payne's 1968 article. This is not to say, however, that Payne's has become the prevailing view, for Warren's contentions, at least among the critical community, continue to predominate. Even as fact-minded a scholar as C. Vann Woodward has emphasized the fictional more than historical in the novel; as he sees it, even though "[t]he life and death, the career and tragedy of Huey Long unavoidably suggest the life, death, career, and tragedy of Willie Stark," that "by no means converts Warren's novel into fictional history with the names changed." In the end, he concludes, the "resemblances" are merely "external." William C. Havard would seem to concur: history, he argues, is for Warren only a means to an end. Those who find him a historical novelist who just happens to be a philosophical novelist are mistaken, Havard implies, for Warren is instead "a novelist who accepts historical experience as fundamental to philosophical understanding as that understanding is unfolded through the creative imagination." Garrett Epps, in "Politics as Metaphor," elaborates: "despite its narrative of the rise and fall of a populist-dictator closely modeled on Long, *All the King's Men* is not, in fact, a *political* novel at all." Its author's "deepest concerns are philosophical, and the 'political' story he tells is no more than a diversion

15. Robert Penn Warren, "A Special Message to Subscribers," in *All the King's Men* (1946; reprint, Franklin Center, Pa.: Franklin Library, 1977), n.p.; Warren, "Time of *All the King's Men*," 9, 40.

. . . designed to allow him to explore his philosophical themes in a uniquely compelling setting." What the debate over Stark-Long parallels lacks, then, is not what Louisa Foulke Newlin calls for in "Robert Penn Warren's Use of History in *All the King's Men*"—not an examination of "the way in which history can be illuminated by imaginative literature"[16]—but, quite the opposite, an examination of the way in which imaginative literature can be illuminated by history, the way in which fact can inspire creation, not duplication, the way in which historical referents can aid, but not unseat, what Turner calls authorial autonomy. In addition to considering to what degree Stark is Huey Long, such an appraisal must also consider to what degree Stark is not, but is nonetheless inspired by, Huey Long. Warren claimed time and again that he was not "privy to the secret of Long's soul," that he "had no idea what . . . Huey P. Long had been." He did know what Long had done, though, and he did know what Long had said—and, as a result, Willie Stark not only does much of what Long did, says much of what Long said, but at times as much as embodies what Warren referred to as the secrets of Long's soul inherent in those very words and deeds.

Unlike most of those that follow, the early years of Stark's life bear only passing resemblance to the corresponding years of Long's. The novel never names the state in which he spends those years, but with its proximity to Texas and Arkansas, its cypress-filled southern bayous and economic reliance on oil and agriculture, it can be only Louisiana. In a 1959 interview, in fact, Warren perhaps slipped in commenting that the scene in which Burden meets Stark takes place, at least in his mind, in New Orleans. Stark's Mason City, moreover, looks much like Long's Winnfield. Both are small, primarily agricultural centers of

---

16. C. Vann Woodward, "History in Robert Penn Warren's Fiction," in *The Future of the Past* (New York: Oxford University Press, 1989), 226; William C. Havard, "The Burden of the Literary Mind: Some Meditations on Robert Penn Warren as Historian," in *Robert Penn Warren: A Collection of Critical Essays*, ed. Richard Gray, Twentieth-Century Views (Englewood Cliffs, N.J.: Prentice-Hall, 1980), 185; Garrett Epps, "Politics as Metaphor," *Virginia Quarterly Review* 55 (1979): 90; Louisa Foulke Newlin, "Robert Penn Warren's Use of History in *All the King's Men*" (Ph.D. diss., American University, 1979), 4.

what were pine forests at the north end of the state before the arrival of Northern lumber companies, little more than red clay hills after their departure. Payne, on the contrary, sees Mason City as the fictional twin of Morgan City, just as he takes Okaloosa, Marston, and Harmonville as the fictional twins of Opelousas, Ruston, and Hammond.[17] As Morgan City is located in southern rather than northern Louisiana, however, it has more in common alphabetically than geographically with Mason City. Because Burden, not his boss, narrates the story, we get little insight into what Willie might have done in Mason City as a child. Given the fact that he grew up on a farm, we might well assume that, like Brand and Martin before him, he helped his father with the crops and livestock. In one early scene, we hear Willie, standing in the barnyard behind his father's house, tell Jack that "I bet I dumped ten thousand gallons of swill into that trough. . . . I bet I slopped five hundred head of hogs out of [it]" (34). He fails to specify whether he did so as a boy, a young man, or both, but if his spitting into it implies anything, it is that he enjoyed his time at it as much as Long, Brand, and Martin did their own. What Stark and Long share at this point is only the most general experience. So far, Warren seems more intent on portraying Stark as the product of a poor, white, rural southern upbringing than as a character who lives any life other than his own.

Stark's young adulthood, though, is both more detailed and more analogous to Long's. At some unspecified point before the 1939 of the novel's immediate present, Stark spent a year at a Baptist college like that Long at least considered attending, a college Burden considered not "much more than a glorified grade school." Shortly thereafter, he spent a year in an Oklahoma military camp and, after the war, returned home to work his father's farm and study "the big names" in "the big books" his one year of college had taught him to appreciate (72). As one of Long's favorite texts was John Clark Ridpath's ubiquitous *History of the World* (*HL* 21), one of Stark's was an unspecified American history text. Showing it to Burden one day, he told him, "I durn near memorized every durn word in it. I could name you every name. I could name you every date." From this and similar volumes he com-

17. "An Interview with Flannery O'Connor and Robert Penn Warren," in Watkins, Hiers, and Weeks, 57; Payne, 582–83.

piled one of his own, a ledger into which he copied words from the likes of Emerson, Macaulay, Franklin, and Shakespeare. Warren is still more vague about the dates of the next significant events in Stark's biography, the beginnings of his lives as husband, father, and politician. As Burden so imprecisely puts it, "Lucy came into the picture, and then the kid Tom . . . and later the courthouse" (72). More the result of blood than books, his political career began because of his father's kinship to Dolph Pillsbury, Chairman of the Board of Mason County Commissioners. After a rift with his county treasurer, Pillsbury had simply inserted Willie into the vacant slot. Stark may thus have found a far easier start in politics than Long did, but both, at roughly the same point in their lives, followed roughly the same path. Both were assiduous self-motivators who refused to let circumstances stand in the way of their desire to one day become big names in the big books themselves. But again, such experience is more general than specific, perhaps as much that of Horatio Alger as of Huey Long.

In 1922, when the *Chronicle*'s Jack Burden first met Willie Stark, the reporter hardly thought the treasurer would ever be a name in any kind of book. Jack's first impression is of a man closer to Long in appearance than in his personal history. He is five foot eleven, heavy chested and short legged, and sports a cheap seersucker suit, a shirt more befitting a Sunday school superintendent than a small-time politician, a striped tie no doubt neglected until his trip to the city, a sweat-stained gray felt hat, and long-unpolished shoes. As Payne sees it, this ensemble "reproduces almost exactly" an oft-published photo of the young Long as a traveling salesman.[18] But "reproduces almost exactly" is far too strong a phrase. The shirt is the same, and the man inside it is roughly the same size, but the suit in the photo, though cheap, is not seersucker, the tie not striped. The photo could nevertheless have inspired the image. The remainder of Jack's impressions, offered as he continues his description of the same meeting, read more like contemporary impressions of Long. Once the two are seated across a table from each other, Jack notices that Willie's lips are "a little bit meaty," but not "loose." His face is "a little bit meaty, too, but thinskinned" and freckled. His eyes are "big, big and brown," and his "dark

18. Payne, 583.

brown" hair is "thick" and "tousled and crinkled down over his fore-head." This, Jack writes, was "little Willie . . . Cousin Willie from the country, from up at Mason City, with his Christmas tie" (21), and his first impressions of him are largely like those that viewers take away from pictures of Long in his late teens and early twenties, those Payne contends inspired Warren's descriptions of Stark. "You could look at Willie," Burden thinks, as many may well have thought of Long, "and see that he never had been and never would be in politics."

Yet just as Long, at roughly the same point in his own career, served as railroad commissioner for the northern district of Louisiana, Stark serves as Mason County treasurer. Not just "in politics," he is perhaps the key figure in a growing dispute over an upcoming bond issue. As he explains to Jack some two months later, county commissioners had tried to force on him a higher bid than he could countenance for the construction of a new schoolhouse. His refusal quickly cast him as what Burden calls "the one-man leper colony of Mason City" (62). Pillsbury called him "biggety," while the general populace, ignoring the fact that the company he favored had a lower asking price, focused instead on the fact that it employed African American laborers, calling him a "nigger-lover" (61). The dispute soon cost the Starks Lucy's teaching post and any possibility of a second term for Willie. He ran nonetheless, even wrote up and distributed his views on the issue—as Long did his on any number of concerns, circulating hand-bills—but lost the election. The county awarded the costlier company the contract, and Pillsbury earned the kickback about which Willie had warned the populace. The circumstances of their early battles may be different—Stark's involving a schoolhouse, Long's oil and other natural resources—but both win early attention for their campaigns against legislative corruption. These correspondences, though, are still far from absolute.

In dramatizing Willie's postelection plans, Warren seems to find inspiration in—but, again, does not quite duplicate—further details from Long's biography. Though Stark tells the *Chronicle* only that "I am going back to Pappy's farm and milk the cows and study some more law for it looks like I am going to need it" (68), he also takes up traveling sales. His route is similar to Long's, Brand's, Crawford's, and Martin's—door-to-door, farmhouse-to-farmhouse, small community to small community—but he sold a household fix-it kit rather than a cooking agent or small appliances. At night, he studied law. The first description of the dogged, solitary scholar he becomes follows Jack's imagining the lonely nights his wife and father must have spent downstairs by the fire. Upstairs, apart from them as from the rest of the world, Willie was in his bedroom devouring the law, but was "not even in that room, either, but in a room, a world, inside himself where something was swelling and growing painfully and dully and imperceptibly like a great potato in a dark, damp cellar" (27). Inside him, Jack imagines, "something would be big and coiling slow and clotting till he would hold his breath and the blood would beat in his head with a hollow sound as though his head were a cave as big as the dark outside." He had no name for it, but there was something "big inside him" (31–32). Largely because of his unflagging dedication to this nameless something, when he took the bar exam three years later he found the questions almost laughable. Warren may have professed an interest in myth rather than fact, but he here seems more interested in portraying Stark as a singularly dedicated, remarkably driven figure than as a character similar to either the mythical or historical Huey Long. He may walk his miles as a traveling salesman, but he never so much as attends law school, neither as the eight-month wonder of myth nor the assiduous "special" student of record. Warren follows the basic outline of the corresponding period in Long's life but diverges from it to portray Stark as a more admirable, far more sympathetic figure than his ostensible archetype was at the time.

Economic and educational issues aside, the most politically significant events of these years bear little if any relation to the corresponding years of Long's life. Warren again attempts to humanize Stark more than to portray him as the masterful, and therefore unsympathetic, politician Long was almost from the beginning. Amid the public disintegration of the machine that had defeated him, Stark becomes "the boy upon the burning deck and the boy who put his finger in the dike and the boy who replies 'I can' when Duty whispers low 'Thou must'" (68). During a fire drill at the schoolhouse that, despite his protests, the administration's preferred contractors built with bricks fired in a notoriously faulty kiln, an external fire escape pulled loose from the outer wall, and three children were killed, some dozen injured. As Burden cynically puts it, though, the disaster was "a piece of luck for Willie," who became still more of a local hero, even an object of sympathy and solicitude, for denouncing the machine responsible for the contract. As a grieving father cried out at the triple funeral following the tragedy, "I am punished for accepting iniquity and voting against an honest man!" Soon thereafter, as Burden would write, Willie—as a result of events with no parallel whatever in Long's biography—would have Mason County "in the palm of his hand" (70).

Because of his new status as spokesman for "the tongue-tied population of honest men," Willie drew the notice of Joe Harrison, a contender in the upcoming democratic gubernatorial primary—which, according to Jack, may as well have been the gubernatorial race itself. As Jack explains, Harrison's henchmen talked Willie into running not because of his reputation as a champion of right, but because a dummy candidate with strong rural appeal could split the country vote, traditionally the constituency of his opponent MacMurfee. Convinced by the big-city big-talkers that he could literally save the state, Willie sanctimoniously accepted what he saw as his mission and started campaigning, hammering flyers into trees, barns, whatever would support them. Much as Long first approached the stump—Williams writes that Long's first speeches ranged from a "composite of pompous nonsense" to a "bor[ing] . . . recital of facts and figures" (HL 198–99)—Stark, though forever attempting the next Gettysburg Address, utterly failed to inspire. In the words of Burden, who covered the campaign for the *Chronicle,* his speeches were an odd combination of the kind of material he copied into his ledger and facts and figures about his tax and road programs. Sadie Burke, one of Harrison's lieutenants, commented that he would hardly have been able to "steal a vote from Abe Lincoln in the Cradle of the Confederacy" (80). Willie's devastated rage at later learning the truth, at finding out that he had been called in only to split the country vote, may lack an absolute parallel in Long's career, but his naïve entrance into politics bears at least some resemblance to Long's first venture into oil speculation. As Williams explains, Long lost thousands of dollars in late 1918 when Standard Oil refused to continue business with a company in which he had invested (HL 118). Both Long and Stark entered unaware and soon ended up exploited and insulted. Nevertheless, at this point Warren is still more intent on evoking our sympathy for Stark than attributing to him the thoughts and actions of any one particular figure.

Warren wants us to sympathize with Willie a little longer, for after Sadie's revelation of his dummy status, he rebels against those who had set him up. At the same time, his actions more closely resemble those of Long, who openly threatened the oil executives he thought had tricked him: "You've done this before and got by with it," Long cried, "but this time . . . do it and see when you hear the last of it" (*HL* 119). Though expecting his standard speech when Willie mounts the platform the next day, Jack and Sadie instead hear something far more politically savvy. "I have a speech here," Willie begins, "a speech about what this state needs. But there's no use telling you what this state needs. You are the state. You know what you need. Look at your pants. Have they got holes in the knee? Listen to your belly. Did it ever rumble for emptiness? Look at your crop. Did it ever rot in the field because the road was so bad you couldn't get it to market? Look at your kids. Are they growing up ignorant as you and dirt because there isn't any school for them?" (97). Instinctively switching from objective facts and figures to the subjective immediacy of rumbling stomachs and rotting crops, Willie—much as Long had done by focusing on his followers' tattered socks—for the first time truly touches his audience. Instead of only appealing to the downtrodden, moreover, he characterizes himself as one of their own, and far more convincingly than either Chuck Crawford or Hank Martin. He tells them that he too has been tired and hungry; he too has felt their suffering. At the same time, though, he characterizes himself as someone removed, someone who wants more but, because of forces even more daunting than those his listeners face, still has not received it. He tells them that he had spent years studying "[s]o he could change things some. For himself and for folks like him" (97). Yet just when it seemed he was reaching his goal, big-city politicians had tricked him into believing he could be governor. After detailing this "foul truth which stinks in the nostrils of the Most High" (98), he first pushes Tiny Duffy, the Harrison henchman posing as his campaign manager, off the platform, then resigns from the race, describing himself as a "hick" who would not again be fooled by sweet-talking suits in a fancy car. The situation may be different— Long, as an independent investor, had been duped by oil executives,

Stark, a popular hero, by more sophisticated politicians—but the notes they sound are much the same. Both incite their fellows to rise up against those who have held them down, those who have tricked them much as they had tricked him, and both exhort their followers to make sure it never happens again. Williams's description of Long at this point in his career applies equally well to Stark: "he liked to give the impression that he was acting out of revenge, that he was only paying back those who had defrauded a poor 'country yap'" (*HL* 119). What had earlier been only general parallels, in short, now begin to seem metaphorical equals.

Thus also begins Stark's battle against the big man. Before he steps off the platform that afternoon, he vows to unite the underprivileged to defeat their common foe. He threatens to "kill Joe Harrison so dead he'll never even run for dogcatcher in this state," later campaigning statewide to spread the message to as many voters as possible. Mounting a stump tour as wide-ranging as one of Long's own, he delivers equally indignant speeches all over the state. "Friends, red-necks, suckers, and fellow hicks," he begins one in particular,

> that's what you are, and you needn't get mad at me for telling you. Well, get mad, but I'm telling you. That's what you are. And me— I'm one, too. Oh, I'm a red-neck, for the sun has beat down on me. Oh, I'm a sucker, for I fell for that sweet-talking fellow in the fine automobile. Oh, I took the sugar tit and hushed my crying. Oh, I'm a hick and I am the hick they were going to try to use and split the hick vote. But I'm standing here on my own hind legs, for even a dog can learn to do that, give him time. I learned. It took me a time but I learned, and here I am on my own hind legs. . . . Are you, are you on your hind legs? Have you learned that much yet? You think you can learn that much? (101)

Apparently they could, for as a result of these exhortations—which come across much more authentically than Crawford's or Martin's—an unprecedented number of similarly tricked hicks unite to defeat the "sweet-talking fellow in the fine automobile." Even after the election, Willie continues his fight. The relative lull between races gives him time to return to his law office, and though he has to live almost a year on what Burden calls chicken-stealing and stray hog cases, he soon strikes out against more sweet-talkers in fancy cars. As did Long, he finds his first real success as an attorney with workers' compensation cases and by suing a large oil company on behalf of independent lease-holders. The details may be different, the chronology a bit scrambled, but both Long and Stark, as both politicians and lawyers, fought similar opponents for similar constituents.

Spending little more time in the law office and courthouse, Willie enters the democratic gubernatorial primary in 1930. Instead of working within the party as one of its own, however, he works not just independently of but in opposition to it, arguing that it had long outlived its efficacy. As a result, by the time of the primary, the party is no more. "There was just Willie," Burden writes, "with his hair in his eyes and his shirt sticking to his stomach with sweat. And he had a meat ax in his hand and was screaming for blood" (103).[19] Though now the most powerful man in the state, Willie does not change his loyalties after winning the election. One of his greatest obstacles while governor is therefore the patrician hegemony that, as in *A Lion Is in the Streets,* had ruled the state for decades. As Warren—anticipating Key's *Southern Politics*—would write elsewhere, the "real power" in Louisiana, "for many generations, had rested in the hands of a tight oligarchy of rich and sometimes well-born, and even well-meaning, planters, merchants and corporation lawyers." The state "was their fief, lock, stock and barrel," and as a result of their self-serving social myopia, "[r]oads were foul, schools farcical, illiteracy a national scandal, per capita income abysmal and social services nonexistent."[20] Stark fights to overhaul much the same situation, and as a result, Jack often finds himself defending his new boss against the oligarchs in his own hometown, patricians who find Willie giving the state away to every "wool-hat jackass" around (131). His position is as follows: "Doesn't it all boil down to this? If the government of this state for quite a long time back had been doing anything for the folks in it, would Stark have been able to

19. Polk's restored edition reads, "and his shirt sticking to his stomach with sweat. And he had a hammer in his hand and was screaming for somebody to open the keg of ten-pennies" (136). The line refers to Willie's earlier threat not to "Nail up" Harrison and his henchmen (102)—as the first edition has it—but to "Crucify 'em!" (134).

20. Warren, "World of Huey Long," 5.

get out there with his bare hands and bust the boys?" (133). We hear more along these same lines upon the resignation of Hugh Miller, Stark's attorney general. Willie reminisces that Miller had sat in his law office for fifteen years "and watched the sons-of-bitches warm chairs in this state and not do a thing, and the rich get richer and the pore get porer." But when Stark appeared, he reminds Miller, he "slipped a Louisville Slugger in your hand and whispered low, 'You want to step in there and lay round you a little?' And you did. You had a wonderful time. You made the fur fly and you put nine tin-horn grafters in the pen" (146). Though Warren often denied that Stark *is* Long, that his state *is* Louisiana, fiction now begins more clearly to mirror fact. The battle Stark wages against the patricians of his un-named state is the same Warren and others would describe Long wag-ing against those of 1920s and 1930s Louisiana. As Warren was to admit time and again, without Huey Long, without 1930s Louisiana, there would be no *All the King's Men*.

Largely because of Willie's war against these patricians, their pup-pets in the state legislature attempt to impeach him. What follows is one of the rare sections of the novel that approaches as closely as Dos Passos's account of the Struck Oil Corporation what Woodward has called "fictional history with the names changed." The impeachment effort is far from unwarranted, for Willie, like Long, runs a machine lubricated, if not fueled outright, by illegality, blackmail in particular. Just before the proceedings begin, in fact, Willie assures himself the continued obedience of state auditor Byram B. White by forcing him to sign an undated resignation. The measure is hardly unusual for Stark, for as he explains to an almost cowering White, he, like Long, has a stack of such documents. But these tactics do not go unchal-lenged, even by members of his own administration: the Byram B. White episode leads directly to Hugh Miller's resignation, in spite of Willie's contention that politics often necessitates, occasionally even demands, just such illegalities. "The law is always too short and too tight for growing humankind," he rationalizes. "The best you can do is do something and then make up some law to fit" (146). Payne cor-rectly finds Warren in this case paraphrasing one of Long's more infa-mous statements. "Unconstitutional?" Long once asked. "Hell, when I want something done I do it and tell my attorney general to dig up a law to cover it."[21] The more Stark starts to employ tactics of the sort, the more his story begins to read like Long's.

Because of the way his modus operandi evinces itself in cases like White's, pro-impeachment forces charge Stark with trying to bully, blackmail, and corrupt the state legislature. Stark responds as Long did, frantically scrambling for public support but, more importantly, bribing his way to a series of under-the-table commitments. What the public sees are two weeks of six, seven, as many as eight speeches a day in which Stark downplays the "leetle mite of trouble" erupting among "that Legislature-ful of hyena-headed, feist-faced, belly-dragging sons of slack-gutted she-wolves" (155). No one who knows him well is worried, for they know even then what is going on behind the public's back: late-night visits to legislators' houses to trade potentially damaging information for votes against impeachment. Just as Long cajoled fifteen state legislators into signing the so-called Round Robin, Willie acquires a full complement of signatures on a similar document stipulating essentially what Long's did, that each of its signers finds the proceedings unjustified and will vote against them regardless of the evidence. Stark and Long are essentially twins here: both face impeachment because of similar heavy-handed tactics and then circumvent the charges with public claims of innocence bolstered by private threats of retribution. Stark will not again look so much like Long (though he will continue to mirror him occasionally, of course) until his assassination several chapters later.

Though their paths diverge at this point—Stark, like Martin, wins a second term as governor, while Long made his way to the U.S. Senate—many of their actions, both public and private, are markedly similar. Stark spends much of his remaining time fulfilling promises he had made during his first term. After announcing his victory at a rally the night of the impeachment vote, he confides to those assembled,

> I tell you what I am going to do. I am going to build a hospital. The biggest and the finest money can buy. It will belong to you. Any man or woman or child who is sick or in pain can go in those doors and know that all will be done that man can do. To heal sick-

ness. To ease pain. Free. Not as charity. But as a right. It is your right. Do you hear? It is your right! . . .

. . . And it is your right that every child shall have a complete education. That no person aged and infirm shall want or beg for bread. That the man who produces something shall be able to carry it to market without miring to the hub, without toll. That no poor man's house or land shall be taxed. That the rich men and the great companies that draw wealth from this state shall pay this state a fair share. That you shall not be deprived of hope! (277)

Long both made and fulfilled the same promises, built a charity hospital and, even today, remains perhaps best known as the man who paved Louisiana. Stark similarly lives up to his word. The hospital becomes for him an all-consuming project as his search for a developer and director becomes a nearly endless pursuit. Jack, meanwhile, praises the new roads stretching across the state. "You'll have to say this for the Boss," he comments at one point: "when he got through you could drive out for a breath of air and still keep your bridgework in place" (55). On a more private note, Stark's after-hours activities also look like Long's. His infidelities to Lucy, who, like Rose Long, eventually leaves her husband to return to her family, begin during his first term, when, on a business trip to Chicago, he had begun a brief affair with a showgirl. His philandering later turns more flagrant as he ends an affair with Sadie—like Long's with Alice Lee Grosjean—to begin one with Anne Stanton, society belle and sister of Adam Stanton, the surgeon he so doggedly courts to run his new hospital. Even his less scandalous pastimes resemble Long's own, particularly his fanaticism for football at what is never called LSU, but which Jack often refers to by such tags as "Dear old State" (389). Though Stark has a more personal reason than Long did for his contact with the team—his son Tom has become one of its standouts—his presence is almost as intrusive. Williams writes that Long often interfered at practices, intervened, during games, from his seat on the sidelines, occasionally even attempted to coach the team (*HL* 504–12). Stark, similarly, makes half-time speeches in the locker room, bullies the coaching staff, even threatens a player or two. Both politically and personally, the Stark of his second gubernatorial term is much the Long of his overlapping terms as governor and U.S. senator.

Despite the fact that Willie at least attempts a reformation after Tom suffers a paralyzing, soon fatal football injury, his past catches up with him and, as did Long, he meets an early and violent end. As several critics have noted, the scene in which an enraged Adam Stanton fires two shots into a surprised Willie Stark is closer to the September 8, 1935, meeting of Carl Austin Weiss and Huey Pierce Long than comparable scenes in any other novel. As did Long's assassination, Willie's takes place immediately following a hastily called legislative session. Jack and Willie walk out into the capitol's domed lobby, where both are surprised to see Adam Stanton. Though initially put at ease by the fact that Adam, like Weiss, seems to be reaching up only to shake the politician's hand, Jack notices the pistol just before it erupts in two shots. The guns of Willie's driver/bodyguard Sugar-Boy O'Sheean and an unnamed highway patrolman then respond more cataclysmically, and Dr. Stanton, as was Dr. Weiss, is killed on the spot. Willie, on the other hand, survives, but no longer than Long did. After an operation at first considered a success, an infection sets in that claims his life soon after the shooting. Before he dies, he asks Jack a question almost identical to that the *New Orleans Times-Picayune* reported Long asking at roughly the same time. Willie asks Jack, "Why did he do it to me?" (424). Long reportedly asked one of his lieutenants, "I wonder why he shot me?"[22] The funeral that follows also sounds much like Long's. As Burden describes it, it is "a hell of a big funeral," one that jams the streets with everyone from courthouse regulars to "red-necks and wool-hat boys" on pavement for the first time in their lives (425). Stark thus dies, as he had often—but not always—lived: like Huey Long himself.

Payne's argument, therefore, is valid: *All the King's Men* is "much more directly based on the historical Huey Long than the words 'suggested,' 'atmosphere,' 'line of thinking and feeling' and 'world of myth' can possibly imply." Stark grows up in Long's surroundings; farms, peddles, studies, and practices law like Long; initially speaks, like Long, for "the tongue-tied population of honest men"; is carried into the governor-

---

22. David Zinman, *The Day Huey Long Was Shot: September 8, 1935*, rev. ed. (Jackson: University Press of Mississippi, 1993), 128.

ship, like Long, on the shoulders of a mostly rural following; and builds a corrupt machine that wields unprecedented political power. If such a sketch sounds like that of what Langley called the universal demagogue, Stark, like Crawford—but far less strictly, it must be said—has characteristics that point toward one and only one demagogue. He bribes his way around impeachment, primarily by means of blackmail; is assassinated under circumstances almost identical to those of Long's last days; and, still more strictly, both looks and talks like Long. Several critics point to the similarity between, for instance, Long's "I know the hearts of the people, because I have not colored my own" and Stark's "My study is the heart of the people," and to the fact that they even share the same memory. As Jack puts it at one point, Willie, like both Long and Martin, is "like the circus elephant," for "he never forgot anything" (18). Two critics take such correspondences still farther, arguing that *All the King's Men* is more a *roman à clef* than any kind of more purely imaginative work. Payne finds Tiny Duffy "a reasonably accurate portrait" of O. K. Allen, Sadie Burke "clearly a modified picture" of Alice Lee Grosjean, Lucy Stark a character "similar in many ways" to Rose Long, Sugar-Boy O'Sheean a "composite" of bodyguard/drivers Joe Messina and Murphy Roden, and Adam Stanton a character "recognizably like" Carl Austin Weiss. Louisa Foulke Newlin, who cites every relevant study but Payne's, corroborates his claims about Sadie and Sugar-Boy but finds Tiny Duffy a composite of Long lieutenants O. K. Allen, James Noe, John Fournet, and Richard Leche. She also finds Adam Stanton a composite of Carl Weiss and Urban Maes, a young doctor who accepted an appointment as head of surgery at the LSU medical school only upon securing from Long a promise, like that Stanton demands from Stark, that the state would not interfere with his office.[23] Yet even more than turning *All the King's Men* into a biography and Robert Penn Warren into a biographer, what these studies do, to their discredit, is ignore the more creative aspects of the novel, rob it of what sets it so far apart from Basso's *Cinnamon Seed* and Dos Passos's *Number One*, not to mention Williams's *Huey Long* and Hair's *The Kingfish and His Realm*. More than just a dry translation of fact into fiction, *All the King's Men* is a

23. Payne, 585, 590, 591, 593; Newlin, 36–37, 41–42.

novel that succeeds not because of the facts it appropriates from Long's life, but because of the fictional life that arises from—sometimes even in spite of—that same material. It succeeds, even excels, in other words, because of the fictional character who is, not the historical figure who was.

Even in light of its indisputable bulk, critics have made claims against the ultimate relevance of the history incorporated into *All the King's Men.* In one of the first articles published on the novel, Robert B. Heilman argues that, though Warren "begins with history and politics," his "real subject" is "the nature of man." Warren "is no more discussing American politics," he claims, "than *Hamlet* is discussing Danish politics." What Warren *is* discussing, Garrett Epps has written, is "the nature of time, God, reality, and the human soul." What all too few have noticed, though, is the irrefutable link between the historical fact on which Payne focuses and the ahistorical fiction on which Heilman and Epps focus. Indeed, in *All the King's Men,* Long's biography becomes the means to something somewhere between fact and fiction, but something that, at the same time, is also more than their mere combination: an intersection in which the fiction, especially compared to that in the other novels examined here, is just as inspired by, but, paradoxically, is more independent of, the incorporated historical fact. In *The Achievement of Robert Penn Warren,* James H. Justus suggests connections between Long's practice of collecting blackmail material and what he refers to as Stark's "pungent doctrine of man." What began with Long's "son-of-a-bitch book," his record of offenses that demanded retaliation,[24] and led to what Williams asserts was a lockbox full of information that could be used to accomplish that revenge (*HL* 751) clearly becomes, in *All the King's Men,* Jack's safety deposit box filled with little black books full of information potentially damaging to any number of sons of bitches. Warren's appropriation of Long's performance on the bar exam, for instance, leads to little more

24. Robert B. Heilman, "*All the King's Men* as Tragedy," in Beebe and Field, 80; Epps, 90; James H. Justus, *The Achievement of Robert Penn Warren* (Baton Rouge: Louisiana State University Press, 1981), 193; Raymond Gram Swing, "Forerunner of American Fascism," in *Huey Long,* ed. Hugh Davis Graham (Englewood Cliffs: Prentice-Hall, 1970), 98.

than a dramatization of Stark's unique motivation and intelligence; his appropriation of Long's lockbox, however, explodes into Stark's all-encompassing belief in the ever-presence and unending repercussions of wrongdoing. Williams might tell us that Long too believed that he could always find the proverbial skeleton in the back of his opponents' closets (*HL* 751), but what Warren articulates by translating this one particular fact into fiction is nothing less than the center of Stark's being. He does so not to create a realistic backdrop for his story, and certainly not to try his hand at the then-popular Huey Long novel, but to create and examine a character whose oft-voiced beliefs on the subject of good and evil constitute a cohesive individual philosophy—one whose implications, far more than those of any other element from the life of Huey Long, eventually expand to become the central concerns of *All the King's Men*.

By the time Warren wrote *All the King's Men* around Stark's philosophy, he had been addressing its component parts for decades. He called himself a naturalist and often denied belief in God, but Warren often confessed a lifelong interest in the Bible, the Old Testament in particular. According to Joseph Blotner, his primary biographer, Warren was a man "without religious faith," but "of religious temperament." He told one interviewer that, when he was a child, his family had been "very un-churchy": his father had not joined the church until late in his life, and he only did so then, Warren suspected, out of a sense of social obligation. At the same time, though, because he considered it one of the "foundation[s] of society," he paid his young son to read the Bible. Over the next several years, Warren would read it at least three times through, a great rarity, it would seem, for such an avowed nonbeliever. He told another interviewer that, as a Vanderbilt undergraduate required to attend chapel, he had "tried to talk myself into some religion . . . but no dice. Vice won. But I kept on reading the Old Testament." The influence would remain apparent all around him for much, if not all, of his life. Blotner reports that Warren nicknamed his 1931 Studebaker "Original Sin," for he found it "damn near" as "indestructible," and several years later his daughter Rosanna would recall that "Original Sin" was one of the first phrases she heard her father utter. The term was "pounded into" her ears, she explains. "He was constantly joking about it"—but that, she emphasizes, means "he believed in it." One of the most predominant themes in his work, consequently, concerns just that notion—or, even if not articulated precisely so, then a nonetheless orthodox belief in pervasive personal guilt and the fear of eventual accountability for it. Whether one calls it sin, crime, or simple wrongdoing, it resurfaces in Warren's works, no matter how long, how deeply, or how long ago buried. As he wrote in 1924 to friend and fellow Fugitive Allen Tate, "The past, though trivial, has often long fingers that follow us in the dark."[25]

The works Warren published before *All the King's Men* are often rife with guilt-ridden figures who flee these fingers and the retribution trailing behind them. One of the first is Big Jim Todd, the "slick black buck" at the heart of his 1928 poem "Pondy Woods." Big Jim spends most of the poem on his belly in a swamp listening for horse hooves and footfalls on a nearby road. His specific crime is never revealed, but the ominous vulture that berates him for much of the poem has no doubt of his guilt and therefore advises him to run, for "The posse will get you . . . / There's a fellow behind you with a big shot-gun." The "long fingers" come closer to the subject of Warren's sole biography, *John Brown: The Making of a Martyr*. Warren's Brown is frequently forced to account for his part in a number of crimes, among them the small but bloody 1856 massacre of five proslavery settlers outside the Kansas Territory's Pottawatomie Creek. He begins denying direct involvement almost immediately afterward, but as late as three and a half years later, as he awaits his date with the sour apple tree for his actions at Harper's Ferry, questions about Pottawatomie continue to hound him. No matter how "trivial" it may seem, one's past, as Warren shows us, is inescapable. Evil will out, for the "long fingers" will follow their prey until they find it. At the center of *Night Rider,* Warren's first novel, are multiple acts of economic terrorism that, though intended to be anonymous, eventually subject their perpetrators to the same kind of pursuit. The wife of a murdered farmer was not to know who

---

25. Blotner, *Robert Penn Warren,* 450, 379, 32, 141, 373; David Farrell, "Reminiscences: A Conversation with Robert Penn Warren," in Watkins, Hiers, and Weeks, 286–87; William Bedford Clark, ed., *Selected Letters of Robert Penn Warren,* vol. 1, *The Apprentice Years, 1924–1934* (Baton Rouge: Louisiana State University Press, 2000), 32.

took her husband from her at gunpoint, nor were several farmers to know who burned their barns and destroyed their tobacco beds. Evil again begins to out, though, and the novel's central character, Percy Munn, soon finds himself the subject of more than the usual amount of local gossip. Soon thereafter, he finds his own farm torched, is forced to flee his home county and hide elsewhere, and ultimately exits the novel only with federal troops at his heels.[26] Because of those indefatigable fingers, wrongdoing in Warren's early works cannot remain anonymous, simply will not go unpunished.

Crimes become more general, criminals more universal, as Warren continues to write his way toward *All the King's Men.* The wrongdoing at the heart of two companion poems from the early 1940s varies with their readers—for we, in short, are the culprits they incriminate. At the beginning of "Crime" (1940), we are told not to pity but to envy "the mad killer who lies in the ditch and grieves," for he has already forgotten "what it was he buried under the leaves." Whether it was an elderly woman, a stranger who asked him for a match, or a child he saw in the park, Warren's psychopath simply cannot remember. Yet despite the blood that stains the killer's hands, the speaker repeats that we should envy him, for "what he buried is buried" and will remain so until someone else happens upon it. What we have buried, though— and the poem, as would Willie Stark, implies that we all have something buried—will not stay buried, for our healthier consciences, more susceptible than the killer's to guilt, will not let us forget it. No matter how assiduously we try to hide it in the metaphorical attic of the final stanza, the letter—the record, whether literal or figurative, that remains of our crime—still "Names over your name." The guilt to which Warren subjects Big Jim Todd and Percy Munn is now yours, now mine, now everyone's but the mad killer's, our common payment for common crimes committed alongside one another. Warren further foregrounds these beliefs in "Original Sin: A Short Story," a poem he

26. Robert Penn Warren, "Pondy Woods," in *The Collected Poems of Robert Penn Warren,* ed. John Burt (Baton Rouge: Louisiana State University Press, 1998), 39–40; Robert Penn Warren, *John Brown: The Making of a Martyr* (1929; reprint, Nashville: J. S. Sanders, 1992); Robert Penn Warren, *Night Rider* (1939; reprint, Nashville: J. S. Sanders, 1992).

first published in 1942. The hero of the piece is "you," the villain, of sorts, a vividly drawn personification of Original Sin. The poem begins,

> Nodding, its great head rattling like a gourd,
> And locks like seaweed strung on stinking stone,
> The nightmare shambles past. . . .

You have encountered it constantly, heard it trying to get at you nearly everywhere you've lived, no matter how far away or how often you may have moved: "it thought no bed too narrow." The two of you, however, are on more congenial terms than one might expect. Despite its frightful persistence, you tolerate it almost complacently. In the last stanza, it tries to get at you while you sleep in yet another bed, but since there is "nothing remarkable in that sound at the door," you hardly stir, leaving it to wander the house and yard acknowledged but not necessarily feared.[27] Warren had implicated only his own characters in previous works, but he implicates us all in "Crime" and "Original Sin." Our common legacy, as he sees it, is a past riddled with wrong that so eludes our attempts to evade or erase it that the best we can hope for is insanity, oblivion, or hard-won indifference.

When Warren turns from his readers to point fingers again at his characters, he comes strikingly close to issues later to be found at the heart of *All the King's Men*. *At Heaven's Gate* so often prefigures *All the King's Men* that Warren described writing the latter novel as a "continuation of the experience of writing" the former. Ashby Wyndham, certainly, lives every day of his life with the kind of guilt that permeates *All the King's Men*. Unlike Todd, Brown, Munn, and the universal addressees of "Crime" and "Original Sin," however, Wyndham never becomes accustomed to it. In the jailhouse statement that punctuates so much of the novel, he confesses to one assault after another, as well as to abandoning his wife upon the death of their young son. His tortured consideration of one moral lapse in particular, his sexual affair with the woman he would marry only after the fact, comes close to prefiguring *All the King's Men*'s central image:

27. Robert Penn Warren, "Crime," in Burt, 68–69; Robert Penn Warren, "Original Sin: A Short Story," in Burt, 69–70.

I taken no thought and it was my sin. I ain't never said it was Maries sin. When a man ever does a sin he ain't done it secret and him
private. He has done taken his own sin on his shoulders, but another mans sin too to bear him down. You throw a rock in a pond
and it don't make but one splash but they is ripples runs out from
it. I sinned and taken Maries sin on my shoulders for Judgemint.
It was my fault she taken spot and had blemish laid on to her.

Other authors have put this image to similar use. In *I Henry VI*, for
instance, Shakespeare's Joan la Pucelle compares glory to

> a circle in the water,
> Which never ceaseth to enlarge itself
> Till by broad spreading it disperse to naught

but Wyndham's use of the image to embody ever-replicating "sin" is
so similar to Burden's, as we shall see, as to be almost identical. *At
Heaven's Gate* foreshadows *All the King's Men* even more notably in
that, toward the end of the novel, this figurative image becomes literal.
Previous Warren works may also reify the image—Brown's guilt, for
instance, infects his sons, Munn's his wife—but this is the first time in
Warren's works that ripples reach those so far removed from the
stone's throw. The example Wyndham sets by refusing all opportunity
to evade responsibility for his crime so unsettles Milt Porsum, a war
hero turned bank president, that he shames himself into confessing the
scheme by which he and his business associates—one of whom has
what Warren called "points of essential similarity" to Willie Stark—are
attempting to defraud an entire state.[28] Given the "essential similarity"
not only between Bogan Murdock and Willie Stark but between the
representations and repercussions of crime at the heart of each novel,
All the King's Men, it seems, was but the next natural step for Warren.

One of Stark's most overriding beliefs is in the wrongdoing of which
he suspects all guilty, the wrongdoing central to so many of Warren's
previous works. At the beginning of *All the King's Men*, when he first

28. Warren, introduction to *All the King's Men* (1953), iii; Robert Penn Warren, *At
Heaven's Gate* (1943; reprint, New York: New Directions, 1985), 120; *I Henry VI* 1.2.133–35.

asks Jack to look into Montague Irwin's past, Jack, exhibiting his decades-long allegiance to the old judge, demands, "[S]uppose there isn't
anything to find?" Stark answers, "There is always something." When
Jack responds, "Maybe not on the Judge," Willie launches for the first
time into what will become for him something of a mantra: "Man is
conceived in sin and born in corruption and he passeth from the stink
of the didie to the stench of the shroud. There is always something"
(54). The significance of this contention can hardly be overstated. Jack
repeats his boss's particular expression of it twice, and much later,
when he and Willie revisit the subject of Judge Irwin, we hear echoes
of it again. In response to Jack's refusal to frame the judge, Willie responds,

> "Boy . . . I'm not asking you to frame him. I never asked you to
> frame anybody. Did I?"
> "No."
> "I never did ask you to frame anybody. And you know why?"
> "No."
> "Because it ain't ever necessary. You don't ever have to frame
> anybody, because the truth is always sufficient."
> "You sure take a high view of human nature . . ."
> "Boy . . . I went to a Presbyterian Sunday school back in the
> days when they still had some theology, and that much of it stuck."
> (358)

What stuck, it seems clear—influenced as Stark is by concepts like
man's birth in "corruption"—is the doctrine of Original Sin. Just as
"God made little green apples with worms in them" (65), as Jack is
fond of saying, He also, according to Willie, created men and women
with innate predispositions toward wrongdoing. Warren, from "Pondy
Woods" to *Night Rider*, from "Original Sin" to *At Heaven's Gate*, had
been saying the same for decades.

The corollary to this belief in the ever-presence of what Willie calls
dirt is that the knowledge of that dirt has a definite pragmatic value.
After commenting on how much of the Presbyterian theology from his
childhood still maintains its hold on him, Willie smirks, adding that
he had found its implications "very valuable" (358). In *All the King's
Men*, this value most often derives from dirt's usefulness as ammuni-

tion in battles between opposing politicians. Trying to change Judge Irwin's opinion of one opponent in particular, for instance, Willie suggests that his record might not be as spotless as the old man believes. "Callahan's been playing round for a long time," he insinuates, "and he who touches pitch shall be defiled, and little boys just will walk barefoot in the cow pasture" (51). Such assertions on Stark's part are rarely just empty claims. After another opponent speaks a bit too freely of him on Capitol Hill, Willie offers a nationwide radio audience a none-too-flattering version of his biography, one in which, as Jack sardonically puts it, he "didn't come off too well" (245). The most significant use to which Willie puts dirt, though, is in extending his tenure in the governor's mansion. Jack's most vivid recollections of the late nights after the six-, seven-, and eight-speech days of the impeachment proceedings are of his boss, sitting in the Cadillac, sending for whichever legislators happened to be sleeping in one darkened house after another. "Tell him to come out. I know he's there. Tell him he better come out and talk to me," Stark would threaten. "If he won't come, just say you're a friend of Ella Lou. That'll bring him" (156). That, or something of the sort, would always bring them, and there would soon be standing next to the car a white-faced, pajama-clad man shivering in the darkness. Or if they were indoors, in Willie's office, perhaps, he would say, "Bring the bastard in. Bring him in." And when they brought him in, Willie would look him over, explain, "This is your last chance," then quickly lean forward and holler, "God damn you, do you know what I can do to you?" "And he could do it, too," Jack adds, for "he had the goods" (157). Willie, then, knows not only that "there is always something," but that that "something" can be useful—that it, in short, *is* "the goods." Knowledge, as Jack puts it, "is power" (331).

Yet Willie does more with this dirt than just safeguard his stay in the governor's mansion. When he speaks of its varied uses, in fact, he rarely speaks of its baser applications. Dirt, he declares, is the stuff of all creation. To Judge Irwin, at one point, he philosophizes: "Dirt's a funny thing. . . . Come to think of it, there ain't a thing but dirt on this green God's globe except what's under water, and that's dirt too. It's dirt makes the grass grow. A diamond ain't a thing in the world but a piece of dirt that got awful hot. And God-a-Mighty picked up a handful of dirt and blew on it and made you and me and George

Washington and mankind blessed in faculty and apprehension" (50). Several metaphors continue this line of reasoning: just as "you don't make omelettes without breaking eggs" (132), just as you don't make bricks without straw—"and most of the time all the straw you got is secondhand straw from the cowpen" (145–46)—you cannot make good without bad, as Willie sees it. "[T]here isn't anything else to make it out of" (272), he claims at one point, an assertion *All the King's Men* corroborates on several occasions. Were it not for the death of three and the crippling of nine schoolchildren, for example, Willie might not have returned to politics to improve the schools of their former classmates; were it not for his blackmailing of one politician after another, he would not have survived impeachment to promise their constituents a charity hospital. Looking back on his boss's career some three years after the assassination, Jack begins to piece together his understanding of Willie's approach to this process:

> The theory of historical costs, you might put it. All change costs something. You have to write off the costs against the gain. Maybe in our state change could only come in the terms in which it was taking place, and it was sure due for some change. The theory of the moral neutrality of history, you might call it. Process as process is neither morally good nor morally bad. We may judge results but not process. The morally bad agent may perform the deed which is good. The morally good agent may perform the deed which is bad. Maybe a man has to sell his soul to get the power to do good.
>
> The theory of historical costs. The theory of the moral neutrality of history. All that was a high historical view from a chilly pinnacle. Maybe it took a genius to see it. To really see it. Maybe you had to get chained to the high pinnacle with the buzzards pecking at your liver and lights before you could see it. Maybe it took a genius to see it. Maybe it took a hero to act on it. (417–18)

From a distance of years, Jack thereby rationalizes his boss's immoral, if not illegal acts of office, forgiving Willie's often unethical means in the name of his nonetheless noble ends. Since we can "judge results but not process," and have to "write off the costs against the gain," we as readers, if we agree with Jack, must see Willie as a man who, although a "morally bad agent," is, in the end, also something of "a hero."

Yet, even if we accept this verdict, we must also realize that while Willie may identify, employ, and even benefit from the laws he so often elucidates, he still tries to defy one of their central tenets. Willie may teach Jack that "there is always something," and that that "something" often has a concrete pragmatic application, but he misses the fact that, as Jack learns only upon returning to his once-abandoned doctoral dissertation, every act—not just the morally corrupt act—can set in motion an unforeseen series of events. Summarizing for us the lesson of Cass Mastern, the guilt-ridden subject of his long-neglected dissertation, Jack writes that

> Cass Mastern lived for a few years and in that time he learned that the world is all of one piece. He learned that the world is like an enormous spider web and if you touch it, however lightly, at any point, the vibration ripples to the remotest perimeter and the drowsy spider feels the tingle and is drowsy no more but springs out to fling the gossamer coils about you who have touched the web and then inject the black, numbing poison under your hide. It does not matter whether or not you meant to brush the web of things. Your happy foot or your gay wing may have brushed it ever so lightly, but what happens always happens and there is the spider, bearded black and with his great faceted eyes glittering like mirrors in the sun, or like God's eye, and the fangs dripping. (200)

What Jack learns from Cass is but a slight modification of what he learns from Willie—but whereas Willie's depends upon moral considerations, Jack's ignores morality altogether. While Willie asserts that one immoral act by one hand can lead to further immoral acts by another, Cass convinces Jack that all acts, no matter what their moral character, can unleash a chaotic series of further acts whose end may never be known. The difference, though subtle, is significant.

Though we have no way of knowing whether Willie recognizes this distinction on his deathbed, we can say that a demonstration of Mastern's perspective, as well as Willie's attempt to defy one of his own laws, is what lands him on that deathbed in the first place. That attempt comes when Willie, as governor, refuses to let Tiny Duffy oversee the contracts for the construction of the new hospital. Jack notes the incongruity between this and Willie's standard approach to such transactions on two separate occasions. "If he believed that you had to make the good out of the bad because there wasn't anything else to make it out of," Jack asks, "why did he stir up such a fuss about keeping Tiny's hands off the Willie Stark Hospital?" (278). "Why did he get so heated up just because Tiny's brand of Bad might get mixed in the raw materials from which he was going to make some Good?" (276).[29] Eventually, Willie has no choice but to let Duffy make the arrangements. After his son Tom's accident, though, at the beginning of his short-lived reformation, he reneges on his commitment. The web then vibrates and, ironically, ripples all the way back to the moment when Willie first asked Jack to dig for dirt on Judge Irwin. For in the process of researching the "Case of the Upright Judge," Jack had uncovered dirt on both Irwin and his friend the former governor, Anne and Adam's father—which he then uses to alter the Stantons' opinion of their late father so dramatically that Adam accepts the directorship of the hospital, and Anne becomes Willie's mistress. Upon Willie's revocation of the hospital contracts, Duffy exposes to Adam the dirt on his sister and his new boss, and the doctor fires two shots into Willie. By trying to defy the law he seemed to understand so completely—by trying to keep bad from producing good—Willie thus brushes the spider web that he himself had spun by demanding dirt on Judge Irwin so many years before. The law thus proves more tenacious than its propounder, and because of Willie's simultaneous applications of and attempts to defy the laws he had come so close to mastering, he meets his early end.

Jack's recognition of this miscalculation notwithstanding, he labels Willie, as we have seen, "[m]aybe . . . a hero." His final judgment, initially almost as halfhearted, is ultimately somewhat more firm. When Lucy asserts at the end of the novel that "Willie was a great man," Jack tells us that he "nodded, I suppose." Later, though, perhaps as late as the novel's composition some three years after the fact, Jack, for reasons he does not divulge, comes closer to fully agreeing. Still, like the "[m]aybe" that precedes the "hero," his acknowledgment seems

---

29. This line has no counterpart in Polk's restored edition.

coerced, like something he has made himself affirm: "I must believe that Willie Stark was a great man. What happened to his greatness is not the question. Perhaps he spilled it on the ground the way you spill a liquid when the bottle breaks. Perhaps he piled up his greatness and burnt it in one great blaze in the dark like a bonfire and then there wasn't anything but dark and the embers winking. Perhaps he could not tell his greatness from ungreatness and so mixed them together that what was adulterated got lost. But he had it. I must believe that" (452). Jack's ambivalence is checked, however, by way of an unlikely agent: Ellis Burden, the man he had been raised to believe his father, a man who has little positive to say about his putative son's employer. "Foulness" and "All foulness" are the comments Stark's name elicits from him earlier in the novel (214, 215). Years later, though, toward the end of *All the King's Men*, the so-called Scholarly Attorney, with Jack's assistance, works to complete a religious tract that contains the following paragraph:

> The creation of man whom God in His foreknowledge knew doomed to sin was the awful index of God's omnipotence. For it would have been a thing of trifling and contemptible ease for Perfection to create mere perfection. To do so would, to speak truth, be not creation but extension. Separateness is identity and the only way for God to create, truly create, man was to make him separate from God Himself, and to be separate from God is to be sinful. The creation of evil is therefore the index of God's glory and His power. That had to be so that the creation of good might be the index of man's glory and power. But by God's help. By His help and in His wisdom. (462–63)

Incorporation, in the end, implies endorsement. By writing the paragraph into his record, Jack indirectly bestows on Willie a kind of praise he could not otherwise offer. And if, in the end, this passage too contains a qualifier—for few would argue that Willie had lived "by God's help . . . and in His wisdom"—the words that precede it praise him in terms of which Jack himself is hardly capable. His belief that Willie turned bad into good, coupled with the Scholarly Attorney's assertion that doing so demonstrates "the index of man's glory and power," equals an implied argument on Jack's part that Willie Stark—on the final pages of the novel, at least—is something of a god among men, an earthly creator wielding the utmost forces at humanity's disposal. Warren's decades of arguments to the contrary, much of *All the King's Men* amounts to an incorporation of detail from Long's biography into the story of a man who, although much like him, is at the same time as much unlike him. Out of the shared facts of their lives arises a character who is not Huey Long, for, as Warren argued time and again, he did not know Huey Long, and therefore could not—and anyway had no desire to—replicate him in fiction. The sixth and, as of this point, final disguised fictionalization of Long is thus a character who, though he does much what his predecessors do, is also much more than what they are. At various points he too is an American dictator, a dismantler of the old order, a manipulator of "ruined words," and a husband and father gone far astray. As much as anything else, though, Stark is not just a politician who wields an unprecedented amount of personal power but an amateur philosopher who studies that power with an assiduity and, ultimately, an understanding that far surpasses that of his predecessors—as well as, as best we can tell, Huey Long himself. *All the King's Men*, consequently, is the one such novel to transcend its historical particulars enough to earn the designation "philosophical novel" as Warren himself defined it. According to his oft-quoted introduction to the 1954 Modern Library edition of Joseph Conrad's *Nostromo*, such a novel is one in which "the documentation of the world is constantly striving to rise to the level of generalization about values," in which "the image strives to rise to symbol" and "the urgency of experience, no matter how vividly and strongly experience may enchant, is the urgency to know the meaning of experience." More than any other author examined here, Warren transcends "the urgency of experience, no matter how vividly and strongly" it may have "enchant[ed]" Lewis, Basso, Dos Passos, and Langley, to examine "the meaning of experience" as a whole. As he wrote in his first introduction to the novel, *All the King's Men* "was never intended to be a book about politics. Politics merely provided the framework story in which the deeper concerns . . . might work themselves out."[30] Stark's primary

---

30. Robert Penn Warren, introduction to *Nostromo*, by Joseph Conrad (1904; reprint, New York: Modern Library, 1951), xxxviii; Warren, introduction to *All the King's Men* (1953), vi.

interest, of course—as it is also Windrip's, Brand's, Slade's, Crawford's, and Martin's—is amassing and maintaining personal power, but
in that Warren shows him studying how one does so, especially as that
effort involves the dirt he assures us blackens all moral ledgers, what
many take as only an "image" of Huey Long "rise[s] to symbol[ize]"
much more, even the full metaphysical potential of all humanity. In
that he transforms evil into good, Stark demonstrates to its fullest extent—and far more completely than his predecessors—what Ellis Burden refers to as "the index of man's glory and power."

Conclusion
The Fiction and the Myth

IN 1995, AMERICAN CRIME WRITER MAX ALLAN COLLINS published *Blood and Thunder,* the most recent indication of novelists' enduring fascination with the life and assassination of Huey Pierce Long. Beginning in late August 1935, the novel tells the story of Nathan Heller, a Chicago-based private detective hired to deliver Long a bulletproof vest. The senator angrily refuses the gift but, because of recent assassination rumors and his respect for Heller's work (three years earlier, during the 1932 Democratic National Convention, he had served as police liaison for Long and his cadre of bodyguards) he retains the detective to track down his would-be assassins. Returning to Louisiana from Harrisburg, Pennsylvania, where Long had secured a publisher for *My First Days in the White House,* his former mistress, Alice Jean Crosley, briefs Heller on the rumors and each of several potential suspects. (As Long biographer Thomas O. Harris had put it, Louisiana "was filled with them" at the time. Any of those who "suffered" under his "dictatorship"—and Harris catalogues dozens—"were potential slayers of Huey P. Long.")[1] After a week of investigation in Baton Rouge and New Orleans, though, Heller not only uncovers no assassination plots but fails to protect his client at the moment he most needs it: just after a special legislative session on the night of Sunday, September 8, in his one and only encounter with a young surgeon named Carl Austin Weiss.

In addition to dramatizing still further chapters from the life of Long, *Blood and Thunder* illustrates again the difference between historical fiction and fictionalized history. Because it inserts fictional characters into a background so historically accurate that its Huey

---

1. Thomas O. Harris, *The Kingfish: Huey P. Long, Dictator* (1938; reprint, Baton Rouge: Claitor's, 1968), 257.

Long character is named Huey Long, *Blood and Thunder* is the former more than the latter. As Collins himself explains, the novel has an "extensive basis in history." He confesses to taking occasional liberties with the facts—no one named Nathan Heller drove the wounded Huey Long to the hospital that night, for instance—but insists that he takes as few of them as possible.[2] The statement is ultimately superfluous, however, for what we see of Long in *Blood and Thunder* is much what we see of him in the sources Collins cites in his bibliography: Long's *Every Man a King,* Williams's *Huey Long,* and Hair's *The Kingfish and His Realm* only three among dozens. Collins may have to remind us that Long did once refuse a bulletproof vest delivered him from Chicago, but for the most part his characterization of Long and his dramatization of the last week of his life are so close to the record—though they cannot, of course, duplicate or reproduce it—that they need no such justification. Upon deciding to call his character Huey Long, it seems, Collins also decided to forfeit much of his artistic license: he might select from and arrange an array of factual detail—as would the historian—but when Long himself walks into any particular scene, Collins becomes almost as much biographer as novelist.

In the case of Long's former mistress, though, Collins freely employs the license he earns by using what Turner calls a disguise. In a prefatory note to the novel, Collins explains that, on the pages that follow, historical figures walk side by side with composite as well as entirely fictional characters. While Long is the best example of the former, Heller the best example of the latter, Alice Jean Crosley is the best example of a composite. Collins asserts that Crosley is a fictional character but also admits that she has a "real-life counterpart."[3] For as is Alice Jean Crosley, Alice Lee Grosjean—also the inspiration for Langley's Sunny Lou McMenimee, it would seem, as well as, perhaps, Warren's Sadie Burke—was a beautiful, brilliant brunette who, at the age of only eighteen, signed on with Long's gubernatorial campaign staff. She too became Long's confidential secretary, then possibly his mistress and, briefly, his secretary of state. By referring to the character by a fictional name, Collins is free to embellish or even ignore alto-

2. Max Allan Collins, *Blood and Thunder* (New York: Dutton, 1995), 313.
3. Collins, 314.

gether her archetype's appearances in the factual record. When Long asks Heller to keep Alice Jean occupied, for instance—the presence of a woman rumored to be his mistress would not reflect well on a man planning to run for the White House, after all—Collins is free to depict the two in scene after scene that did not, in fact, take place. Collins's respect for the historical record forces him not just to attribute to his Huey Long only the words and actions of the historical Huey Long (or reasonable approximations thereof) but to alter the name of Long's alleged mistress lest he attribute fictional words and actions to a historical figure. *Blood and Thunder*'s lesson about historical fiction and fictionalized history, then, is that, while writers forgoing disguises often feel compelled to represent history as recorded (but not always—see Robert Coover's *The Public Burning* [1977], for instance), those who employ disguises can free themselves from the demands of historicity to present scenes of their own creation in addition to, or even instead of, the scenes history records.

Between 1934 and 1946, five American novelists employed this strategy in a handful of novels that fictionalize, to a greater or lesser degree, the life and career of Huey Pierce Long. Not one of the five refers to the Long character as Huey Long. Most, in fact, try to dissuade readers from making any connection between factual figure and fictional character—a move that gives them license to use history as a means to whatever narrative ends they desire. In what he later described as an overt attempt to sabotage Long's designs on the White House, Sinclair Lewis cast his Long character as an American incarnation of the 1930s totalitarian menace, a sort of homegrown Hitler. To dramatize the lamentable but inevitable decline he found the transition from Old South to New, Hamilton Basso created two Long characters, each a rabble-rousing affront to what remained of the old order. To warn Americans of the pitfalls inherent in the politician-constituent contract, John Dos Passos created a Long character who manipulates his followers with once-revered, but increasingly empty words and phrases. Adria Locke Langley's fictionalized Long embodies faults both public and private, in the end becoming the single such figure most completely condemned for political as well as spousal and parental failings. Robert Penn Warren's Long, finally, is almost as much philosopher as politician: though considered for several decades now *the* fictional incarnation of the Kingfish, Willie Stark, ironically, is much less based on the historical Huey Long than many of his now largely forgotten predecessors. His reputation, it would seem, lies in the fact that, though he is among the least historical of Huey Long figures, he is undoubtedly the most compelling fictional character of the lot.

In "The Value of Narrativity in the Representation of Reality," Hayden White addresses not fiction but fact. His primary contention is that it is not novelists but historians who cannot help but impose closure on their narratives, cannot help but submit to the somehow irrepressible desire to have history conclude as tidily as fiction. "Has any historical narrative ever been written," White asks, "that was not informed not only by moral awareness but specifically by the moral authority of the narrator?" Considered in light of this question, the Huey Long novels—though not quite the kind of narratives White had in mind—should not have so infuriated Long's son Russell. When the Long figure leaves the periphery of *Cinnamon Seed* to approach the center of *It Can't Happen Here*, the novel's "moral awareness," its narrator's "moral authority," casts him as a villain who selects as his victim nothing less than the whole of American democracy. The figure becomes a similarly villainous madman, one who takes a tangible role in the piecemeal dismantling of a long-standing and long-cherished social tradition, in *Sun in Capricorn*. Like Lewis's before him, Dos Passos's Long also threatens American democracy—but not, in the end, in its entirety. Less than a decade after its appearance, then, the Long figure's threat had already begun to diminish. Like those ever-widening ripples around the stone's throw Ashby Wyndham describes in *At Heaven's Gate*, the repercussions were already dissipating. Langley's Long not only poses a still more localized threat but, all too human, succumbs to temptation more than simply degenerating into such a one-dimensional embodiment of evil as Windrip or Slade. Willie Stark, finally, even if not entirely sympathetic, is ultimately elevated beyond the realm of ordinary human scrutiny. Burden never can quite call him a hero, but he in no way condemns him as the villain so many of his fellow-narrators do their Long figures. What White describes as the almost irrepressible urge to moralize, therefore, had waned. Lewis's Jessup and Basso's Hazzard are both avowed enemies of the Long figures in their lives, but Verity Martin marries Hank, and Jack Burden as much as panegyrizes Willie. When Long departs the pages of the modern American novel, then, he does so not as the villain Basso so often and adamantly asserted he was but as a hero he argued he could not otherwise have become—a hero he should not have become at all. What Basso most laments in "The Huey Long Legend" is what he likens to an "ascending spiral": "book by book," he complains, the Kingfish "has risen . . . out of the muck of his own brand of totalitarian politics until, when last seen in fiction, he was asking Abraham Lincoln to move over and give him room."

Russell Long, therefore, should perhaps have thanked instead of so publicly denouncing his father's fictionalizers. Robert Penn Warren, after all, has more readers than T. Harry Williams, and as C. Vann Woodward once lamented, fiction is in many cases more responsible than recorded history for the "conceptions, interpretations, convictions, or fantasies" we have about the past. Support for this point comes, ironically, from Williams himself. In detailing Long's early performances on the campaign trail, he cites a 1950 *Southwest Review* article in which historian Arthur Marvin Shaw describes a speech he saw the thirty-two-year-old Long deliver on July 4, 1925. Hardly the blistering diatribe he had hoped to hear, it was instead "strangely mechanical and uninspired." Long's voice, Shaw writes, was "without magic," his hand "without cunning," which ultimately makes the story he has to tell us all the more beguiling, for we eventually watch alongside him as the Long of later speeches becomes the mesmerizing speaker who would lead the Louisiana masses. Williams, however, casts immediate doubt on Shaw's impressions, calling them "sharply at variance" with the facts and "probably influenced" more by fictional speeches Shaw had recently read than the actual speeches he had heard some twenty-five years before. Shaw's Long, Williams concludes, is a little too "suspiciously similar to" the wooden rube Jack Burden describes embarking on his first campaign for governor. If we recall Hayden White's definition of myth—he finds it an intersection of the "real" and the "imaginary" that "is under no obligation to keep the two orders of events . . . distinct from one another"[4]—we therefore watch

4. Hayden White, "The Value of Narrativity in the Representation of Reality," in *The Content of the Form: Narrative Discourse and Historical Representation* (Baltimore: Johns

as fiction still further mythologizes fact, even itself becomes, upon incorporation into articles like Shaw's, something that at least passes for recorded history. And if fact alone can inspire such seemingly indestructible myths as that of the eight-month law degree, how long will it be before fictionalized fact again inspires some future Long authority to cite, perhaps, a story of how the Kingfish, while chopping wood one day, accidentally slipped and cut off two of the toes on his left foot? How long will it be, in other words, before Huey Long himself becomes a "Huey-who-isn't-Huey"? Or, after the eight-month law degree began worming its way into recorded history, after *All the King's Men* and its predecessors began to still further mythologize the so-called facts, can we say with absolute certainty that, to at least some degree, he hasn't been one for decades?

Hopkins University Press, 1987), 21; Hamilton Basso, "The Huey Long Legend," *Life*, 9 December 1946, 121, 110; C. Vann Woodward, "Fictional History and Historical Fiction," in *The Future of the Past* (New York: Oxford University Press, 1989), 235; Arthur Marvin Shaw, "The First Time I Saw Huey," *Southwest Review* 35 (1950): 60, 64; T. Harry Williams, *Huey Long* (1969; reprint, New York: Vintage, 1981), 203; White, "Value of Narrativity," 3–4.

Bibliography

Aaron, Daniel. *Writers on the Left: Episodes in American Literary Communism.* 1961. Reprint, New York: Columbia University Press, 1992.

Adams, J. Donald. "America under the Iron Heel: A Novel by Sinclair Lewis Pictures a Fascist Dictatorship." Review of *It Can't Happen Here,* by Sinclair Lewis. *New York Times Book Review,* 20 October 1935, 1, 31.

Austin, Allen. "An Interview with Sinclair Lewis." *University of Kansas City Review* 24 (1958): 199–210.

Basso, Hamilton. *Beauregard: The Great Creole.* New York: Scribner's, 1933.

———. *Cinnamon Seed.* New York: Scribner's, 1934.

———. *Courthouse Square.* New York: Scribner's, 1936.

———. "The Death and Legacy of Huey Long." *New Republic,* 1 January 1936, 215–18.

———. "Der Fuhrer and the Kingfish." Review of *Huey Long's Louisiana Hayride: The American Rehearsal for Dictatorship, 1928–1940,* by Harnett T. Kane. *New Republic,* 4 August 1941, 162–63.

———. "The Future of the South." *New Republic,* 8 November 1939, 70–74.

———. "Huey Long and His Background." *Harper's Monthly,* May 1935, 663–73.

———. "The Huey Long Legend." *Life,* 9 December 1946, 106–21.

———. "Huey P. Long, Kingfish: The American as Demagogue." In *Mainstream.* New York: Reynal and Hitchcock, 1943.

———. "Huey's Louisiana Heritage." *New Republic,* 30 August 1939, 99–100.

———. *In Their Own Image.* New York: Scribner's, 1935.

———. "The Kingfish: In Memoriam." Review of *The Inside Story of Huey Long* [*sic*], by Carleton Beals; *Huey Long: A Candid Biography,* by Forrest Davis; and *My First Days in the White House,* by Huey P. Long. *New Republic,* 18 December 1935, 177.

———. "Let's Look at the Record." *New Republic,* 20 February 1935, 41–42.

———. "Letters in the South." *New Republic,* 19 June 1935, 162–63.

———. "Mr. Senator, Come Clean!" Review of *Every Man a King*, by Huey P. Long. *New Republic*, 21 February 1934, 54.

———. *Relics and Angels*. New York: Macaulay, 1929.

———. "A Spotlight on the South." *New Republic*, 18 April 1934, 287–88.

———. *Sun in Capricorn*. New York: Scribner's, 1942.

———. *The View from Pompey's Head*. Garden City, N.Y.: Doubleday, 1954.

Beals, Carleton. *The Story of Huey P. Long*. Philadelphia: Lippincott, 1935.

Beebe, Keith. "Biblical Motifs in *All the King's Men*." *Journal of Bible and Religion* 30 (April 1962): 123–30.

Beebe, Maurice, and Leslie A. Field, eds. *Robert Penn Warren's "All the King's Men": A Critical Handbook*. Belmont, Calif.: Wadsworth, 1966.

Belkind, Allen, ed. *Dos Passos, the Critics, and the Writer's Intentions*. Carbondale: Southern Illinois University Press, 1971.

Blackmur, R. P. "Utopia, or Uncle Tom's Cabin." Review of *It Can't Happen Here*, by Sinclair Lewis. *The Nation*, 30 October 1935, 516.

Blake, Nelson Manfred. "How to Learn History from Sinclair Lewis and Other Uncommon Sources." In *American Character and Culture in a Changing World: Some Twentieth-Century Perspectives*, edited by John A. Hague. Contributions in American Studies, vol. 42. Westport: Greenwood, 1979.

Blotner, Joseph. *The Modern American Political Novel, 1900–1960*. Austin: University of Texas Press, 1966.

———. *Robert Penn Warren: A Biography*. New York: Random House, 1997.

Boutell, Clip. "A Literary Lion Cleans Up." *New York Post Magazine*, 29 June 1945, 25.

Bradford, Roark. "Life and Death of a Demagogue." Review of *A Lion Is in the Streets*, by Adria Locke Langley. *New York Times Book Review*, 13 May 1945, 3, 20.

Brickell, Herschell. Review of *It Can't Happen Here*, by Sinclair Lewis. *North American Review* 240 (1935): 543–46.

Brinkley, Alan. *Voices of Protest: Huey Long, Father Coughlin, and the Great Depression*. New York: Knopf, 1982.

Bristow, Gwen. "Gilgo Slade of Louisiana." Review of *Sun in Capricorn*, by Hamilton Basso. *Saturday Review of Literature*, 19 September 1942, 16.

Brookhouser, Frank. "Rise and Fall of a Southern Dictator in Tradition of Long." Review of *All the King's Men*, by Robert Penn Warren. *Philadelphia Inquirer*, 18 August 1946.

Brooks, Cleanth. *The Hidden God: Studies in Hemingway, Faulkner, Yeats, Eliot, and Warren.* New Haven: Yale University Press, 1963.

Burns, Ken, and Richard Kilberg. *Huey Long.* RKB/Florentine Films, 1987.

Burt, John, ed. *The Collected Poems of Robert Penn Warren.* Baton Rouge: Louisiana State University Press, 1998.

Carr, Virginia Spencer. *Dos Passos: A Life.* Garden City, N.Y.: Doubleday, 1984.

Cash, W. J. *The Mind of the South.* 1941. Reprint, Garden City, N.Y.: Doubleday, 1954.

Chen, Jue. "Poetics of Historical Referentiality: Roman a Clef and Beyond." Ph.D. diss., Princeton University, 1997.

Clark, William Bedford, ed. *Selected Letters of Robert Penn Warren.* 2 vols. Baton Rouge: Louisiana State University Press, 2000–2001.

Coates, Robert M. "Five New Novels." Review of *Cinnamon Seed,* by Hamilton Basso. *New Republic,* 28 March 1934, 190–91.

Collins, Max Allan. *Blood and Thunder.* New York: Dutton, 1995.

Commins, Saxe. "Some Powerful Variations on a Huey Long Theme." Review of *All the King's Men,* by Robert Penn Warren. *Cleveland News,* 7 September 1946.

Congressional Record. 80th Cong., 1st sess., 1947. Vol. 93, pt. 1: 438–39.

Cowley, Malcolm. "The Writer as Craftsman: The Literary Heroism of Hamilton Basso." *Saturday Review of Literature,* 27 June 1964, 17–18.

Davis, Forrest. *Huey Long: A Candid Biography.* New York: Dodge, 1935.

Davis, Robert Gorham. "Dr. Adam Stanton's Dilemma." Review of *All the King's Men,* by Robert Penn Warren. *New York Times Book Review,* 18 August 1946, 3, 24.

Dexter, Ethel Hathaway. "Robert Penn Warren's *All the King's Men:* Southern Poet's Novel a Dramatic Story Based on the Real Life of a Famous Demagog—Many Characters Add to Interest." Review of *All the King's Men,* by Robert Penn Warren. *Springfield* (Mass.) *Sunday Union and Republican,* 1 September 1946.

Donaldson, Scott. *Archibald MacLeish: An American Life.* Boston: Houghton Mifflin, 1992.

Dos Passos, John. *Adventures of a Young Man.* New York: Harcourt, Brace and Co., 1939.

———. *The Big Money.* 1936. Reprint, New York: Modern Library, 1937.

———. *Chosen Country.* Boston: Houghton Mifflin, 1951.

———. *District of Columbia.* Boston: Houghton Mifflin, 1952.

———. *The 42nd Parallel.* 1930. Reprint, New York: Modern Library, 1937.

———. *The Grand Design.* Boston: Houghton Mifflin, 1949.

———. *Manhattan Transfer.* 1925. Reprint, Boston: Houghton Mifflin, 1953.

———. *Nineteen Nineteen.* 1932. Reprint, New York: Modern Library, 1937.

———. *Number One.* Boston: Houghton Mifflin, 1943.

———. *Occasions and Protests.* Chicago: Henry Regnery, 1964.

———. *One Man's Initiation: 1917.* 1920. Reprint, Ithaca: Cornell University Press, 1969.

———. Papers. Albert and Shirley Small Special Collections Library. University of Virginia.

———. *Three Soldiers.* 1921. Reprint, New York: Modern Library, 1932.

———. "Washington: The Big Tent." *New Republic,* 14 March 1934, 120–23.

Epps, Garrett. "Politics as Metaphor." *Virginia Quarterly Review* 55 (1979): 75–98.

Fadiman, Clifton. "Red Lewis." Review of *It Can't Happen Here,* by Sinclair Lewis. *New Yorker,* 26 October 1935, 83–84.

Faulkner, William. *Requiem for a Nun.* 1951. Reprint, New York: Vintage, 1975.

Fineran, John Kingston. *The Career of a Tinpot Napoleon: A Political Biography of Huey P. Long.* New Orleans: privately printed, 1932.

Fleishman, Avrom. *The English Historical Novel: Walter Scott to Virginia Woolf.* Baltimore: Johns Hopkins University Press, 1971.

Foley, Barbara. *Telling the Truth: The Theory and Practice of Documentary Fiction.* Ithaca: Cornell University Press, 1986.

Foote, Shelby. "The Novelist's View of History." *Mississippi Quarterly* 17 (1964): 219–25.

Gannett, Lewis. "Books and Things." Review of *All the King's Men,* by Robert Penn Warren. *New York Herald Tribune,* 19 August 1946.

Graham, Hugh Davis, ed. *Huey Long.* Great Lives Observed. Englewood Cliffs, N.J.: Prentice-Hall, 1970.

Gray, Richard. "The American Novelist and American History: A Revaluation of *All the King's Men.*" *Journal of American Studies* 6 (1972): 297–307.

Gregory, Horace. "Dos Passos and the Demagogue." Review of *Number One,* by John Dos Passos. *New York Times Book Review,* 7 March 1943, 1, 18.

Grimshaw, James A., Jr., ed. *Cleanth Brooks and Robert Penn Warren: A Literary Correspondence.* Columbia: University of Missouri Press, 1998.

Grimshaw, James A., Jr., and James A. Perkins, eds. *Robert Penn Warren's "All the King's Men": Three Stage Versions.* Athens: University of Georgia Press, 2000.

Hackett, Alice Payne. "New Novelists of 1945." *Saturday Review of Literature,* 16 February 1946, 8–10.

Hair, William Ivy. *The Kingfish and His Realm: The Life and Times of Huey P. Long.* Baton Rouge: Louisiana State University Press, 1991.

Harris, Thomas O. *The Kingfish: Huey P. Long, Dictator.* 1938. Reprint, Baton Rouge: Claitor's, 1968.

Havard, William C. "The Burden of the Literary Mind: Some Meditations on Robert Penn Warren as Historian." In *Robert Penn Warren: A Collection of Critical Essays,* edited by Richard Gray. Twentieth-Century Views. Englewood Cliffs, N.J.: Prentice-Hall, 1980.

Hemingway, Ernest. *A Farewell to Arms.* 1929. Reprint, New York: Scribner, 1953.

Hicks, Granville. "Sinclair Lewis: Anti-Fascist." Review of *It Can't Happen Here,* by Sinclair Lewis. *New Masses,* 29 October 1935, 22–23.

Hutchens, John K. "On the Books." *New York Herald Tribune Weekly Book Review,* 30 January 1949, 10.

Hutcheon, Linda. *A Poetics of Postmodernism: History, Theory, Fiction.* New York: Routledge, 1988.

Ikerd, Clarence Frye. "Hamilton Basso: A Critical Biography." Ph.D. diss., University of North Carolina, 1974.

Jones, Howard Mumford. "Sound-Truck Caesar." Review of *Number One,* by John Dos Passos. *Saturday Review of Literature,* 6 March 1943, 7–8.

Justus, James H. *The Achievement of Robert Penn Warren.* Baton Rouge: Louisiana State University Press, 1981.

Kane, Harnett T. *Huey Long's Louisiana Hayride: The American Rehearsal for Dictatorship, 1928–1940.* 1941. Reprint, Gretna, La.: Pelican, 1971.

Key, V. O., Jr. *Southern Politics in State and Nation.* New York: Vintage, 1949.

Knoenagel, Axel. "The Historical Context of Sinclair Lewis' *It Can't Happen Here.*" *Southern Humanities Review* 29 (1995): 221–36.

Krieger, Murray. *The Classic Vision: The Retreat from Extremity in Modern Literature.* Baltimore: Johns Hopkins University Press, 1971.

Kurth, Peter. *American Cassandra: The Life of Dorothy Thompson.* Boston: Little, Brown, 1990.

Lake, Inez Hollander. *The Road from Pompey's Head: The Life and Work of Hamilton Basso.* Baton Rouge: Louisiana State University Press, 1999.

Landsberg, Melvin, ed. *John Dos Passos' Correspondence with Arthur K. Mc-Comb, or, "Learn to Sing the Carmagnole."* Niwot: University Press of Colorado, 1991.

Lane, Anthony. "Warring Fictions." *New Yorker,* 26 June 1995, 60–73.

Langley, Adria Locke. *A Lion Is in the Streets.* New York: Whittlesey House, 1945.

Lewis, Sinclair. *Ann Vickers.* 1933. Reprint, New York: Collier, n.d.

———. *Babbitt.* 1922. Reprint, New York: Harcourt Brace Jovanovich, 1950.

———. *Elmer Gantry.* 1927. Reprint, United States of America: Signet, 1967.

———. *It Can't Happen Here.* Garden City, N.Y.: Doubleday-Doran, 1935.

———. *Main Street.* 1920. Reprint, New York: Harcourt Brace Jovanovich, 1948.

———. *The Prodigal Parents.* New York: Doubleday-Doran, 1938.

Lingeman, Richard R. *Sinclair Lewis: Rebel from Main Street.* New York: Random House, 2002.

Long, Huey P. *Every Man a King.* 1933. Reprint, Chicago: Quadrangle, 1964.

———. *My First Days in the White House.* Harrisburg: Telegraph, 1935.

Lovett, Robert Morss. "Mr. Lewis Says It Can." Review of *It Can't Happen Here,* by Sinclair Lewis. *New Republic,* 6 November 1935, 366–67.

Lukács, György. *The Historical Novel.* 1937. Translated by Hannah and Stanley Mitchell. Lincoln: University of Nebraska Press, 1983.

Ludington, Townsend. *John Dos Passos: A Twentieth-Century Odyssey.* New York: Dutton, 1980.

———, ed. *The Fourteenth Chronicle: Letters and Diaries of John Dos Passos.* Boston: Gambit, 1973.

Lundquist, James. *The Merrill Guide to Sinclair Lewis.* Columbus: Merrill, 1970.

Lydenberg, John. "Dos Passos and the Ruined Words." *Pacific Spectator* 5 (1951): 316–27.

MacLeish, Archibald. "Post-War Writers and Pre-War Readers." *New Republic,* 10 June 1940, 789–91.

Manchester, William. *The Glory and the Dream: A Narrative History of America, 1932–1972.* Vol. 1. Boston: Little, Brown and Co., 1974.

Mann, Robert. *Legacy to Power: Senator Russell Long of Louisiana.* New York: Paragon House, 1992.

Mansfield, Luther Stearns. "History and the Historical Process in *All the King's Men.*" *Centennial Review* 22 (1978): 214–30.

Marsh, Fred. "Demagogue's Progress: A Novel of American Politics Following the Huey Long Story and Legend." Review of *All the King's Men*, by Robert Penn Warren. *New York Herald Tribune Weekly Book Review*, 18 August 1946, 2.

Millichap, Joseph R. *Hamilton Basso*. Twayne's United States Authors, vol. 331. Boston: Twayne, 1979.

Milne, Gordon. *The American Political Novel*. Norman: University of Oklahoma Press, 1966.

Montesi, Albert J. "Huey Long and *The Southern Review*." *Journal of Modern Literature* 3 (1973): 63–74.

Moore, L. Hugh, Jr. *Robert Penn Warren and History: "The Big Myth We Live."* The Hague: Mouton, 1970.

Murry, John Middleton. "The Hell It Can't." Review of *It Can't Happen Here*, by Sinclair Lewis. *Adelphi* 11.6 (1936): 321–27.

Newlin, Louisa Foulke. "Robert Penn Warren's Use of History in *All the King's Men*." Ph.D. diss., American University, 1979.

Opotowsky, Stan. *The Longs of Louisiana*. New York: Dutton, 1960.

Payne, Ladell. "Willie Stark and Huey Long: Atmosphere, Myth, or Suggestion?" *American Quarterly* 20 (1968): 580–95.

Pizer, Donald. *Dos Passos' "U.S.A.": A Critical Study*. Charlottesville: University Press of Virginia, 1988.

———, ed. *John Dos Passos: The Major Nonfictional Prose*. Detroit: Wayne State University Press, 1988.

Prescott, Orville. *In My Opinion: An Inquiry into the Contemporary Novel*. Indianapolis: Bobbs-Merrill, 1952.

Redding, J. Saunders. "Whey Down South." Review of *A Lion Is in the Streets*, by Adria Locke Langley. *New Republic*, 18 June 1945, 852–53.

Review of *A Lion Is in the Streets*, by Adria Locke Langley. *Booklist*, 15 May 1945, 269–70.

Review of *A Lion Is in the Streets*, by Adria Locke Langley. *Commonweal*, 7 September 1945, 506.

Rocks, James E. "Hamilton Basso and the World View from Pompey's Head." *South Atlantic Quarterly* 71 (1972): 326–41.

Rohmer, Sax. *President Fu Manchu*. Garden City, N.Y.: Doubleday, Doran, 1936.

Rosen, Robert C. "Dos Passos' Other Trilogy." *Modern Fiction Studies* 26 (1980): 483–502.

———. *John Dos Passos: Politics and the Writer*. Lincoln: University of Nebraska Press, 1981.

Rothman, N. L. "Dictator, American Style." Review of *A Lion Is in the Streets*, by Adria Locke Langley. *Saturday Review of Literature*, 12 May 1945, 8.

Rubin, Louis D., Jr. "All the King's Meanings." In *The Curious Death of the Novel: Essays in American Literature*. Baton Rouge: Louisiana State University Press, 1967. First published in *Georgia Review* 8 (1954), 422–34.

Sanders, Marion K. *Dorothy Thompson: A Legend in Her Time*. Boston: Houghton Mifflin, 1973.

Scarborough, Dorothy. "A Louisiana Senator." Review of *Cinnamon Seed*, by Hamilton Basso. *New York Times Book Review*, 25 February 1934, 8–9.

Schlesinger, Arthur M., Jr. *The Politics of Upheaval*. Vol. 3 of *The Age of Roosevelt*. Boston: Houghton Mifflin, 1960.

Schorer, Mark. *Sinclair Lewis: An American Life*. New York: McGraw-Hill, 1969.

Schulberg, Budd. "Lewis: Big Wind from Sauk Centre." *Esquire*, December 1960, 110–14.

Scouten, Arthur H. "Warren, Huey Long, and *All the King's Men*." *Four Quarters* 21 (May 1972): 23–26.

Seldes, George. "To Americans Facing Fascism." In *Sawdust Caesar: The Untold History of Mussolini and Fascism*. New York: Harper, 1935.

Sheean, Vincent. *Dorothy and Red*. Boston: Houghton Mifflin, 1963.

Sinclair, Upton. *Money Writes!* London: Laurie, 1931.

Sindler, Allan P. *Huey Long's Louisiana: State Politics, 1920–1952*. Baltimore: Johns Hopkins University Press, 1956.

Smith, Laban C. "A Wily Political Boss: From Lincolnesque to Huey Long–Like Role." Review of *All the King's Men*, by Robert Penn Warren. *Chicago Sun Book Week*, 18 August 1946, 3.

Smith, Webster [pseud.]. *The Kingfish: A Biography of Huey P. Long*. New York: Putnam, 1933.

Snyder, Robert E. "The Concept of Demagoguery: Huey Long and His Literary Critics." *Louisiana Studies* 15 (1976): 61–83.

Sochatoff, A. Fred. "Some Treatments of the Huey Long Theme." In *All the King's Men: A Symposium*. Carnegie Series in English, vol. 3. Pittsburgh: Carnegie Institute of Technology, 1957.

Streator, George. Review of *Sun in Capricorn*, by Hamilton Basso. *Commonweal*, 2 October 1942, 570.

Swing, Raymond Gram. *Forerunners of American Fascism.* New York: Julian Messner, 1935.

Tanner, Stephen L. "Sinclair Lewis and Fascism." *Studies in the Novel* 22 (1990): 57–66.

Thompson, Dorothy. *I Saw Hitler!* New York: Farrar and Rinehart, 1932.

———. "The Boy and Man from Sauk Centre." *Atlantic Monthly,* November 1960, 39–48.

Thorp, Willard. *American Writing in the Twentieth Century.* Cambridge: Harvard University Press, 1960.

Tolson, Jay, ed. *The Correspondence of Shelby Foote and Walker Percy.* New York: Norton, 1997.

Turner, Joseph W. "The Kinds of Historical Fiction: An Essay in Definition and Methodology." *Genre* 12 (1979): 333–55.

Tyler, Parker. "Novel into Film: *All the King's Men.*" *Kenyon Review* 12, no. 2 (1950): 369–76.

Vanderwerken, David L. "*Manhattan Transfer:* Dos Passos' Babel Story." *American Literature* 49 (1977): 253–67.

———. "*U.S.A.:* Dos Passos and the 'Old Words.'" *Twentieth Century Literature* 23 (1977): 195–228.

Wagner, Linda W. *Dos Passos: Artist as American.* Austin: University of Texas Press, 1979.

Warren, Robert Penn. *All the King's Men.* New York: Harcourt, Brace and Co., 1946.

———. *All the King's Men.* Restored edition. Edited by Noel Polk. New York: Harcourt, 2001.

———. "*All the King's Men:* The Matrix of Experience." *Yale Review* 53 (1963): 161–67.

———. *At Heaven's Gate.* 1943. Reprint, New York: New Directions, 1985.

———. "In the Time of *All the King's Men.*" *New York Times Book Review,* 31 May 1981, 9, 39–42.

———. Introduction to *All the King's Men.* 1946. Reprint, New York: Modern Library, 1953.

———. Introduction to *All the King's Men.* 1946. Reprint, New York: Time, 1963.

———. Introduction to *Nostromo,* by Joseph Conrad. 1904. Reprint, New York: Modern Library, 1951.

———. *John Brown: The Making of a Martyr.* 1929. Reprint, Nashville: J. S. Sanders, 1993.

———. *Night Rider.* 1939. Reprint, Nashville: J. S. Sanders, 1992.

———. "A Special Message to Subscribers." In *All the King's Men.* 1946. Reprint, Franklin Center, Pa.: Franklin Library, 1977.

———. "The World of Huey Long." *London Times,* 5 January 1974.

Watkins, Floyd C. *The Flesh and the Word: Eliot, Hemingway, Faulkner.* Nashville: Vanderbilt University Press, 1971.

Watkins, Floyd C., and John T. Hiers, eds. *Robert Penn Warren Talking: Interviews, 1950–1978.* New York: Random House, 1980.

Watkins, Floyd C., John T. Hiers, and Mary Louise Weaks, eds. *Talking with Robert Penn Warren.* Athens: University of Georgia Press, 1990.

White, Hayden. *The Content of the Form: Narrative Discourse and Historical Representation.* Baltimore: Johns Hopkins University Press, 1987.

———. "The Fictions of Factual Representation." In *The Literature of Fact: Selected Papers from the English Institute,* edited by Angus Fletcher. New York: Columbia University Press, 1976.

Williams, T. Harry. *Huey Long.* 1969. Reprint, New York: Vintage, 1981.

———. *Romance and Realism in Southern Politics.* Athens: University of Georgia Press, 1961.

Wilson, Edmund. "Archibald MacLeish and the Word." *New Republic,* 1 July 1940, 30–32.

Woodward, C. Vann. *The Future of the Past.* New York: Oxford University Press, 1989.

Zinman, David. *The Day Huey Long Was Shot: September 8, 1935.* Rev. ed. Jackson: University Press of Mississippi, 1993.

Index

Messina, Joe, 208
Milton, John, 83
Morgan, J. P., Jr., 72
Mussolini, Benito, 55, 77, 189, 190

Night Rider (Warren), 211–12, 213, 214, 215
Nineteen Nineteen (Dos Passos), 125, 127, 152
Noe, James, 208
Nostromo (Conrad), 221
Number One (Dos Passos): as political novel, 34; as documentary novel, 36; as *roman à clef*, 37; and the politician's "double life," 130–31; and "the people," 133–35, 136, 137, 138–40, 141, 143; Crawford/Long parallels in, 135–52; mentioned, 4, 33, 42, 95, 132, 160–61, 162, 163, 165, 168, 170, 172, 176, 182, 198, 201, 204, 208, 222, 225, 226

Oates, Joyce Carol, 181n4
O'Connor, Flannery, 112, 113
One Man's Initiation: 1917 (Dos Passos), 124, 128, 130
"Original Sin: A Short Story" (Warren), 212–13, 215
Overton, John H., 2

Page, Thomas Nelson, 87
Paine, Thomas, 54, 122
Pavy, Benjamin, 30–31
Pelley, William Dudley, 53, 56
Percy, Walker, 119
Perkins, Maxwell, 87, 91
Pipkin, Charles W., 178
Political novel, 33–34, 38
"Pondy Woods" (Warren), 211, 212, 213, 215
President Fu Manchu (Rohmer): as "Yellow Peril thriller," 39–40; Bragg/Long parallels in, 40–42, 61; and Coughlin, 56

Primary Colors (anonymous), 37
Prodigal Parents, The (Lewis), 45
Proud Flesh (Warren), 180–81, 186, 188
Public Burning, The (Coover), 225
"Pudd'nhead Wilson's Calendar," 65

Ransdell, Joseph E., 100, 142
Ransom, John Crowe, 87
Reed, John, 44
Relics and Angels (Basso), 86–87
Requiem for a Nun (Faulkner), 90
Rockefeller, John D., Jr., 72
Roden, Murphy, 208
Rogers, Will, 78
Rohmer, Sax, 39–42. See also *President Fu Manchu*
Roman à clef, 37–38, 57, 109, 158, 208
Roosevelt, Franklin Delano, 17, 26, 29–30, 39, 52–53, 56, 68, 131
Rothstein, Arnold, 38
Ruth, Babe, 25–26

Sacco, Nicola, 125, 126
Sanders, J. Y., 97, 98, 100, 108
Sanders, J. Y., Jr., 100
Sartoris (Faulkner), 92
Scott, Sir Walter, 35, 115
Shakespeare, William, 197. See also *Hamlet; I Henry VI*
Shushan, Abraham, 107, 109
Sinclair, Upton, 44, 45, 53. See also *Jungle, The*
Smith, "General" Art J., 53, 56
Smith, Gerald L. K., 32, 148
Snopes, Clarence, 86
Snopes, Flem, 86, 109, 116
Socialist Party, 44
Song of Solomon, 174
Sound Wagon, The (Stribling), 34
Southern Review, 179, 180, 183–84, 188